LAND, CHURCH, AND PEOPLE

Essays presented to

PROFESSOR H. P. R. FINBERG

BRITISH AGRICULTURAL HISTORY SOCIETY

LAND, CHURCH, AND PEOPLE

ESSAYS PRESENTED TO PROFESSOR H. P. R. FINBERG

Edited by

JOAN THIRSK

MUSEUM OF ENGLISH RURAL LIFE, WHITEKNIGHTS PARK
READING, BERKS
1970

PRINTED IN GREAT BRITAIN
AT THE BROADWATER PRESS, WELWYN GARDEN CITY, HERTFORDSHIRE

CONTENTS

HERBERT FINBERG:
An Appreciation

ERBERT PATRICK REGINALD FINBERG, we are told, was born at Rickmansworth on 21 March 1900. The fact seems as authentic as any in history, although the sprightly figure of spring 1970 taking his constitutional in Chiswick Park might seem to contradict bare chronology; and, indeed, no one would be better placed to outwit us all in a matter of dating than he who for so long pitted his wits successfully against the deceivers and the self-deceivers, the forgers and improvers of Anglo-Saxon charters.

It was provident of him to arrange to be born so neatly poised between the nineteenth and the twentieth centuries: to inherit the developed tools of nineteenth-century historical criticism and to be in time to take advantage of the motor-car—chauffeused by his wife, Joscelyne—as a means of penetrating the countryside that the charters delineated, and of arriving at distant bases from which their explorations on foot could begin. It was provident to be the son of the biographer of the artist, Turner; for, in so far as talents are inherited, he was guaranteed a lively appreciation of the significance of the painter's visual scene as well as the skill of narrative biography. It was also provident to arrange to be born at Rickmansworth, then poised between town and country: for Herbert Finberg, urbane and unmistakably a man of Town libraries, Town clubs, and Town restaurants, was destined to spend the formative years of his working life away from London in the Cotswolds and at Welwyn; and in his second life at Leicester to expound with conviction the doctrine that History is the biography of Little Places as well as of Great Men; to become Head and then Professor in a Department of English Local History set in the very middle of the grassy Midland shires, while retaining a toehold if not a foothold in West London suburbia.

This special number of THE AGRICULTURAL HISTORY REVIEW, made up of essays by Herbert Finberg's friends, colleagues, and fellow students, celebrates the seventieth birthday of an English local historian. It should be noted, however, that Finberg the historian is far from being the whole of Finberg. The 'Bibliography' that follows this 'Appreciation' gives slight clues to these other lives outside History. At Oxford he studied not History but Greats, and his earliest interests were in philosophy and literature, as the publications of 1925 and 1926 indicate; and there is said to be a manuscript of an unpublished book from this period lurking in some Chiswick cupboard. Long before the emergence into public print of Finberg the historian in 1941 and 1942, there had been another career of distinction in publishing and book production where the art interests of his father emerged again in the creative artistry of the printed page. Like Tawney and Housman before him, Finberg had been prevented from post-graduate studies by the examiners' view of his Finals papers although, like Tawney and Housman, he had the later satisfaction of contemplating the predictive quality of a Finals class from the elevated position of his own professorial Chair. Thus the young graduate found himself in a provincial workshop, the printing establishment of the Shakespeare Head Press, directed by Basil Blackwell and Bernard Newdigate, then at Stratford-upon-Avon. From Stratford he moved to Chipping Campden, and there founded his own press, the Alcuin, in a barn. His ambition was to demonstrate that one could live in the twentieth century, taking advantage of the techniques of mechanized printing, and yet achieve high and imaginative standards: from Finberg at the Alcuin Press came the Housman *Poems* in 1929, but all forms of jobbing printing were undertaken. It was at this time also that he became interested in handwriting, as the 1929 item in the 'Bibliography' indicates, achieving an elegant personal hand: on an envelope in brown ink it immediately distinguishes the sender and softens the impact of even the sharpest critical comment. In the age of typewriters one of the few pleasures remaining to a printer must be to set up a piece from Finberg in his manuscript. So far as I know, he types nothing.

In 1935 the Alcuin Press moved to Welwyn Garden City but then encountered the depression in 1936, and Finberg went to work as a director of The Broadwater Press Ltd, where he remained until 1944. In this period the Twickenham *Pope* was launched. At the end of the war he became editorial director of Burns Oates & Washbourne Ltd, no doubt attracted by the prospect of liturgical publishing for Roman Catholic use, but with a fine oecumenical toleration he also took on advisory work for Eyre & Spottiswoode Ltd, H.M. Printers, designing for them the *Coronation Service* of 1953: on the secular side he advised the then Ministry of Works from 1944 to 1948, and takes particular pride in the format of the *Post-war Building Studies: Housing Manual*. Although he ceased to be a director of Burns Oates in 1949, a connection continued, and it was from this press that his *Manual of Catholic Prayer* came in 1962, winning the *Prix Graphica Belgica* in 1965. It should not have surprised me, therefore, when Herbert Finberg visited Leeds some time in the 1950's, and I introduced him to the Brotherton Librarian as "Dr Finberg, the topographer", that I was misheard and stayed to overhear a long technical conversation between Dr Page and Dr Finberg, the typographer.

The second career, the one which this volume celebrates, begins in Dr Hart's bibliography with the short article in *Devon and Cornwall Notes and Queries* in 1941, when Finberg had already passed forty years of age. The unsuspecting agent of the transformation seems to have been Mrs Finberg. In 1933 Finberg married Joscelyne Payne, and together they became interested in the genealogy of her family. Although not published until 1956, his paper on the Gostwicks of Willington was written in 1940, and the researches had taken him—fatally, but happily for us—into the Record Office of the Bedford estate. There he encountered the massive documentation of the dukes' Tavistock Abbey properties. Holidays were taken in Devon and the assimilation of local topography began. The writing began during spells of fire-watching duties in Welwyn, and although I believe that there were no actual fires, the phoenix that arose from the flames of these long candle-watches was *Tavistock Abbey*, completed in 1949 and published in 1951. Except for the *Axel* translation of 1925 it was Finberg's first book, and there can have been few more successful late entries in the academic race. It was a book by a non-professional of which any professional would have been proud, and it must have been the main evidence on which Tawney and Stenton sponsored him in 1952 for the vacant post of Reader and Head of the Department of English Local History at the then University College of Leicester. As he himself later wrote, "what had been a private hobby thus became a professional duty." Like his first master, B. H. Newdigate, he could now be called Scholar-printer.

Finberg's predecessor at Leicester had been W. G. Hoskins. Hoskins was born in Devon, had written about Exeter, and shared many of Finberg's interests. They had begun to correspond after Finberg's early articles in *D.C.N.Q.*, met at the field outings of the Devon Association in 1946, and signalled their own working association with their *Devonshire Studies*, published in the year that Finberg went to Leicester. This volume of essays and studies is a classic, and alongside J. D. Chambers's *Nottinghamshire in the Eighteenth Century* and A. L. Rowse's *Tudor Cornwall* it marked the renaissance of English local history at a level of technique, imagination, and significance equal to that of academic history in more conventional areas of study. As might be expected from two rugged—even jagged—individualists, their collaboration derived its strength from the complementarity of their interests rather than a grand design for essays with two co-operating authors, although the reader with a keen eye may be able to detect cross-influences in the individual essays that made up the volume. The partnership was not broken when Hoskins went to Oxford, for Finberg's *Gloucestershire* of 1955 was one of a series of landscape histories initiated and edited by Hoskins, while Hoskins contributed in 1960 to the series of *Occasional Papers* of the Leicester Department which Finberg had initiated with his own first public lecture at Leicester (November 1952), and which he triumphantly edited until his retirement.

If the selectors at Leicester thought that they had appointed a desk-bound and study-bound medievalist to their academic fellowship they were to be rudely shaken. It is true that Finberg followed Hoskins's example in firmly separating the workplace from the home by the thickness of a railway timetable, but in fact his two bases were used for a double ration of historical enterprise. At Bosworth Richard III had wondered if there were not two Richmonds in the field, but from 1952 to 1965 an observer might have been pardoned for thinking that there were even more Finbergs in the field. The 'Bibliography' shows that it was the period in which he consolidated his own reputation with his work on early charters; and it was the period when (drawing perhaps on his own observations of warfare between critical scholars and of warfare between academics and administrators) he set out to challenge the old assumption that in the Saxon invasions the victors had succeeded in annihilating the vanquished without trace. Finberg's own philosophy of local history placed little weight on the local discipline for 'illuminating' national history, a 'propaedeutic value', as he once dubbed it. "To treat it as an introduction to or a contribution to national history is to invert the true relationship between them." Yet in the historiography of the illumination of the so-called Dark Ages Finberg has assured immortality for the name of one rural Gloucestershire community, Withington.

But the 'Bibliography' which records the scholar's output in the Leicester years (1952–65) necessarily omits, or gives light emphasis to, the other side of the headship of a Department of English Local History, that of entrepreneurship. Here scholar, printer, publisher, and businessman were fused in a succession of enterprises and initiatives. These very pages are the result of one of these enterprises: his editorship of the REVIEW after the Agricultural History Society was founded. Another enterprise, the series of *Occasional Papers of the Department of English Local History*, shows Finberg as the discerning patron of publication, the list of contributors having more than one future Reader or Professor, including the successor to his own Chair. In his *Gloucestershire Studies* (1957) he enlarged the size of the two-man partnership that had produced *Devonshire Studies* five years earlier, and five years later he edited and contributed to a symposium on History itself, the Finberg element being 'The Approach to Local History'. As the diligent reader of the 'Bibliography' will also see, Finberg has never subscribed to the view that a scholar's work, once published in article form, should thereafter blush unseen: in *Lucerna*, in *Local History—Objective and Pursuit*, and latterly in *West-Country Historical Studies* he has made available within hard covers and among the 'proper books' of libraries the majority of his own historical writing that had first appeared in periodicals or become out of print.

But the greatest enterprise of these years was undoubtedly the initiation of *The Agrarian History of England and Wales*. One hopes that among Finberg's fragments of autobiography he has recorded the saga of its making. At times, confronted by the idiosyncrasies of university presses and university contributors he must have thought that it was easier to engineer the making of the

English landscape than the making of an Agrarian History. Yet Volume IV has shown that within a decade a grand idea could be translated into a grand reality. His friends and admirers rejoice that his current objective and pursuit, aided by the patrons of his Cambridge post-retirement fellowship and his Leverhulme Emeritus award, is to edit and also to contribute to the volume that will chronologically be the first of the *Agrarian History*.

The thirteen years at Leicester, first as Reader and then as Professor, continuing and extending the work of Hoskins, the first Head of the Department, saw Finberg—if one may paraphrase Falstaff—not only as enterprising in himself but the occasion of enterprise in others. Some of this was engendered in colleagues and graduate students. Alan Everitt, a contributor to this volume, was colleague and successor in the Chair; Joan Thirsk, another colleague of those Leicester years, was to succeed Hoskins in the Oxford Readership and Finberg in the editorship of the AGRICULTURAL HISTORY REVIEW: and thereby to contribute to and to edit this volume of appreciative essays. As patron of younger scholars Finberg sponsored the annual John Nichols prize in English Local History, a Leicester award but competed for nationally: some fruits of this enterprise will be seen in the *Occasional Papers*. Being himself an amateur historian for so many years, Finberg still retained a close interest in training and improving the standards of amateurs in local history. His work for the Standing Conference on Local History is one aspect of this interest; the John Nichols prize, open to all comers, professional and amateur, is another; the pronouncements on the nature of local history brought together in the 1967 volume are another, an attempt to stimulate thought and action by definition and example; and alongside the solemnities (not over-solemn, however) of these public occasions, there is also that highly recommended piece of calculated and mocking didacticism, 'How Not to Write Local History'.

This particular appreciation of Herbert Finberg, historian, scholar, and friend, is confessedly less than a full appreciation of the man whose portrait faces our title-page. It has dealt only cursorily with his creative work in printing and fine book production, and it would not be appropriate in the context of this REVIEW to treat a further aspect of his work, integral to the man, that of Roman Catholic exposition; although the 'Bibliography'—as complete as could be achieved in the semi-secrecy of a *Festschrift* project—indicates his published work in the field of liturgy and apologetics. This appreciation is also written by someone who has come to work closely with Finberg only in very recent years and who has not had the advantage of the long or intimate contact possessed by some of those who have made other contributions to this volume.

This *Festschrift*, it is intended, will be presented to Professor Finberg on 25 September 1970 at a dinner at Sadler Hall, Leeds, organized jointly by the British Agricultural History Society and the University of Leeds. Leeds is the third of Finberg's universities, where he came in retirement to a humble but honourable part-time appointment. Since my own interest in the subject of petty medieval boroughs sprang from Finberg's earlier treatment of them in Devon and Gloucestershire, it was peculiarly fitting that his retirement from Leicester in 1965 should have coincided with a moment when I was far enough advanced in my study of medieval town plantation to see that a complete hand-list of all medieval boroughs, organic and planted, would be a useful service to urban history; at that moment also I took on a stint of internal academic administration, and, in some measure of compensation for my diversion from research, the University of Leeds made funds available for some assistance in compiling this handlist: and so the Doctor of Oxford and the Emeritus of Leicester became Part-time Research Assistant of Leeds, *serviens servientium*.

Since this 'Appreciation' has now edged itself towards the border of personal involvement, I cannot resist pointing out that the strenuous bibliographer who seems to have pursued Herbert Finberg so zealously down the corridors of time has missed one contribution to our education that is worth mentioning because it relates to another Finbergian Objective and Pursuit, the enlivenment of provincial field work by critical examination of the cellars and tables of country inns. What is the missing reference? In the ceremonial dress of scholarly footnoting it would read, 'Raymond Postgate, ed., *The Good Food Guide, 1969–1970* (1969), p. 304, *sub* South Zeal, and see also p. 280'.

To get one's name as an approver into the footnotes of the *Good Food Guide* may seem as difficult as getting into *Who's Who*. What shall we say of a man who has succeeded not only in getting into the *Guide* twice but also in being directly quoted on the authenticity of an inn's claim to be 'twelfth-century'? It was, one must note, the historian's call of duty which clearly led H. P. R. F. to South Zeal, for is it not one of the petty medieval boroughs of Devon, with twenty burgesses *apud la Sele* in 1315?

On 25 September his hosts will acknowledge this service to the by-ways of local scholarship, for they intend to invite him to exercise this one of his many crafts, and to choose the wine for his celebration dinner.

M. W. BERESFORD

H. P. R. Finberg: A Bibliography

THIS bibliography includes all Professor Finberg's published writings, with the exception of book reviews, letters, etc., of less than one page in length.

Abbreviations: *AHR*   Agricultural History Review
DCNQ   Devonshire and Cornwall Notes and Queries
EHR   English Historical Review
TDA   Transactions of the Devonshire Association

1925

'Francis Thompson', *English Review*, XLI, pp. 822–31.

Axel, by Jean Marie Matthias Philippe Auguste, Count de Villiers de l'Isle-Adam, translated into English by H. P. R. Finberg, with a preface by William Butler Yeats, 296 pp. Edition limited to 500 copies. Jarrolds Publishers (London) Ltd.

1926

'The Filiation of Aesthetic Ideas in the Neoplatonic School', *Classical Quarterly*, XX, pp. 148–51.

1929

'Handwriting, Good and Bad', *Everyman*, 14 February, pp. 21–2.

1937

'Things I badly want to say', *Catholic Herald*, 6 August.

1939

'The Hirsch Collection of Decorated Papers', *Signature*, XII, pp. 47–53.

1941

'Prideaux of Tavistock and Altarnun', *DCNQ*, XXI, pp. 337–45.

1942

'The Cartulary of Tavistock', *DCNQ*, XXII, pp. 55–61.
'A Domesday Identification', *ibid.*, p. 95.
'Bounds of the Devon Stannaries', *ibid.*, pp. 121–3.
'Manumissions by Ordgar', *ibid.*, pp. 135–6.

1943

'The House of Ordgar and the Foundation of Tavistock Abbey', *EHR*, LVIII, pp. 190–201.
'Church and State in Twelfth-Century Devon: some Documentary Illustrations', *TDA*, LXXV, pp. 245–57. Reprinted in *West-Country Historical Studies*, 1969.
Four articles on Tavistock history, *Tavistock Gazette*, 14 May, 21 May, 28 May, 18 June.
'Ancient Demesne in Devonshire', *DCNQ*, XXII, pp. 178–9.
'Abbots of Tavistock', *ibid.*, pp. 159–62, 174–5, 186–8.

1944

'Abbots of Tavistock', *DCNQ*, XXII, pp. 194–7.

'The Bounds of Abbotsham', *ibid.*, pp. 201–2.

'Pillas, an extinct grain', *ibid.*, p. 226.

'The Early History of Werrington', *EHR*, LIX, pp. 237–51. Rewritten as 'The Making of a Boundary' in *Devonshire Studies*, 1952; reprinted in *Lucerna*, 1964.

1945

'Pirate Gore in Scilly', *DCNQ*, XXII, pp. 250–1.

'Illegal Fairs', *ibid.*, pp. 280–1.

'A Vice-Archdeacon's Legacies', *ibid.*, pp. 285–7. Reprinted in *Devonshire Studies*, 1952, and *West-Country Historical Studies*, 1969.

'Morwell', *TDA*, LXXVII, pp. 157–71. Reprinted in *Devonshire Studies*, 1952, and *West-Country Historical Studies*, 1969.

1946

'Childe's Tomb', *TDA*, LXXVIII, pp. 265–80. Reprinted in *Devonshire Studies*, 1952.

'St Rumon', *DCNQ*, XXII, pp. 331–2.

'The Tragi-comedy of Abbot Bonus', *ibid.*, pp. 341–7. Enlarged and reprinted in *Devonshire Studies*, 1952, and *West-Country Historical Studies*, 1969.

'The Skelving-Stool', *DCNQ*, XXII, pp. 368–9.

1947

'Some Early Tavistock Charters', *EHR*, LXII, pp. 352–77.

'St Michael's, Brentnor', *Tavistock Ruridecanal Magazine*, XXXVIII.

'The Devon–Cornwall Boundary', *DCNQ*, XXIII, pp. 104–7.

'The Castle of Cornwall', *ibid.*, p. 123.

'The Borough of Tavistock: its Origin and Early History', *TDA*, LXXIX, pp. 129–53. Reprinted in *Devonshire Studies*, 1952, and *West-Country Historical Studies*, 1969.

1948

'What is a Farleu?', *DCNQ*, XXIII, pp. 133–5. Reprinted in *Devonshire Studies*, 1952, and *West-Country Historical Studies*, 1969.

'Prelude to Abbot Bonus', *DCNQ*, XXIII, pp. 184–7.

'The Manor of Roborough', *ibid.*, p. 241.

'A Cellarer's Account Book', *ibid.*, pp. 253–5. Reprinted in *Devonshire Studies*, 1952, and *West-Country Historical Studies*, 1969.

Review: *Saint Aldhelm*, by Joseph Fowler. *DCNQ*, XXIII, pp. 190–1.

1949

The Missal in Latin and English, being the text of the Missale Romanum with English rubrics and a new translation. Edited by the Rev. J. O'Connell and H. P. R. Finberg. xliv + 1284 + 270 pp. Supplement of 160 pp. containing 'Masses approved by the Holy See for use in England, Scotland, and Wales'. Burns Oates and Washbourne Ltd. Further editions in 1957, 1958, 1960, and 1962.

'The Stannary of Tavistock', *TDA*, LXXXI, pp. 154–84.

'The Open Field in Devonshire', *Antiquity*, XXIII, pp. 180–7. Enlarged and reprinted in *Devonshire Studies*, 1952, and in *West-Country Historical Studies*, 1969.

'The meaning of Barton', *DCNQ*, XXIII, pp. 326–7, 363.

'Lydford Castle', *ibid.*, pp. 386–7.

1950

'The Customs of Stokenham', *DCNQ*, XXIV, pp. 69–70. Reprinted in *Devonshire Studies*, 1952, and *West-Country Historical Studies*, 1969.

'The Ancestry of J. M. W. Turner, R.A.', *ibid.*, p. 97.

'An Unrecorded Stannary Parliament', *TDA*, LXXXII, pp. 295–310.

1951

'Understood by the People', *The Clergy Review*, XXXV, pp. 1–9.

'The Domesday Plough-Team', *EHR*, LXV, pp. 67–71. Reprinted in *Lucerna*, 1964.

Tavistock Abbey, A Study in the Social and Economic History of Devon. xii+320 pp. Cambridge University Press. Second edition, 1969.

'The Boroughs of Devon', *DCNQ*, XXIV, pp. 203–9.

'Church Dedications in Devon', *ibid.*, pp. 225–6.

Review: *B. H. Newdigate, Scholar-Printer, 1869–1944*, by Joseph Thorp. *The Month*, CXCI, pp. 179–81.

1952

'The Place-Names of Devon', *DCNQ*, XXV, pp. 34–8, 69–72.

Devonshire Studies, by W. G. Hoskins and H. P. R. Finberg. 470 pp. Jonathan Cape Ltd.

The Local Historian and his Theme. An introductory lecture delivered at the University College of Leicester, 6 November 1952. Department of English Local History, Occasional Papers, No. 1. 18 pp. University College, Leicester. Reprinted in *Local History—Objective and Pursuit*, 1967.

1953

'Sherborne, Glastonbury, and the Expansion of Wessex', *Transactions of the Royal Historical Society*, 5th ser., III, pp. 101–24. Reprinted in *Lucerna*, 1964.

The Early Charters of Devon and Cornwall. Department of English Local History, Occasional Papers, No. 2. 32 pp. University College, Leicester. Second edition, 1963.

Editorial article: *AHR*, I, pp. 1–3.

'Changes in the Coronation Service', *The Tablet*, 9 May.

Reviews: *The Roman Ritual in Latin and English*, translated and edited by the Rev. Philip T. Weller. *Amen*, May–August.

English Historical Documents, Vol. II, 1042–1189, ed. D. C. Douglas and G. W. Greenaway. *The Month*, CXCV (n.s. IX), pp. 364–6.

1954

'An Early Reference to the Welsh Cattle Trade', *AHR*, II, pp. 12–14.

Review: *Medieval Religious Houses*, by David Knowles and R. Neville Hadcock. *Transactions of the Leicestershire Archaeological Society*, XXX, pp. 135–6.

1955

Roman and Saxon Withington, a Study in Continuity. Department of English Local History, Occasional Papers, No. 8. 40 pp. University College, Leicester. Reprinted in *Lucerna*, 1964.

Gloucestershire, An Illustrated Essay on the History of the Landscape. 128 pp. Hodder and Stoughton.

Reviews: *The Open Fields*, by C. S. and C. S. Orwin (2nd edn). *AHR*, III, pp. 54–5.

> *The Victoria County History of Leicestershire*, Vol. II. *Antiquaries Journal*, XXXV, pp. 114–15.

> *The Domesday Geography of Midland England*, by H. C. Darby and I. B. Terrett. *Transactions of the Leicestershire Archaeological Society*, XXXI, pp. 71–2.

1956

'The Tavistock Scriptorium', *DCNQ*, XXVII, pp. 27–8.

'The Boroughs of Devon', *ibid.*, pp. 54–5.

'An Agrarian History of England', *AHR*, IV, pp. 2–3.

'The Small Ritual', *Clergy Review*, XLI, pp. 578–84.

English in the Liturgy: a Symposium, ed. C. R. A. Cunliffe. vi+154 pp. Burns and Oates. pp. 109–22, 'The Problem of Style', by H. P. R. Finberg.

'The Gostwicks of Willington', *Publications of the Bedfordshire Historical Record Society*, XXXVI, pp. 46–138 (written in 1940, according to the author's note).

Review: *Devon Monastic Lands*, ed. Joyce Youings. *AHR*, IV, pp. 63–4.

1957

Gloucestershire Studies, edited by H. P. R. Finberg. xiv+304 pp. Leicester University Press.

Review: *English Place-Name Elements*, by A. H. Smith. *AHR*, V, pp. 117–18.

1958

'Three Anglo-Saxon Boundaries', *Transactions of the Shropshire Archaeological Society*, LVI, pp. 28–33.

Reviews: *Medieval England, an Aerial Survey*, by M. W. Beresford and J. K. S. St Joseph. *AHR*, VI, pp. 116–17.

> *The Victoria County History of Oxfordshire*, Vol. V. *Economic History Review*, n.s. XI, pp. 170–1.

1959

'The Catholic Historian and his Theme'. An address delivered at Oxford to the Conference on Post-Reformation Catholic History, 16 April 1958. *Downside Review*, LXXVII, pp. 254–65.

Reviews: *The Historical Atlas of Cheshire*, ed. Dorothy Sylvester and G. Nulty. *AHR*, VII, pp. 60–1.

> *Medieval England*, ed. A. L. Poole. *ibid.*, pp. 121–2.

1960

Translation from the Latin of the 'Universal Prayer' attributed to Pope Clement XI. *The Tablet*, 23 July.

The Westward Expansion of Wessex, by W. G. Hoskins. Department of English Local History, Occasional Papers, No. 13. 44 pp. Leicester University Press. pp. 23–44 form a Supplement, by H. P. R. Finberg and others, to *The Early Charters of Devon and Cornwall* (see under 1953).

Review: *Valley on the March*, by Lord Rennell of Rodd. *EHR*, LXXV, pp. 328–9.

1961

The Early Charters of the West Midlands. 256 pp. Leicester University Press.

'Recent Progress in English Agrarian History', *Geografiska Annaler* (Stockholm), XLIII, pp. 75–9.

1962

'You *versus* Thou', *The Tablet*, 27 January.

'A Meditation upon Candour', *Search*, I, pp. 49–51.

'Two Cornish Boundaries', *DCNQ*, XXIX, p. 27.

Approaches to History. A symposium edited by H. P. R. Finberg. x+222 pp. Routledge and Kegan Paul. Introduction, p. vii, and 'Local History', pp. 111–25, by the editor. pp. 111–25 reprinted in *Local History—Objective and Pursuit*, 1967.

The Manual of Catholic Prayer for all days and seasons and every circumstance of Christian life: compiled from the holy Scriptures, the Liturgical books of the Latin rite, other Catholic liturgies, and the writings of saintly men and women. xxx+600 pp. Burns and Oates.

1964

The Early Charters of Wessex. 282 pp. Leicester University Press.

Local History in the University. An inaugural lecture delivered at the University of Leicester, 26 May 1964. 20 pp. Leicester University Press. Reprinted in *Local History—Objective and Pursuit*, 1967.

Objections to Roman Catholicism, ed. Michael de la Bedoyère. 190 pp. Constable. pp. 91–109, 'Censorship', by H. P. R. Finberg.

Lucerna. Studies of some Problems in the Early History of England. x+230 pp. Macmillan.

1967

The Agrarian History of England and Wales, edited by H. P. R. Finberg. Vol. IV, 1500–1640, edited by Joan Thirsk. xl+920 pp. Cambridge University Press. Preface, pp. v–vii, by H. P. R. Finberg.

'The Canon of the Mass: an Experimental English Version', *The Tablet*, 27 May.

'St Patrick at Glastonbury'. The O'Donnell Lecture delivered at the University of Oxford, 10 May 1966, *The Irish Ecclesiastical Record*, CVII, pp. 345–61 (attributed by a printer's error to A. N. E. D. Schofield). Reprinted with corrections and additions in *West-Country Historical Studies*, 1969.

Local History—Objective and Pursuit. x+132 pp. David and Charles. pp. vii–ix, 1–86, 128–30 by H. P. R. Finberg; pp. 87–127 by V. H. T. Skipp.

'The Canon in English', *The Tablet*, 18 November.

1968

'The Sunday Masses in English', *The Tablet*, 20 January.

'Some Crediton documents re-examined: with some observations on the criticism of Anglo-Saxon charters', *Antiquaries Journal*, XLVIII, pp. 59–86. Reprinted in *West-Country Historical Studies*, 1969.

1969

West-Country Historical Studies. 232 pp. David and Charles.

The *Codex Wintoniensis* and the King's *Haligdom*[1]

By CYRIL HART

THE *Codex Wintoniensis* is the name commonly given to a cartulary compiled at Winchester Cathedral Priory, otherwise known as the Old Minster, *c.* A.D. 1130 × 1150, during the episcopate of Henry de Blois.[2] Of the surviving English cartularies only three, all from Worcester, were written at an earlier date.[3] Apart from a few late insertions, the contents of the *Codex* are confined to copies of royal charters and other miscellaneous texts relating to lands and privileges, all purporting to have been drawn up before the Norman Conquest; the oldest document entered may be dated 685 × 687,[4] and the most recent 1053.[5]

In all there are 218 entries (a few being duplicated), making the *Codex* by far the most voluminous surviving source of pre-Conquest land charters, embracing as it does well over 10 per cent of the whole corpus. Four out of every five *Codex* entries withstand all modern tests of authenticity; of the remainder, many are basically genuine texts which have been subjected to minor interpolation or touching up at some stage in their transmission. The majority of the spurious charters entered in the *Codex* claim to have been drawn up at some date prior to the accession of King Athelstan in 924; half of the fifty-four charters bearing an earlier date are spurious, or modified in some way, but of the *Codex* texts assigned to the last one and a half centuries of the Anglo-Saxon state, nine out of every ten appear to be wholly authentic. This is a record as good as almost any to be found among surviving English cartularies, and better than most.

Moreover, sufficient Winchester charters survive in the original to establish

---

[1] Abbreviations: DB = Domesday Book; CS = W. de Gray Birch, *Cartularium Saxonicum*, 3 vols., London, 1885–93; Davis = G. R. C. Davis, *Medieval Cartularies of Great Britain*, London, 1958; ECEE = C. Hart, *The Early Charters of Eastern England*, Leicester, 1966; ECW = H. P. R. Finberg, *The Early Charters of Wessex*, Leicester, 1964; ECWM = H. P. R. Finberg, *The Early Charters of the West Midlands*, Leicester, 1961; H = F. E. Harmer, *Anglo-Saxon Writs*, Manchester, 1952; Ha = F. E. Harmer, *Select English Historical Documents*, Cambridge, 1914; K = J. M. Kemble, *Codex Diplomaticus Ævi Saxonici*, 6 vols., London, 1839–48; R = A. J. Robertson, *Anglo-Saxon Charters*, Cambridge, 2nd edn, 1956; W = D. Whitelock, *Anglo-Saxon Wills*, Cambridge, 1930; WCD = *Winchester Cathedral Documents*, ed. W. R. W. Stephens and F. T. Madge, Hants. Record Soc., Vol. II, 1897. Charters are quoted by their number in the respective editions.

[2] Davis, No. 1042.   [3] Davis, Nos. 1068–9.

[4] No. 97. Charters in the *Codex Wintoniensis* are quoted by the numbers assigned to them in Appendix II to this paper.

[5] No. 175.

beyond all doubt that the compilers of the *Codex* made careful and complete transcripts of the materials before them, whether the documents themselves were genuine or not.[1] Usually they transcribed the witness lists completely; their knowledge of Old English enabled them to make accurate renderings of the boundary clauses, and regularly they incorporated the endorsements on the original membranes in their introductory rubrics to the cartulary texts, a laudable custom found elsewhere only in the Wilton cartulary.

All this calls for emphasis because the *Codex Wintoniensis* has come in for more than its fair share of adverse criticism in the past, by an impressive collection of authorities. As long ago as 1871 the great William Stubbs condemned it as being "of the lowest possible character,"[2] a phrase repeated in 1897 by F. W. Maitland, who went on to claim it was "full of lies."[3] W. H. Stevenson in 1904 considered it a "suspicious source;"[4] in 1910 F. M. Stenton referred to "the fraudulent *Codex*;"[5] and as recently as 1955 Miss D. Whitelock described it as "a less reliable source" than "cartularies of good repute."[6] In the same year, F. M. Stenton returned to the attack by including Winchester Cathedral in a list of "centres of proved fabrication" from which "no document . . . should be accepted at its face value without close examination."[7]

It was left to H. P. R. Finberg to commence the process of rehabilitation, by pointing out in 1961 that while the *Codex* "does indeed contain several dubious charters, . . . against this must be set the fact that the compiler has preserved scores of precious and authentic documents."[8] Three years later he published his penetrating study of the Winchester Cathedral endowments, in which the majority of the suspicious charters entered in the *Codex* were shown to have been forged as a group within the half-century following the Benedictine reform of 964.[9] The forgeries, he maintained convincingly, were carried out not in order to acquire estates and liberties to which the monks were not entitled, but merely "to provide a background of precedent for the scheme of renewal and restitution" of the cathedral endowments carried out by King Edgar after the displacement of the Winchester clerks by a body of monks. Some of these properties had first come into the possession of the see before the advent of the solemn royal diploma in the second half of the seventh century; for others acquired in later years the original donation charters had been lost, or were in-

---

[1] The following *Codex* entries are copies of charters of which the originals or pseudo-originals still survive: Nos. 28, 41, 44, 110, 136, 138, 141–3, 150, 171, 191, 215. Of these, Nos. 44, 171, and 191 are known to have been at Winchester in 1640, along with many other *Codex* originals since lost.

[2] A. W. Haddan and W. Stubbs, *Councils and Ecclesiastical Documents*, III, Oxford, 1871, p. 638.

[3] F. W. Maitland, *Domesday Book and Beyond*, Fontana edn, 1960, p. 387.

[4] W. H. Stevenson, *Asser's Life of King Alfred*, Oxford, 1959 reprint, p. lxv, n. 3.

[5] F. M. Stenton, *Types of Manorial Structure in the Northern Danelaw*, Oxford, 1910, p. 79n.

[6] D. Whitelock, *English Historical Documents*, I, London, 1955, p. 338.

[7] F. M. Stenton, *The Latin Charters of the Anglo-Saxon Period*, Oxford, 1955, p. 11.

[8] ECWM, p. 21.   [9] ECW, ch. VII.

sufficiently explicit as to the privileges conveyed; the Benedictine reform supplied both the motive and the opportunity for the fabrication of fresh title
deeds.

Finberg's essay was followed in 1965 by a paper by E. John, in which the
diplomatic of several of the more important items of the *Codex* was studied in
the context of the monastic revival.[1] This review upheld the authenticity of a
number of charters previously suspect, among them those numbered 15–23 in
the Appendix II to the present paper. It is not my purpose here to develop the
study of the cathedral endowments initiated in these two essays by John and
Finberg, except to put forward the suggestion—it is no more than that—that
each of the estates "restored" by charters Nos. 15–23 represented in fact an
individual prebend once held by a Winchester clerk of the unreformed foundation.[2]

Our indebtedness to Professor Finberg for fresh light on the *Codex* is not
confined to his work on the cathedral endowments, for in 1961 he pointed out
that several of the cartulary entries related to estates which were very unlikely
ever to have been in the possession of the Old Minster.[3] He noted that of four
charters entered on fols. 108ᵛ–111 relating to estates called *Wudetune*, only one
concerned the priory estate at Wootton St Lawrence, Hants. Of the three
others, two related to places of the same name in Oxfordshire and Gloucestershire. Similarly, he noted that of the six entries on fols. 72ᵛ–75 relating to
places called *Eastun*, two only belonged to estates in Hampshire which may
have belonged to the priory; the remainder were located as far apart as Shropshire and Berkshire. Finally he cited consecutive entries relating to places
called *Heantun*, one being the Winchester estate at Hinton Ampner, Hants, and
the other no less than Wolverhampton in Staffordshire. "It begins to look,"
continued Finberg, "as if the Winchester scribes took the opportunity to
copy out as many Old English charters as they could lay their hands on. And
where, we may ask, did they find all these documents recording grants of land
in distant shires, grants made by kings to laymen? Where, if not in the royal
archives, which in their day, let us remember, were still housed at Winchester?"

Professor Finberg modestly claimed this discovery to be no more than a
hypothesis, for others to test by more detailed examination of the contents of
the *Codex*, a suggestion I found sufficiently attractive to cause me to attempt
the present study. Let us now explore, in the light of Finberg's hypothesis, the
charters entered in the *Codex*, as listed in the appendix to this paper.

[1] E. John, 'The Church of Winchester and the Tenth Century Reformation', *Bull. John Rylands
Library*, 47, 1965, pp. 404–29.

[2] Professor M. Deansley has pointed out that a prebendal system was established at Christ Church,
Canterbury, as early as 832.—*The Pre-Conquest Church in England*, London, 1961, p. 314.

[3] ECWM, pp. 21–2.

There can be no doubt that most of the charters were grouped according to the names of the places conveyed. Thus entries 28–34 relate to Ebbesborne, 35–9 to Alresford, 40–52 to Taunton and its members, 53–5 to Pitminster, 56–61 to places called *Clere*, 62–7 to places called *Meon(e)*, 68–70 to Poolhampton, and so on. No. 89 concerning an estate called *Risctun* was misread by the cartulary compiler as *Rimtun* and included therefore in the group 87–90, relating (apart from this entry) to the latter estate. One suspects that Nos. 164–5 relating to Enford, Wilts., (*Enedforda*) are grouped with Nos. 163 and 166 relating to Wroughton and Lydiard Millicent, Wilts., (*Ellendune*) because of a superficial similarity in the O.E. names.

Note that while the arrangement is topographical, it is not alphabetical; evidently the compilers thought that all the charters grouped under a single name referred to the same place. With these examples in mind, let us pass on now to consideration of the interesting groups of charters which relate in fact to *different* estates bearing the same name.

Nos. 71–3 and No. 75 concern places called *Mordune*. The last-mentioned text is the will of the ætheling Athelstan, by which Morden in Cambridgeshire was given to the Old Minster; the location is confirmed by the DB entry for this estate. Nos. 71–3, however, are royal grants to thegns of Moredon in Rodbourne Cheney, near Swindon, Wilts., which also became for a while a Winchester property;[1] at other times it was in the possession of Malmesbury[2] and Abingdon.[3]

Nos. 118–24 concern places named *Stoce*. The two first have been located at Longstock, Hants, the next at South Stoke, Sussex;[4] the next at Alverstoke, Hants; the next at Odstock, Wilts.; and the last at Stoke by Hurstbourne, Hants. (No. 123, the famous diploma of Hurstbourne Priors, was included in this group because of its relationship to this last charter, No. 124.[5]) Of these, only Stoke by Hurstbourne is known to have been at any time a Winchester property. Odstock was possibly included within the hundred of Downton (No. 29). All the remainder are royal landbooks issued to thegns.

Nos. 125–30 relate to places named *Eastun*. The first is Easton near Winchester, which was a cathedral property. No. 126 has not yet been located, but the occurrence of a *crundel* in the bounds points to somewhere in the West country. Nos. 127 and 128 concern Church Aston and Aston in Wellington respectively, both in Shropshire; the second of these two charters was issued at Glastonbury at the request of a monk who came, presumably, from that house. Next comes a diploma of Little Aston, Staffs. The group is then completed by a charter of another cathedral property named *Eastun*, comprising

---

[1] R LIII.   [2] CS 185.   [3] K 1305.
[4] This charter was issued to replace one that had been burnt.
[5] Discussed by H. P. R. Finberg in *Lucerna*, London, 1964, p. 141.

the eastern part of Avington, near Winchester. Apart from the two charters issued for Winchester cathedral estates, all the others in this group are royal landbooks to thegns; again, there is no evidence that Winchester ever possessed the estates concerned.

Nos. 139 and 140 are charters for places called *Heantune*. As we have seen already, the first of these is Wolverhampton in Staffordshire, the second Hinton Ampner in Hampshire, which came into the possession of the church of Winchester. Nos. 147–51 form a second group of related texts. No. 147 is a charter granting Hinton Ampner to the church of South Stoneham, near Southampton. No. 148 also concerns South Stoneham. No. 149 relates to *Wenbeorg(en)*, *que modo Hynyton dicitur*, and the bounds are of Little Hinton, Wilts. Nos. 150 and 151 deal with the same estate, which was also a Winchester property.

Of the *Hammes* in Nos. 141–4, all but the last relate to Ham in Wiltshire, and derive ultimately from two membranes attached to each other. The estate was given to the Old Minster 933 × 939. No. 144 however conveys land at East and West Ham, Essex, to Ealdorman Athelstan.[1]

Nos. 187–90 deal with places called *Wudetune*; they relate to Wootton, Oxon., Wootton St Lawrence, Hants, an estate as yet unidentified,[2] and Wootton-under-Edge, Glos., in that order. The Hampshire property descended to the Old Minster; but the estates conveyed by the other three, all royal grants to thegns, were never Winchester property as far as can be ascertained.

Finally, No. 215 concerning *Uferantun* (East Overton, Wilts.) is followed by No. 216 concerning *Ofærtune* (Orton Waterville, Hunts.[3]). The former belonged to Winchester by the time of DB, but the latter estate is unlikely ever to have been Winchester property, and one may hazard a guess that both these charters were included in the cartulary simply because the Old Minster possessed a prebendal estate at *Uferantun* or Overton, Hants (Nos. 17, 56).

Here we have ample vindication of Professor Finberg's hypothesis, for there can be but one satisfactory explanation of all these remarkable coincidences. The materials entered in the *Codex* are derived from two distinct sources, the

---

[1] In *The Early Charters of Essex: The Saxon Period*, Leicester, 1957, p. 14, I gave a misleading account of this charter, which I am pleased to take this opportunity to rectify. The recipient of East and West Ham was not Ealdorman Athelstan of East Anglia, the "Half King," who was dead by 958; he must have been Athelstan "Rota," who became Ealdorman of Essex in 956. Furthermore, there are no "errors in the witness list" for which I blamed the copyist of the *Codex*; the error was in fact my own, due to a careless misreading of a comment of Miss Robertson in R, p. 338. East and West Ham passed into the possession of Westminster, probably before the end of the tenth century; CS 1264, the charter recording this, is spurious as it stands but there is no need to question the information it conveys.

[2] On the location, see my forthcoming *Early Charters of Northern England and the North Midlands*.

[3] On the location, see ECEE, pp. 22–3.

original title deeds to the Old Minster estates being supplemented extensively by charters drawn from a large and comprehensive collection, which can only have been that forming the archives of the Anglo-Saxon royal house.[1]

Whoever made this selection were presumably under the impression that these royal diplomas recorded the earlier history of estates that had since become cathedral property, and in this assumption they were often correct. But not always, for they failed to take into account two fundamental characteristics of Old English topography, which continue to bedevil scholarship to the present day. The first is that place-names like *Mordune*, *Stoce*, *Eastun(e)*, *Heantune*, *Hamme*, *Wudetune*, and *Uferantun* were very common, each being applied to a substantial number of sites scattered widely over the English countryside. Secondly, right up to the time of the Norman Conquest, individual settlements along valleys such as those of the *Ebbesburna*, *Cleare*, *Meone*, and *Wylye* often named themselves after the parent river, without any distinguishing prefixes or suffixes.

The repercussions of the former circumstance on the structure of the *Codex* we have examined already; it remains now to be seen if the second factor was also at play as the royal collection was searched for charters to reinforce the cathedral archives.

Let us open this section of our inquiry with a consideration of charters Nos. 30–4 in the *Codex*, five diplomas issued between 947 and 986, each relating to 5 hides at *Ebbesburna*, each being a conveyance to a thegn. Writing in 1955, Professor Darlington stated "the grants . . . presumably relate to Bishopstone, since the preservation of the documents in the *Codex Wintoniensis* raises the presumption that the lands were subsequently given to Winchester."[2] We have shown already how dangerous such an assumption can be, but as a matter of fact these estates *did* descend to Winchester Cathedral, all being included within the 45 hides at Ebbesborne restored to the Old Minster in 997 by the authentic No. 29. Evidently they had been alienated some time between 901 (No. 106) and 947 (No. 31). As to the locations, the boundary clauses show that Nos. 31 and 33 indeed related to Bishopstone; but No. 30 concerned Odstock, No. 32 part of Stratford Tony, and No. 34 Coombe Bissett.[3] It seems likely that all five of these charters were drawn from the royal collection.

Turning now to Nos. 56–61 relating to places called *Cle(a)re*, the key charter is No. 57, which appears to be authentic, with bounds describing the eastern half of Highclere. By this diploma, dated 955, the estate was given to the bishop

---

[1] That such a selection was possible implies that the charters in the royal collection were filed in alphabetical order according to the estates conveyed. See Appendix I for the filing process of the royal archives.

[2] *VCH Wilts.*, II, p. 84.

[3] ECW, Nos. 265, 279, 287, 292, and 320. The bounds rule out Coombe Bissett and Homington for No. 279, leaving Odstock.

of Winchester, who bequeathed it to his kinsmen some time before 959.[1] The property was back in the possession of Winchester Cathedral by the time of Domesday; it may be presumed that the restoration dates from the time of King Edgar. Two other entries in this group, Nos. 59 and 60, have bounds which are copies of those of No. 57. Both charters seem to be Winchester forgeries, the text of the former being copied *verbatim* from the genuine No. 195.[2] We are left with three charters, Nos. 56, 58, and 61, which relate to estates which had no known connection with the Old Minster; they concern land in the western half of Highclere, at Burghclere, and at Ecchinswell. Of these, No. 61 is one of the important *flebilia fortiter* diplomas discussed recently by Eric John.[3] It was witnessed at Colchester in 931, and conveys Ecchinswell to an abbot named Ælfric whose house was probably New Minster; certainly the Old Minster had no abbot at this or at any other time.[4] The religious lady Ælfswith, the recipient of Burghclere by No. 58, was presumably connected with Wilton.

The *Cle(a)re* group of charters is followed in the *Codex* by six entries relating to *Meon(e)*, Nos. 62–7. East Meon was held at the time of DB by the bishop of Winchester, but there is no evidence that he or his predecessors ever held the land at West Meon, conveyed to a thegn by No. 65.

In 946 Ealdorman Æthelwold left 12 hides at *Wilig* to the Old Minster (No. 153). The estate is probably to be equated with the 10 hides at Codford and Stockton in the Wylye valley which belonged to Winchester Cathedral at the time of Domesday.[5] The *Codex* group of charters concerning lands in the Wylye valley includes one dated 901 by which this estate was granted to someone called Æthelwulf (No. 155).[6] Two later charters in this group (Nos. 152 and 154), both grants to thegns, concern estates which do not appear ever to have been Winchester property.

So far we have not discussed the date at which selection may have been made of deeds from the royal muniments to reinforce those of the cathedral. Professor Finberg postulated that this occurred at the time that the *Codex* was being compiled, i.e. *c.* 1130×1150, and so far the present investigation has yielded

---

[1] W IV; ECW, p. 228.

[2] The bounds of No. 59 are in O.E., an anachronism for the date claimed, A.D. 749.

[3] E. John, *Orbis Britanniae*, Leicester, 1966, pp. 49–51.

[4] Ælfric heads the abbots witnessing the following charters of the period 931 × 934: CS 674–7, 689, 691–2, 635 (a New Minster charter of Athelstan dated 11 Jan. 933, which has been amended by the substitution of King Edward's name), 695, and 702. In the *Codex* rubric to No. 61 he is "promoted" to bishop, no doubt to support the inference that this is an Old Minster estate. See footnote 6 below for a similar "promotion."

[5] ECW, p. 88.

[6] The rubric claims him to be a bishop, but there is no known bishop of this name alive in 901, either at Winchester or elsewhere. In the body of the charter, the failure to give any title to Æthelwulf the recipient is most unusual, and I suspect that some such word as minister has been deleted from the original text by the *Codex* copyist, so that the rubric should not be contradicted.

nothing to contradict this view. If we consider Nos. 53–5 relating to Pitminster for instance, two of these diplomas were issued to a thegn in 938 and 941, and, from analogy with other groups of charters in the *Codex*, we would expect these to have been drawn from the royal muniments. The third charter in the group, however, records the gift of this property to the Old Minster in 1044, so that the two earlier charters are unlikely to have been transferred from one set of muniments to the other before that date. Similar considerations apply to Nos. 68–70 relating to Poolhampton, to Nos. 76–7 relating to Witney, to Nos. 136–8 relating to Millbrook, and to Nos 139–40 relating to places called *Heantune*; in all of these cases the transfer of muniments is unlikely to have occurred before the mid-eleventh century.

The possibility remains, however, that some transfers of this kind had been taking place for many years prior to the compilation of the *Codex*. The process may have been initiated soon after the Benedictine reform. Three charters Nos. 81–3 relating to Harwell, Berkshire, are a case in point. All three are grants to thegns, of the type commonly selected from the royal collection to reinforce evidence of the cathedral's ownership. Presumably therefore the Old Minster acquired land at Harwell some time between 985 (the date of No. 82) and the Norman Conquest, for it was a Domesday possession of the cathedral. But if we examine No. 83 in detail, we find that it underwent some revision before its entry into the *Codex*. Its text is similar to that of CS 968, a diploma of King Eadwig dated 956.[1] In the Harwell charter, however, King Edgar's name has been substituted for that of the donor, King Eadwig, and two resulting substitutions appear in the witness list.[2]

There is a simple reason for these alterations, for the titles of many charters issued in the troubled years of King Eadwig's reign were suspect in the generation after his death, and it appears to have been a common practice of the Benedictine reformers to amend them.[3] With this in mind, there can be little doubt that the rehabilitated text of No. 83, with the original personal names restored, represents a genuine charter issued by King Eadwig in 956, the first year of his

[1] This charter is entered in a fourteenth-century hand on fol. 27ᵛ of BM Cott. Tib. B. v, an early eleventh-century miscellany of Winchester origin, which was at Battle Abbey in the twelfth and thirteenth centuries; cf. N. Ker, *Catalogue of MSS Containing Anglo-Saxon*, Oxford, 1957, pp. 255–6. The estate conveyed was at Zeal and Donhead, Wilts.; cf. ECW, No. 280.

[2] Dunstan takes the place of Oda as archbishop of Canterbury, and the name of Ealdorman Ælfhere has been substituted for that of the ætheling Edgar, the later king.

[3] CS 1022 from Abingdon, issued in 958 some time after 2 June, has Eadwig's name displaced by that of King Eadred. So has CS 1024 from Evesham, dated by the witness list 956. CS 1150, a *Codex* charter (No. 15), ascribes to King Eadred a transaction recorded in CS 938, another *Codex* charter (No. 37) which is in fact a diploma of King Eadwig; cf. ECW, p. 238, n. 3. CS 1005, a charter of Eadwig dated 957, is ascribed to King Edgar in the rubric to its entry in the Abingdon cartulary. CS 1023 is a charter from the Wells archives, issued by Edgar while king of the Mercians, and dated 5 May 957 × 2 June 958, in which Edgar's name has been ousted by that of Eadred. A similar substitution is made in CS 1021 dated 958, a charter which found its way into the Burton muniments.

reign. The amendments recorded in the *Codex* version were concerned with preserving the charter's validity as a title deed, a question unlikely to have been of more than academic importance after the first quarter of the eleventh century. Moreover, they could hardly have been made while the charter was filed in the royal archives, for King Eadwig's successors stood to gain nothing from such an alteration. Validity of title was the concern of the holder of the land; it seems likely therefore that the substitutions in the text were made after the deed had been transferred from the royal muniments to those of the cathedral, possibly at the turn of the tenth century.

Just the same argument applies in the case of No. 179, one of a group of *Codex* charters relating to Woolstone, Berks., another Domesday estate of Winchester Cathedral which must have been acquired in or before the reign of the Confessor. Here again, an authentic diploma of King Eadwig dated 958 has been amended, by the substitution of the name of King Eadred as the donor. But the most important example for our purpose is that of No. 129, one of the *Eastun* charters that has been discussed already. It relates to land in Staffordshire which could never have belonged to Winchester, and the strong supposition is that this charter was originally in the royal collection. As with No. 179, the name of the donor, King Eadwig, has been altered to Eadred. The amendment may have been made when the charter was transferred to the cathedral muniments, possibly in this case soon after the reformation of the chapter in 964, for Easton near Winchester had been given to the bishop in 961 (No. 125).

Evidence of a rather different kind, but pointing to the same conclusion, comes from the *Codex* entries concerning a certain Æthelgeard, who was one of the most powerful Wessex thegns of the mid-tenth century. His interests were centred on Winchester where he held considerable property, especially at the eastern end of the town,[1] and he left land to the New Minster for the souls of himself and his wife; it seems likely that they were buried there, and that he is the Æthelgeard *preñg* whose name appears in a list of benefactors to that house.[2] No less than eight charters survive in the *Codex*,[3] and one in the Hyde Abbey Register (formerly New Minster),[4] by which successive kings from Athelstan to Eadwig grant him over 70 hides in the Thames valley near Wallingford, and in East Hampshire, mostly in the Meon valley. In addition, he received 5 hides at *Niwantun* (possibly Newtown, Berks, near Sotwell),[5] and another 5 hides in the Isle of Wight which he probably gave to Evesham, for Evesham owned the estate at the time of Domesday and it is in the Evesham

---

[1] *Codex* Nos. 184, 86.

[2] W VI; *Liber Vitæ: Register and Martyrology of New Minster and Hyde Abbey*, Winchester, ed. W. de Gray Birch, Hampshire Record Society, 1892, p. 22.

[3] *Codex* Nos. 65, 184, 85–6, 78, 80, 91, 116.   [4] CS 988.

[5] CS 944, a charter which strayed into the archives of Wulfric Spot's eleventh-century foundation at Burton-on-Trent. Other charters in this abbey's register relate to lands in Oxfordshire and Wiltshire.

cartulary that the text of the grant is preserved.[1] Towards the end of his career, Æthelgeard rose to third in the hierarchy of thegns in constant attendance upon the king. Some of his charters show evidence of this special service to the royal family;[2] he knew the æthelings in their childhood,[3] and King Eadwig called him his *carus*.[4] It is noteworthy that Æthelgeard remained true to Eadwig after Edgar's revolt in 957;[5] when Eadwig died and Edgar succeeded, Æthelgeard disappeared from the pages of history, whether by death or disgrace we do not know.[6]

Æthelgeard's estates near Wallingford had once been the property of the bishops of Winchester, having formed part of King Æthelwulf's Second Decimation of 854.[7] In return the bishop was to bear the cost of entertaining distinguished foreign visitors to Winchester, an indication of the town's importance as the West Saxon capital. Alienation occurred, however, before the end of the first half of the tenth century, and the estates were given piecemeal to Æthelgeard; in 947 he received 10 hides at Brightwell (No. 80), a year later 5 hides at Sotwell and 5 more at Mackney (No. 91), and finally in 957 a further 15 hides at Sotwell (CS 988). One can only speculate whether with the receipt of these properties Æthelgeard inherited the duties of entertaining foreign visitors. Certainly his extensive Winchester possessions would have enabled him to do this without difficulty. Serjeantry in England was not unknown before the Norman Conquest.

When he died Æthelgeard left the reversion of his Sotwell estate to New Minster, and the remaining 20 hides near Wallingford descended to the Old Minster, so restoring to the cathedral most of the land there originally granted by King Æthelwulf a century previously. Æthelgeard's Exton property (*Codex* No. 184) also came into the cathedral's possession,[8] presumably at the same time as the Brightwell estate;[9] both were retained by Winchester after the Norman Conquest.

---

[1] CS 1025. The formulas of the proem, dispositive, and immunity clauses of this undated fragment were not evolved until 958 (CS 1023, 1034–5), to which year it should be assigned.

[2] E.g. the dispositive clauses of *Codex* Nos. 65, 80.

[3] *Codex* No. 78, a charter of King Eadred wrongly dated 945. See p. 17, n. 3.

[4] CS 944.   [5] He witnesses several of Eadwig's charters, but none of Edgar's, in that year.

[6] In addition to those charters already discussed, Æthelgeard witnesses the following royal diplomas: CS 705, R xxv (934); CS 707 (935); CS 775 (942); CS 783, 787, 789 (943); CS 791–2, 795, 798, 802 (944); CS 808 (945); CS 814, 818 (946); CS 820–1, 824, 830, 832–4 (947); CS 866, 868–71 (948); CS 875, 877, 879, 882–3, 888 (949); CS 891–2 (951); CS 895 (952); CS 905, 917 (955); CS 919, 921, 924–5, 927, 930, 932, 934–5, 938, 942–3, 948–9, 952–3, 955, 957–66, 970–1, 973–4, 977, 979, 981–3, 985, 1024 (956); CS 1002 (*c.* 956); CS 1009 (956 × 957); CS 987, 992, 994, 997–9, 1001, 1003–4 (957); CS 1032 (before 2 June 958). In the text of CS 976 (*Codex* No. 116) he is given the title of an ealdorman, but the rubric correctly calls him a thegn.

[7] *Codex* No. 79; ECW, p. 203.   [8] It was given by King Edgar, cf. WCD, p. 64.

[9] Possibly the 30 hides at Brightwell given to the bishop of Winchester in 854 formed part of the hundred of Cholsey, all of which was in Winchester's possession in 879 × 899, when it was returned to the king in exchange for 50 hides at Chisledon and 60 at Hurstbourne Priors (No. 196).

One may suppose that some, if not all, of Æthelgeard's charters reached the *Codex* via the royal collection, for the lands conveyed by Nos. 65, 85–6, and 116 appear never to have become Winchester property.[1] Yet Æthelgeard's No. 80, as Professor Finberg has established, was used as an exemplar for the attestations to the spurious *Codex* entries Nos. 28 and 42, composed by the Winchester monks at the end of the tenth century or soon afterwards.[2] The witness list appears also to have been utilized when No. 78 was fabricated, probably at about the same period.[3]

More detailed work of this sort is needed before the *Codex* yields all its secrets, but the general pattern is beginning to emerge. Soon after the Bene-

[1] Nos. 85–6 are two very interesting charters by King Edmund for Æthelgeard, relating to 7 hides at West Tisted, Hants. The former was issued in 941 from the royal estate at Cheddar, Somerset, and utilizes formulas common in the early diplomas of King Athelstan, whence the detailed dating clause, constructed from an Easter table. Evidently the transcriber could not read the incarnation date clearly, so he supplied it from the indiction; unfortunately he chose the wrong decennovenal cycle, giving 960 for the supplied date instead of 941. The epact is two years out for either 941 or 960, but such an error is all too easy to make when reading an Easter table, and in no way invalidates the record of this transaction. The indiction, concurrent, and regnal year are all right for 941, and the witness list is compatible. This is a wholly convincing charter, and I see no good reason why Professor Whitelock should have stigmatized it as "doubtful" (*Anglo-Saxon Charters*, ed. P. H. Sawyer, Roy. Hist. Soc., 1968, p. 192, No. 511). The second West Tisted charter, No. 86, was issued two years later because the former one had been mislaid—"*ideo scripsimus novam cartulam quia antiquum librum non habebamus,*" (a phrase repeated in CS 757, 801, and with variations in Nos. 123 and 162), so the whole thing had to be done again, including the drawing up of a completely fresh set of bounds for this estate. It looks as if the "lost" charter was stored away in the king's *haligdom* all the time.

[2] ECW, p. 236, n. 7.

[3] The four charters relating to Æthelgeard's estates near Wallingford must be considered as a group (*Codex* Nos. 78, 80, 86, and the New Minster text CS 988). Of these, the surviving texts of No. 80 and CS 988 may be accepted as wholly authentic. No. 86 is also basically authentic, but has two late interpolations, discussed below. No. 78, however, bears all the marks of forgery. The witness list has been lifted from No. 80, and is incompatible with the ostensible date, 945. Incidentally, the forms of attestation of the witnesses do not appear elsewhere in authentic charters of a date earlier than 946, e.g. CS 818. The boundary clause is in three parts, the first describing the land conveyed by No. 80, and the second that of CS 988; the third section repeats part of the boundary clause of No. 86, relating to property within the town of Wallingford, and land just to the north of the ancient town wall (for a reconstructed map of Wallingford at the time of the Norman Conquest, see *VCH Berks.*, I, p. 365). It seems therefore that the 30 hides said to be conveyed by this charter comprise the 10 hides of No. 80 plus the 15 hides of CS 988, plus the unhidated portion of No. 86. The reason for making all this come to 30 hides is plain enough; the conveyance is intended to represent the same territory as in King Æthelwulf's Decimation Charter, the authentic No. 79. Yet it does appear possible that No. 78 is a heavily modified version of a lost authentic diploma issued by King Eadwig in 957–8 to confirm the three donations recorded in Nos. 80, 86, and CS 988. The invocation to the surviving text, for example, is found elsewhere only in a few charters of the years 995 × 997 (CS 909, 949, 956–7, 995), and the reference in the dispositive clause to the king's childhood is convincing. Whether No. 78 is completely fabricated or just a heavily amended version of an authentic charter, the surviving form of the text is likely to be due to the activities of Benedictine revisionists in the late tenth century. Unhappily, the matter is further complicated by a much later interpolation in the texts of both No. 78 and No. 86, referring to the *castellum* at Wallingford. Wallingford castle was a Norman structure, so these interpolations are probably due to the compilers of the *Codex*. To the same period must be assigned the anachronistic reference to Bishop Æthelwold introduced into the boundary clause of No. 86.

dictine reformation of 964, the Winchester monks began to reconstruct the cathedral muniments to bring them into line with their newly acquired endowment of lands and liberties. Undoubtedly the driving force was their great bishop Æthelwold, whose influence with the young King Edgar enabled him to bring about substantial changes in land tenure and in seignorial jurisdiction over the estates of his new monastic foundations. In their turn these innovations resulted in a considerable development of the work and organization of the monastic scriptoria and muniment rooms. It seems likely that at the Old Minster, the heart of the reform movement, the monks were uniquely placed as custodians of the royal *haligdom*, from which they abstracted earlier landbooks concerning (as they thought) their newly acquired estates, both in order to supplement the evidence of the cathedral archives, and also possibly to make it more difficult for descendants of previous owners to re-establish claims to their ancestors' property. This transfer of old land titles from the royal repository to the cathedral's own muniment collection soon became a routine process, which was repeated right up to the Norman Conquest every time a property was newly acquired by the cathedral.

This theory postulates first that the later Anglo-Saxon kings kept copies of the royal landbooks issued by them, and secondly that this royal collection was housed at Winchester, at least during the last century of the Anglo-Saxon state. As to the first assumption, in the tenth and eleventh centuries the royal diplomas themselves are silent on this matter; but in the ninth century the Mercian royal house kept a collection of its land charters stored at Winchcombe (CS 384; cf. ECWM p. 229), and *Codex* No. 198 shows that the West Saxon kings similarly kept duplicates of diplomas issued by them, which they filed with "the charters of the royal inheritance." In an appendix to this paper I argue that the Old English endorsements to the royal land charters were made for ease of reference when they came to be filed in the royal archives, and that the custom originated in Wessex in 854 and was perpetuated until the Norman Conquest. For the period 995 × 1053 we have evidence that vernacular copies of wills and of monastic and private charters were often placed *æt thæs cinges haligdome*.[1] The *haligdom* was the royal sanctuary or chapel where holy relics were kept; if private titles to land were preserved there, we may be sure that so too were the solemn royal diplomas, the sacredness of which was protected by the most formidable anathemas.

But was the *haligdom* at Winchester, at some other place, or peripatetic with the king? There are good grounds for believing that by the end of the tenth

---

[1] W XVI, XXX; R LXXV, CXV. Similar references occur in late Latin translations of O.E. vernacular documents, e.g. *Liber Eliensis*, ed. E. O. Blake, Roy. Hist. Soc., 1962, pp. 157–8, and *Chronicon Abbatiæ Rameseiensis*, ed W. Dunn Macray, London, 1886, p. 172. The topic was discussed recently by Professor F. Barlow in *The English Church, 1000–1066*, London, 1963, pp. 122–4.

century the collection of royal diplomas was large and comprehensive, covering bookland in the whole of England south of the Humber.[1] At a conservative estimate it must have numbered several thousand charters, and it seems to me highly unlikely that it was carried about on the royal perambulations.

It was from the Winchester scriptorium (surely that of the Old Minster) that the scribes came who drafted the royal landbooks of the period 931–63,[2] and the Anglo-Saxon Chronicle was being compiled there by the same group of people at this period. What happened to the production of royal diplomas during the last century before the Norman Conquest is still a matter for debate, but we know that the king's treasury was established at Winchester by 1036, and that Domesday Book was compiled and kept there. Sometimes kings were consecrated and buried at the Old Minster; sometimes they held their councils and wore their crown there. If the evidence of the *Codex* has been interpreted correctly, the royal charter collection was undoubtedly kept at Winchester at some time between 1045 and 1150,[3] and the same evidence suggests that the former date should be amended to 964. There is indeed a good case for supposing that the royal charter archives (first for Wessex only, later for all England south of the Humber) were stored at Winchester during the whole of the three centuries following King Æthelwulf's famous Second Decimation of 854. Support on general grounds for such a conclusion is forthcoming from the growing evidence for the development in England of a strong and sophisticated machinery of central government from the time of Edward the Elder onwards. It can confidently be predicted that closer examination of the structure and contents of the *Codex* will shed further light on these and related themes.

It would be wrong however to conclude this review without noticing that the *Codex* is far from being a comprehensive record of all the Anglo-Saxon charters available at the Old Minster at the time of its compilation. The cathedral muniments suffered disastrous depredation at the hands of Cromwell's soldiers, and when in 1643 John Chase, the chapter clerk, catalogued such few title deeds as had been salvaged by the townsfolk, of the thirty listed items of pre-Conquest date no less than half refer to texts which had not been entered in the *Codex*.[4] Many of these of course may have come originally from the royal archive collection—for example, diplomas relating to Conington, Hunts.,[5] to Newnham

---

[1] If we have interpreted the *Codex* correctly, the royal collection was sufficiently large to include several charters conveying lands in different places having the same place-name such as *Eaton*, *Stoce*, etc. Of the charters entered in the *Codex*, no less than 86 could possibly have been drawn from the royal archives; these are marked "k" in the handlist forming Appendix II to this paper.

[2] P. Chaplais 'The Origin and Authenticity of the Royal Anglo-Saxon Diploma', *Jnl Soc. of Archivists*, III, 1965, particularly pp. 59–61.

[3] See, further, the references cited in ECWM, p. 22, n. 3.   [4] WCD, pp. 59–64.

[5] †CS 1003.

Murren, Oxon.,[1] and to Madeley near Newcastle under Lyme in Staffordshire.[2] In the same category we may place the remarkable diploma by which King Æthelwulf booked to himself land at South Hams, Devon; although this does not appear in Chase's Catalogue, he certainly recovered it for the chapter muniments, for it is endorsed in his own hand.[3] But several of the charters listed by Chase must have been kept in the Old Minster's own muniment collection from the outset, and among these appear such major items as a copy of King Æthelwulf's First Decimation, and a diploma of King Alfred relating to the hundred of Chilcomb, as well as several straightforward grants to the minster, such as those of *Wolferdyngton* (possibly Wolverton, Hants) and Exton, Hants.

We may note too that some Old Minster charters which reached the Cottonian collection were neither entered in the *Codex* nor listed by Chase.[4] The same applies to at least two charters that came into the possession of Harley,[5] and also to a number of O.E. writs.[6] The *Codex* is indeed notably deficient in O.E. material, although there must have been large numbers of wills and private charters sent to the Old Minster for safe keeping in the king's *haligdom*. One has only to recall the masses of vernacular texts surviving to a late date at Bury St Edmunds, and underlying the Latin transcripts preserved in the Liber Eliensis and the Ramsey Chronicle, to appreciate just how much similar material at the Old Minster has been lost irretrievably.

APPENDIX I

CONTEMPORARY ENDORSEMENTS TO THE ROYAL LANDBOOKS

When the scribe of a royal diploma of the Anglo-Saxon period had finished writing the last name of the witness list and ensured that the ink was dry, he would habitually fold it several times horizontally and vertically. In so doing, two purposes would be served; the dimensions of the membrane would be reduced, so facilitating transportation and storage, and the writing itself would be protected from dirt, rubbing, and fading, for the folds were always made inwards. And in the course of time, so that one folded membrane could be distinguished from another without going to the trouble of unfolding it, the scribes evolved the custom of endorsing one of the outside panels as soon as the charter had been folded.

Little is known about contemporary endorsements to royal diplomas issued before

---

[1] †CS 1176.   [2] †CS 1312.

[3] †CS 451. This charter has recently been discussed by Professor Finberg, in *West-Country Historical Studies*, 1969, pp. 11–23.

[4] The collection of Cotton Charters at the British Museum includes original Anglo-Saxon texts from Evesham, Westminster, Rochester, and Winchester (Old Minster), with a single late item from Canterbury (K 742). The charters which are probably of Old Minster provenance include CS 181, 225, 451, 469, 1083, and W III and R cxviii.

[5] *CS 1145, ***K 1335.   [6] H, Nos. 109, 110, 111.

the reign of Athelstan. With the exception of two examples from the East Saxon diocese (CS 81, 111), our earliest evidence is confined to charters preserved by the see of Canterbury; in the first quarter of the ninth century these were sometimes endorsed with the name of the place conveyed, followed by the word *bo[e]c* (e.g. CS 289, 326, 343, 400; and see E. John, *Orbis Britanniae*, Leicester, 1966, p. 74). A small subgroup of these Kentish texts has endorsements with rather more detailed topographical descriptions (CS 373, 380–1), and in the earliest of these the word *landboc* first appears. CS 416 shows that Mercian charters of a slightly later date could bear still more elaborate endorsements, but these did not, apparently, keep to any fixed formula, and we have to return to Kentish evidence to trace the next steps in the development of the stereotyped phraseology which characterizes contemporary endorsements to royal charters issued in the last two centuries of the Anglo-Saxon state.

CS 467 is an original diploma which should probably be dated 853 and is endorsed ✠*ðis sindan ðes landesbec et uluham, ealdheres landes* in a contemporary hand. CS 496 dated 858 is another original Kentish diploma, famous for its reference to folkland, with a contemporary endorsement commencing ✠*ðis siondan ðes landesboec et Wassingwellan ðet Eðelbearht cyning Wullafe sealde his ðegne. . .*[1] We need have no difficulty, therefore, in accepting the evidence of a late copyist that CS 469, concerning land in Wiltshire, was originally endorsed ✠*ðis seondan ðes landes bec ðe Æðelulf cyning Wiferde his ðegne salde*, an important prototype formula which we shall call F₁. Professor Finberg has shown this text to be an authentic copy of one of King Æthelwulf's famous

'Second Decimation' charters of 22 April 854,[2] and the *Codex Wintoniensis* also preserves copies of two authentic charters in this series (Nos. 79 and 160), headed respectively by the rubrics *ðis is thara. xxx. hida boc æt Brihtanwylle th(æt) Athelwlf cing gæbocade into Ealdan Mynstræ*, and *this is ðara. iii. hida boc to Worðie ðae Æthelwulf cing bocode Hunsie his thegne on ece yrfe*. This second version forms another important prototype which we shall call F₂.

A full examination has yet to be made of the part played by the text of Æthelwulf's Second Decimation in the development of charter diplomatic, but already there can be no doubt as to its importance; the invocation, for example, immediately became the normal form for West Saxon diplomas issued in the second half of the ninth century. It will now be shown how the two prototypes F₁ and F₂ guided the evolution of the formulas of endorsement to the royal Anglo-Saxon land charters.

Within two decades of F₁ we have the following *Codex* rubric (No. 159):[3] *ðis seond ðæs landes boc thæ Æðelred cing Hunsige his thegen saldæ æt Worðie*. The rubric to a further *Codex* charter, dated 901 (No. 155), runs: *ðis is thæra land boc to biWilig thæ Eadweard cing gebocade Aðelwulf biscope on æce yrfe*; another, dated 928 (No. 122), runs: *ðis is seo land boc to Stoce the Edelstan cing gebocade Byrhtferthæ his thegne on ece yrfæ*. Nine years later, the rubric to a Wilton charter (CS 714)[4] reads as follows: *This is Brydancumbes land boc the Æthelstan cing gebocade tham hiwan at Wiltane . . . on eche yrfe*, which led the following year to the fully developed formula of yet another *Codex* entry (No. 90), which we shall label F₃: *This is Rimtunes land boc de Æthelstan cing gebocade Ætherede his thegne on ece yrfæ*. From 938 onwards, formula F₃ was endorsed on *Codex* charters

---

[1] Cf John, *op. cit.*, pp. 106, 112–13. *Sealde* comes from the verb *sellan*, which meant 'to give' at this date, without necessarily implying a money transaction.

[2] ECW, ch. vi, a fundamental contribution to our knowledge of the development of the Anglo-Saxon royal diploma.

[3] The rubrics prefacing charters entered in the *Codex* are accurate copies of the endorsements on the original membranes of these landbooks, as they lay before the cartulary scribes. This is established by comparison of the *Codex* entries with those charters of which the originals or pseudo-originals have survived (see p. 8, n. 1 above). Because of this, the *Codex* greatly increases the evidence otherwise available for investigating the development of contemporary endorsements to royal diplomas of the Anglo-Saxon period.

[4] As with the *Codex*, rubrics to entries in the Wilton cartulary reproduce the endorsements to the charters concerned.

Nos. 176, 184, and 190, and also on the following originals from Kent and Wiltshire: CS 734, 741, and 743, and on two Wilton charters, CS 756 and 782. In diplomas of this group issued after the year 939 the word *landboc* was replaced by *boc*, and the whole formula was discontinued after the year 943.

Turning now to prototype F₂, we have an early development in No. 181 from the *Codex*, dated 856: *ðis is thara. xx. hida boc to Æscesbyrig the Ædelwulf cing gebocade Aldrede his thegne on ece yrfe*, which we shall call formula F₄. This version is not to be found again until 940 (CS 757 from Wilton, and *Codex* charter No. 70),[1] but it was destined to continue unaltered as the main form from then onwards until 961, and sporadically thereafter right up to the Norman Conquest. During this period it is represented by no less than fifty-three examples from the *Codex*,[2] and another thirteen from the Wilton cartulary;[3] the formula appears also in a group of thirteen original charters (and copies of originals) relating to lands in Kent, Berkshire, Oxfordshire, Huntingdonshire, Northamptonshire, Staffordshire, Warwickshire, Cornwall, and Devon.[4]

In 961 an interesting original diploma, CS 1072, which is also entered in the *Codex* (No. 44), was endorsed with the following variant of formula F₄: *This is thæra feower hyda landboc æt Withiglea the Eadgar cing hæfð gebocod*

Cenulfe on ece yrfe.[5] As far as can be ascertained, the substitution of *hæfð gebocod* for *gebocade* occurs only once elsewhere, in another original charter CS 1165 dated 965, relating to land in Dorset.[6] Both these charters also omit the words *his thegne* after the name of the recipient, and they substitute the compound *landboc* for the simple *boc* of earlier charters in the series. This last modification was retained by the majority of contemporary endorsements from 965 onwards, producing a formula we shall call F₅, for which the original CS 1101, a Canterbury charter relating to land in Essex and dated 963, may be quoted as exemplar: *⊹this is thara. vii. hida land boc æt Fengge the Eadgar cyning gebocode Ingerame his thegne on ece yrfe.*

Formula F₅ is well represented in endorsements to royal diplomas issued throughout the last century of the Anglo-Saxon period. Six examples are preserved in the *Codex*,[7] eight in copies of charters from other centres,[8] and a further seven survive as originals.[9] These landbooks relate to properties scattered over Suffolk, Bedfordshire, Middlesex, Oxfordshire, Berkshire, Hampshire, Wiltshire, Somerset, Dorset, and Devon. It should be noted that the three Devon examples have unusual forms in place of the verb *gebocode* which appears elsewhere;[10] it is possible that these were all written at Crediton, but the topic requires further investigation before a firm conclusion

---

[1] I omit three slightly modified examples from the *Codex*, Nos. 65, 54, and 157 (dated 932 × 939), and CS 734, an original Wiltshire charter dated 939 which also has a small modification to the formula.

[2] These are, in chonological order, Nos. 85, 55, 86, 58, 73, 180, 78, 80, 31, 91, 121, 179, 57, 110, 87, 37, 163, 177, 40, 30, 189, 68, 116, 174, 66, 71, 33, 117, 144, 187, 56, 194, 34, 93, 64, 83, 72, 76, 81, 62, 118, 134, 135, 182, 139, 32, 183, 152, 188, 186, 156, 209, 77.

[3] These are, in chronological order, CS 795, 818, 870, 879, 934, 958, 992, 998, 1030, 1031, 1053, 1216, K 778.

[4] These are, in chronological order, CS 791 from Canterbury, CS 877, 892, 895, 965, 966 from Abingdon, CS 986 from Bath, CS 1003 from Winchester, CS 1056 from Bodmin, CS 1295 from Rochester, CS 1303 (repository unknown), CS 1312 probably from Winchester, and K 705 which is possibly from Evesham. The F₄ formula was also doubtless used to endorse the lost charter of King Æthelred concerning East Oakley in Wooton St Lawrence, Hants. ECW, No. 143. WCD, p. 62.

[5] A much later endorsement in the hand of John Chase, the chapter clerk, shows that this charter was at Winchester as late as 1643. WCD, p. 63.

[6] Provenance unknown.

[7] These are, in chronological order, Nos. 125, 126, 145, 82, 53, and 115.

[8] These are, in chronological order, CS 1116 from Wells, CS 1145 and 1176 from Winchester, CS 1221 from Abingdon, CS 1269 from Ely, CS 1309 from Westminster, and K 1318 and 1332 from Sherborne.

[9] These are, in chronological order, CS 1083 probably from Winchester, CS 1085 from Westminster, CS 1103 from Exeter (thought by some to be a later copy), CS 1229 from Worcester, K 744 and 770 of unknown provenance, and K 781 from Winchester.

[10] K 744 *het gebocian*, K 770 *let gebecean*, and K 1332 *let gebocygean*.

can be reached. Another feature of formula F_5 endorsements is that the word *thegne* is often replaced by a more descriptive appellative such as *mæge* (CS 1085), *burhthegne* (CS 1083), *hunta(n)* (K 648), and *huskarle* (K 1318). CS 1229 shows a further elaboration; the recipient, who is described as the king's *leofan, getreowan thegne*, was in fact Ælfwold, the brother of Ealdorman Æthelwine of East Anglia, and a notable supporter of the Benedictine reform.

There remains for consideration a small group of charters bearing unusual endorsements, or having no contemporary endorsement at all. It is surprising how few there are. CS 1040 from Wells, an original issued in 958 and conveying land in Herefordshire, is endorsed *Her is stantunes boc*; a *Codex* entry (No. 127) dated 963 and relating to land in Shropshire is similarly entitled *Her is Eastunes boc and Plesces*. Two more *Codex* texts, concerning lands in Hampshire and Sussex (Nos. 64 and 120, dated 967 and 975), are headed by the rubrics *ðis is seo boc æt Meone* and *ðis is seo boc æt Stoce*. CS 536 is an original Kentish landbook composed in 873; it purports to be a royal diploma, but in fact it was written at Christ Church by someone who was a poor Latinist; it is endorsed *ðis is sia boc æt Gildincge*.[1] Similarly, *Codex* No. 128 dated 975, another text cast in the form of a royal landbook, seems to be a copy of a product of the Glastonbury scriptorium; it was endorsed *this is Ealhhelmes land boc the Eadgar cing him gebocode on ece yrfe æt Eastun*.[2] Crawford Charter No. VIII, an original dated 998 from Evesham, bears a contemporary endorsement using a rather archaic formula: *ðis is thæra landda boc to Sulthham and to Hlodbroce and to Hreodburnan the Æthelred cyninge sealde Leofwine ealdorman on ece yrfe*. Finally, CS 792, 964, 968, 1066, 1082, 1231, and ECDC 37, are original charters which appear not to have been endorsed at the time they were composed; they all come from different sources and the lands conveyed are widely scattered, from Suffolk to Cornwall.

What has emerged from this study is that the great majority of the royal diplomas issued from the reign of Athelstan to that of Edward the Confessor were endorsed at the time of their composition by brief summaries in Old English, following a stereotyped formula. The endorsement gave the names of the estate, the donor, and the recipient, and very often the hidage of the estate conveyed; the date of the transaction was invariably omitted. It would appear that the custom originated in Wessex in the reign of King Æthelwulf, probably as a result of his Second Decimation in 854. There is a strong presumption that these endorsements were made for ease of reference when the charters came to be filed in the royal archives. When copies of the diplomas were made for recipients or for third parties, the

---

[1] This text calls for more attention than has been devoted to it in the past. The scribe was recording a transaction by which the archbishop of Canterbury, with King Alfred's consent, sold to a thegn the life lease of a Kentish estate, with reversion to the *familia*. He made a clumsy job of it, utilizing for his exemplar what purported to be a royal diploma concerning the estate, issued by King Æthelwulf of Wessex in 839 × 851; but this exemplar was itself written by a member of the Christ Church *familia*, for in the boundary clause reference is made to land held by another member of the *familia* who is called *mona[c]hus nostri (sic)*. The witness list to the surviving text is in three parts; the first, from Æthelwulf *rex* to Wulfred, has the attestations followed by *consensi et subscripsi*, and derives from the text of the exemplar. These names are repeated, minus this phrase, in the second part of the list, and I suggest that this section came from a small piece of parchment attached physically to the exemplar, as in CS 442. The third section of the list, from Ceolnoð *archiepiscopus* onwards, contains names which (with one exception) do not appear in the other two sections, and I suspect that these also were originally listed on the attached parchment.

[2] This charter was drawn up at the request of the king's relative, a monk named Ælfwine. The transaction was enacted at Glastonbury and witnessed by all the *familia* there. The remainder of the witness list differs sharply from that of other charters of the period, the names being confined to those of the bishop of Hereford, the ealdorman of Mercia, the abbots of St Albans, Bath, Glastonbury, St Augustines (probably), and Milton, and three thegns, of whom at least one, Ordulf, was probably from the West country. It looks as if the king was visiting Glastonbury with a small retinue, and the transaction was completed on the spot at the request of his relative, a monk there. The text utilized a regular diploma of King Edgar for its exemplar (see CS 1314, 1351 for the formulas). The *Codex* version derives presumably from a copy made for inclusion in the king's *haligdom*.

endorsements were usually copied also, but this was not invariably done, for the recipients would rarely have assembled a large enough set of charters of their own to require the sophisticated filing methods used for the royal collection.[1]

[1] Examples of such local copies survive in the Burton archives preserved at the William Salt Library at Stafford. An unpublished original charter of King Æthelred to his thegn Morcar, granting land in Derbyshire in 1009, is endorsed in capitals: ✠*Westunes Landbóc*. An earlier original granting land to Bishop Wulfric in 968 (CS 1211) is endorsed: *wulfrices boc bisc[eop] æt stantune ā on ece erfe*. Two late eleventh-century copies of charters issued in 956 (CS 954) and 993 (unpublished; Abbots Bromley, Staffs.) are endorsed: ✠*deorlafestunes boc* and ✠*Bedintunes boc*, in each case in the main hand.

APPENDIX II

THE CONTENTS OF THE *CODEX WINTONIENSIS*[1]

Charter No.	Folio No.	Edition	Date	Description
1	6	*H 107	984 × 1001	Chilcomb, Hants. Writ.
2	6	*CS 1160	N.D.	Chilcomb. List of lands forming the hundred.
3	6	*CS 1161	N.D.	List of lands belonging to the Old Minster.
4	6ᵛ	*K 1291	996	A messuage in Winchester to the Old Minster.
5	7	*K 626	980	1½ hides at Calshot, Hants, to the Old Minster.
6	7	***H 112	1053 × 1066	Portland, Dorset. Writ (late insertion).
7	7ᵛ	Unpublished	13th c.	Crondall and Itchell, Hants. Bounds (late insertion).
8	8	*K 1347; R LIII	975 × 979	Exchange by bishop and *familia* of Old Minster: 12 hides at Moreden in Rodbourne Cheney, Hants, for 2 acres in Winchester.
9	8	*CS 605, 1338; Ha XVI	?900	Exchange of land in Winchester.
10	8ᵛ	*CS 1302	968 × 970	Grant of land in Winchester to the three minsters.
11	8ᵛ	*R XLIX	?970 × 975	Exchange of lands etc. in Winchester.

[1] Code of Asterisks: †Original charter extant. *Wholly authentic. **Basically authentic, but incorporating some spurious material. ***Basically spurious, but incorporating some authentic material. For further details, see ECEE, p. 17. All charters are grants by the reigning monarch, unless otherwise stated. Those prefixed by the letter k *possibly* came from the royal archives.

Charter No.	Folio No.	Edition	Date	Description
12	9	**CS 1146	c. 964 × 975	Restoration to Old Minster of 100 hides at Downton, Wilts., and 30 at Bowcombe, I.O.W. Renewal of title of Chilcomb, Hants.
13	9v–10	*CS 1147; R xxxviii	?964 × 975	Renewal of beneficial hidation of Chilcomb.
14	10	*CS 1149	c. 964 × 975	Confirmation to bishopric of Winchester of 100 hides at Taunton, 20 at Stoke by Shalbourne, Wilts., and 30 at Banwell and 10 at Crowcombe, both in Som.
15	10v–11	*CS 1150	?964 × 975	Restoration to Old Minster of 40 hides at Alresford, Hants.
16	11	*CS 1151	?964 × 975	Restoration to Old Minster of 10 hides at *Clere* (High Clere), Hants.
17	11rv	*CS 1152	?964 × 975	Confirmation to Old Minster of 20 hides at Overton, 15 at North Waltham, and 5 at Bradley, all in Hants.
18	11v	*CS 1153	?964 × 975	Confirmation to Old Minster of 60 hides at Tichborne, Beauworth, and Ovington, all in Hants.
19	11v–12	*CS 1154	?964 × 975	Confirmation to Old Minster of 60 hides at Farnham, Surrey, and 10 at Bentley, Hants.
20	12	*CS 1155	?964 × 975	Confirmation to Old Minster of 70 hides at Beddington, Surrey, with appurtenant woodland.
21	12rv	*CS 1156	?964 × 975	Confirmation to Old Minster of 30 hides at Fareham, Hants.
22	12v	*CS 1157	?964 × 975	Confirmation to Old Minster of 28 hides at Bishops Waltham, Hants.
23	12v	*CS 1158	?964 × 975	Confirmation to Old Minster of 64 hides at Twyford, Crawley, Owslebury, Hensting, Horton or Houghton, Bishopstoke, Otterbourne, Chilland, Easton, and Hunton, all in Hants.
24	12v–13v	*CS 1159	?964 × 975	Summary and confirmation of charters 12–23 above.
25	13v–14	***CS 27	?793 × 796	100 hides at Downton, Wilts., to Winchester Cathedral.
26	14rv	***CS 391	826	55 hides at Downton, and 45 at Ebbesborne, Wilts., to Winchester (confirmation of No. 25).
27	14v–15	***CS 690	931 × 933	Renewal of liberty of Downton, as granted in No. 25.

Charter No.	Folio No.	Edition	Date	Description
28	15ᵛ–16	***CS 862	948	Confirmation of title to Downton and Ebbesborne, as in Nos. 25–6.
29	16–17	*K 698	997	Restoration to the Old Minster of 55 hides at Downton, and 45 at Ebbesborne, with reference to Nos. 12, 25, and 27–8.
k 30	17ʳᵛ	*CS 962	956	5 hides at Ebbesborne to the thegn Wulfric (Odstock, Wilts.).
k 31	17ᵛ–18	*CS 832	947	5 hides at Ebbesborne to the thegn Ælfsige (Bishopstone, Wilts.).
k 32	18–19	*K 655	986	5 hides at Ebbesborne to the thegn Ælfgar (part of Stratford Tony, Wilts.).
k 33	19ʳᵛ	*CS 1004	957	5 hides at Ebbesborne to the thegn Ælfric (Bishopstone).
k 34	19ᵛ–20	*CS 1071	961	5 hides at Ebbesborne to the thegn Byrnsige (Coombe Bissett, Wilts.).
35	20ʳᵛ	***CS 623	909	Confirmation to the bishop of Winchester of 40 hides at Alresford, Hants.
36	20ᵛ–21	***CS 102	701	Restoration to Winchester Cathedral of 40 hides at Alresford (as in No. 39).
k 37	21ʳᵛ	*CS 938	956	40 hides at Alresford to the thegn Ælfric.
38	21ᵛ–22	*CS 939	956	Repetition of bounds of No. 37.
39	22	***CS 398	824 × 833	Restoration to Winchester Cathedral of 40 hides at Alresford (as in No. 36).
40	22ᵛ	*CS 960	956	4 hides at Withiel Florey, Som., to the thegn Ælfwold.
41	22ᵛ–23ᵛ	***CS 727	938	Confirmation of 4 hides at Withiel Florey, and 3 at Charmouth, Dorset, to the Old Minster.
42	23ᵛ–24	***CS 831	947	Restoration of 130 hides at Taunton, Som., to the Old Minster and the bishopric of Winchester.
43	24–26	**CS 1219, 1220; R xlv	968	Renewal of freedom of Taunton (2 Latin and 1 O.E. versions).
k 44	25ʳᵛ	†CS 1072	961	4 hides at Withiel Florey to the thegn Cenwulf.
45	26ʳᵛ	*H 108	995 × 1002	Ruishton, Som. (member of Taunton). Writ.

Charter No.	Folio No.	Edition	Date	Description
46	26ᵛ–27	*CS 611	904	The bishop and *familia* of Winchester give 20 hides at Stoke by Shalbourne, Wilts., to the king in return for privileges for Taunton.
47	27ᵛ	*CS 549	879	Ruishton, Somerset. Bounds of No. 89.
48	27ᵛ	ECW 417–19	c. 890	Notes of 3 leases of members of Taunton.
49	27ᵛ	*ECW 547	N.D.	Bounds of Kingston, near Taunton.
50	27ᵛ–28	***CS 476	854	Bounds of Hundred of Taunton Deane (see No. 100).
51	28	**CS 158	737	Bounds of Withiel Florey, Som., and of Charmouth, Dorset (see No. 102).
52	28	*ECW 548	N.D.	Bounds of Washford in Old Cleeve, and of Kentsford, near Watchet, Som.
53	28ᵛ–29	*K 774	1044	15 hides at Pitminster, Som., to the Old Minster.
k 54	29–30	*CS 729	938	16 hides at Pitminster to the thegn Ælfheah.
k 55	30–31	*CS 770	941	16 hides at Pitminster to the thegn Ælfheah.
k 56	31ʳᵛ	*CS 1051	959	10 hides at the western half of Highclere, Hants, to the thegn Ælfwine.
57	31ᵛ–32	*CS 905	955	Lease of 10 hides at the eastern half of Highclere to the bishop of Winchester, with reversion to the Old Minster after 4 lives.
k 58	32–33	*CS 787	943	15 hides at Burghclere, Hants, to the religious lady Ælfswith.
59	33ʳᵛ	***CS 179	749	10 hides at *Cleran* to Winchester Cathedral.
60	33ᵛ–34	***CS 628	c. 909	Confirmation to the bishop of Winchester of 10 hides at Highclere.
k 61	34–5	*CS 674	931	10 hides at *Clere* (Ecchinswell, Hants) to the abbot Ælfric (witnessed at Colchester, Essex).
k 62	35ᵛ–36	*CS 1319	959 × 963	Confirmation of 65 hides at *Meone* (East Meon, Farnfield in Privett, Froxfield, Steep, and Langrish, all in Hants), to Queen Eadgifu.
k 63	36ᵛ	*CS 1114	963	8 hides at Ambersham, Sussex, to the church of St Andrew, Meon.
k 64	37ʳᵛ	*CS 1200	967	8 hides at East and West Meon and Farnfield to Winflæd.

Charter No.	Folio No.	Edition	Date	Description
k 65	37ᵛ–38ᵛ	*CS 689	932	12 hides at West Meon to the thegn Æthelgeard.
k 66	38ᵛ–39	*CS 982	956	50 hides at *Meone* (part of East Meon, with Steep, Langrish, and Oakshott in Froxfield) to the thegn Eadric.
k 67	39ᵛ–40	**CS 377	824	22 hides on both sides of the river Meon (East Meon and Froxfield) to the thegn Wulfheard.
k 68	40ʳᵛ	*CS 974	956	5 hides at Poolhampton (in Overton, Hants) to the thegn Byrnric.
k 69	40ᵛ–41	*CS 752	1033	10 hides at Poolhampton to Earl Godwin.
k 70	41ʳᵛ	*CS 763	940	5 hides at Poolhampton to the nun Ætheldryth.
k 71	41ᵛ–42	*CS 983	956	20 hides at Moredon in Rodbourne Cheney, Wilts., to the thegn Wynsige.
k 72	42–43	*CS 1217	968	20 hides at Moredon in Rodbourne Cheney to the thegn Eadwine.
k 73	43ʳᵛ	*CS 788	943	20 hides at Moredon in Rodbourne Cheney to the thegn Ælfsige.
74	43ᵛ	*R xcviii	1043–4	The bishop and *familia* of the Old Minster to the thegn Osgod: life lease of Adderbury, Oxon., in return for (5 hides at) Wroxall, I.O.W.
75	43ᵛ–44	†W xx	1015	Will of the ætheling Athelstan: Adderbury (Oxon.), Marlow (Bucks.), and Morden (Cambs.) to the Old Minster. See also No. 84.
k 76	44ᵛ–45	*CS 1230	969	30 hides at Witney, Oxon., to the thegn Ælfhelm.
77	45–46	*K 775	1044	30 hides at Witney, Oxon., to the bishop of Winchester.
78	46–47	*CS 810	945	30 hides at Brightwell, Sotwell, Mackney, and Wallingford, all in Berks., to the thegn Æthelgeard.
79	47ʳᵛ	*CS 474	854	30 hides at Brightwell to the bishop of Winchester.
k 80	47ᵛ–48	*CS 830	947	10 hides at Brightwell to the thegn Æthelgeard.

Charter No.	Folio No.	Edition	Date	Description
k 81	48ʳᵛ	*CS 1292	973	7 hides at Harwell, Berks., to the thegn Ælfric.
k 82	48ᵛ–49ᵛ	*K 648	985	17 hides at Harwell to the huntsman Æthelric.
k 83	49ᵛ–50	**CS 1183	956	7 hides at Harwell to the thegn Ælfstan.
84	50ʳᵛ	†W xx	1015	Copy of No. 75.
k 85	50ᵛ–51	*CS 765	941	7 hides at West Tisted, Hants, to the thegn Æthelgeard.
k 86	51–52	*CS 786	943	7 hides at West Tisted to the thegn Æthelgeard.
k 87	52ʳᵛ	*CS 931	953 × 955	5 hides at *Rimtun* (Rimpton, Som.) to the thegn Brihtric (Grim).
88	52ᵛ	*W vii	964 × 980	Will of Brihtric Grim. *Rimtun* (5 hides + 1 hide) to the Old Minster.
89	52ᵛ–53	*CS 549	?879	8 hides at *Risctun* (Ruishton, Som.) to the bishop of Winchester.
k 90	53ʳᵛ	*CS 730	938	5 hides at *Rimtun* to the thegn Æthered.
91	54ʳᵛ	**CS 864	948 (for 947)	5 hides at Mackney and 5 at Sotwell, Berks., to the thegn Æthelgeard.
92	54ᵛ–55ᵛ	***CS 629	909	20 hides at Crawley and 8 at Hunton, Hants, to the bishop of Winchester.
93	55ᵛ	*CS 1077	961	Lease of 10 hides at Kilmeston, Hants, to the thegn Athulf, with reversion to Winchester.
94	56	*R xxxiii	961	Lease of Kilmeston to the thegn Athulf, by the Old Minster.
95	56	***CS 625	?909	20 hides at *Uferantun* (Overton), 15 at Waltham, 5 at Bradley (all in Hants), all to the bishop of Winchester.
96	57ʳᵛ	***CS 626	?909	Another version of No. 95.
97	57ᵛ–58	*CS 72	685–7	60 hides at Farnham, Binton, Churt, and *Cusanweoh*, all in Surrey, to Cedde, Cisi, and Criswa.

Charter No.	Folio No.	Edition	Date	Description
98	58	*CS 324	801 × 805	60 hides at Farnham from the bishop of Winchester to Byrhthelm, in exchange for 33 hides at Wooton Rivers, Mildenhall, Froxfield, and Bedwyn, all in Wilts.
99	58–59	***CS 627	909	60 hides at Farnham and 10 at Bentley confirmed to the bishop of Winchester (see also No. 19).
100	59ʳᵛ	***CS 476	854	133 hides forming the Hundred of Taunton Deane, and 10 hides at Brown, Som., to Winchester Cathedral to augment Taunton. See No. 50.
101	60ʳᵛ	**CS 612	904	Privileges for Taunton to the bishop and *familia* at Winchester, in exchange for 10 hides at Crowcombe, 20 at Compton, 20 at Banwell (all Som.), and 20 at Stoke by Shalbourne, Wilts. See No. 14.
102	60ᵛ–61	**CS 158	737	4 hides at Withiel Florey, Som., and 3 at Charmouth, Dorset, to Winchester Cathedral, to augment Taunton. See No. 51.
103	61	*ECW 352	N.D.	Bounds of Downton, Wilts., and of 30 hides at Calbourne, I.O.W. See No. 107.
104	61ʳᵛ	*R xv	879 × 909	Lease by the bishop and *familia* of Winchester to Alfred: 40 hides at Alresford, Hants.
105	61ᵛ	*W v	10th c.	Will of Ordnoth and his wife. 10 hides at Candover, Hants, to the Old Minster.
106	61ᵛ–62	*Ha xvii	902	Lease by the bishop and *familia* of Winchester to Beornwulf: 15 hides at Ebbesborne, Wilts.
107	62ʳᵛ	*CS 392	826	30 hides at Calbourne, I.O.W., to the bishop of Winchester. See No. 103.
108	62ᵛ	*CS 731	938	25 hides at Tichborne, including 5 at Beauworth, Hants, to the Old Minster.

Charter No.	Folio No.	Edition	Date	Description
109	62ᵛ–63ᵛ	*R xx	*c.* 909	Lease by the *familia* to the bishop of Winchester: 20 hides at Tichborne.
k 110	63ᵛ–64	†CS 926	956	7 hides at Millbrook, Hants, to Ealdorman Wulfric. See No. 136.
111	64ʳᵛ	***CS 475	854	8 hides at Ruishton, and 8 at Stoke St Mary and Orchard Portman, Som., to Winchester Cathedral, to augment Taunton.
k 112	64ᵛ–65	*CS 550	882	15 hides at Creech and 2 at Stoke (?St Mary), Som., to the thegn Athelstan.
113	65ʳᵛ	*CS 590	900	10 hides at Lydiard, Wilts., from the bishop and *familia* of Winchester to Ealdorman Ordlaf, in return for 10 at Fonthill, Wilts., from Ordlaf to the bishop, and 3 at Avington, Hants, from the bishop to the *familia*.
114	65ᵛ–66	*CS 613	904	38 hides at Bishops Waltham, Hants, to the bishop and *familia* of Winchester, in exchange for 40 hides at Porchester, Hants.
115	66–67	*K 776	1045	8 hides at South Stoneham, Hants, to the Old Minster. See No. 148.
k 116	67ʳᵛ	*CS 976	956	10 hides at Chidden in Hambledon, Hants, to 'Ealdorman' Æthelgeard.
k 117	67ᵛ	*CS 1027	958	2½ hides and 25 acres at Ashford in Burlescombe and Boehill in Sampford Peverell, Devon, to the thegn Eadheah.
k 118	67ᵛ–68ᵛ	*K 633	982	3 hides and 30 acres at *Stoce* (Longstock, Hants) to the thegn Leofric. See No. 119.
119	68ᵛ–69	*K 633	982	Copy of No. 118.
k 120	69ʳᵛ	*CS 1314	975	4 hides at *Stoce* (South Stoke, Sussex) to his kinsman Osward.
k 121	69ᵛ–70	*CS 865	948	11 hides at *Stoce* (Alverstoke, Hants) to the thegn Ælfric.

Charter No.	Folio No.	Edition	Date	Description
k 122	70–71	*CS 663	928	12 hides at *Stoce* (Odstock, Wilts.) to the thegn Byrhtferth. Witnessed at Exeter.
123	71^{rv}	*CS 592	900	50 hides at Hurstbourne, Hants, to the *familia* at Winchester.
124	71^v–72	*CS 594; R cx	900	10 hides at *Stoce be Hysseburnan* (Stoke by Hurstbourne, Hants), to the *familia* at Winchester, in exchange for land at Chisledon, Wilts., and at Sparsholt in Lydiard Millicent, Hants.
125	72^v–73	*CS 1076	961	7½ hides at *Eastun* (Easton near Winchester) to the bishop of Winchester.
k 126	73^{rv}	*CS 1199	967	5 hides at *Eastun* (unlocated) to the thegn Ælfsige.
k 127	73^v–74^v	*CS 1119	963	6 hides in *Plesc* (Plaish in Cardington, Salop.) and *Eastun* (Church and Chetwynd Aston, Salop.) to the thegn Wulfric.
k 128	74^v	*CS 1315	975	3 hides at *Eastun* (Aston in Wellington, Salop.), to the thegn Ealhhelm, at the request of the king's kinsman, the monk Ælfwine. Dated from Glastonbury.
k 129	74^v–75	**CS 987	957	5 hides at *Eastun* (Little Aston, Staffs.) and *Bearre* (Great Barr, Staffs.) to the thegn Wulfhelm.
130	75^{rv}	*R xiv	871 × 877	Lease by the bishop and *familia* of Winchester to Ealdorman Cuthred and his wife Wulfthryth: 8 hides at *Eastune* (the eastern part of Alvington, near Winchester).
131	75^v–76^v	***CS 390	825	15 hides at Alton Priors, Wilts., to Winchester Cathedral.
132	76^v	*R cvii	1047 × 1052	Lease by the bishop and *familia* of Winchester to Wulfric: 2 hides and 1 yardland at Alton Priors, and 3 yardlands at Patney, Wilts.
133	76^v–77	*CS 566; R xvii	871 × 899	Ceolwin to the *familia* of Winchester: 15 hides at Alton Priors.
k 134	77^{rv}	*K 636	982	10 hides at Bushton in Clyffe Pypard, Wilts., to Ealdorman Æthelmær.

Charter No.	Folio No.	Edition	Date	Description
k 135	77ᵛ–78	*K 638	983	10 hides at Bushton in Clyffe Pypard to the thegn Æthelwine.
k 136	78ʳᵛ	†CS 926	956	7 hides at Millbrook, Hants, to Ealdorman Wulfric. Copy of No. 110.
k 137	78ᵛ–79ᵛ	ECW 164	1045	7 hides at Millbrook to Ealdorman Godwine. Text identical with No. 138.
138	79ᵛ–80	†K 781	1045	7 hides at Millbrook to the bishop of Winchester. Text identical with No. 137.
k 139	80–81	*K 650	985	9 hides at *Heantune* (Wolverhampton, Staffs.) and 1 at Trescott, Staffs., to the lady Wulfrun.
140	81ʳᵛ	*K 780	1045	8 hides at *Heantun* (Hinton Ampner, Hants) to the bishop of Winchester.
k 141	81ᵛ–82	†CS 677	931	9 hides at *Hamme* (Ham, Wilts.) to the thegn Wulfgar.
142	82ʳᵛ	*CS 679	N.D.	Copy of bounds in No. 141.
143	83	†R xxvi	933–9	Will of Wulfgar: the reversion of Ham, Wilts., to the Old Minster.
k 144	83ʳᵛ	*CS 1037	958	5 hides at *Hamme* (East and West Ham, Essex) to Ealdorman Athelstan (called bishop in rubric).
k 145	83ᵛ–84	*CS 1316	975	5 hides at Fyfield, Hants, to the thegn Ælfweard. See No. 217.
k 146	84ʳᵛ	*CS 1118	963	5 hides at Patney, Wilts., booked by the king to himself.
k 147	84ᵛ–85	*K 712	990	10 hides at *Heantun* (Hinton Ampner, Hants) to the church of South Stoneham.
k 148	85ʳᵛ	*K 713	990	8 hides called *Westun* at (South) Stoneham to ? (given later to the bishopric for the Old Minster). See No. 115.
149	85ᵛ–86	***CS 477	854	20 hides at Wanborough, Wilts., to the church of Winchester. Endorsed *Wenbeorgen que modo Hynyton dicitur*. The bounds are of Little Hinton, Wilts.

Charter No.	Folio No.	Edition	Date	Description
150	86^{rv}	***R VIII	(854)	Late record of No. 149, in O.E. without bounds.
151	86^v	*CS 479	1047 × 1070	Bounds of *Wenbeorgan* (Wanborough and Little Hinton) in the time of Bishop Stigand of Winchester.
k 152	86^v–87	*K 664	988	5 hides at Wylye, Wilts., to the thegn Ælfgar.
153	87^{rv}	*Ha xx	946	Will of Ealdorman Æthelwold. 12 hides at Wylye to the Old Minster (Stockton, west of Wylye; see ECW, p. 88).
k 154	87^v–88	*K 611	977	10 hides at Wylye to the thegn Ælfric (bounds include Bathampton).
k 155	88^{rv}	*CS 595	901	10 hides at Wylye to Ethelwulf (bounds include Codford and Stockton).
k 156	88^v–89^v	*K 743	1026	5 hides at *Worthi* (Abbots Worthy, Hants) to the bishop of Crediton.
k 157	89^v–90	**CS 740	939	8 hides at *Worthige* (Chilland in Martyr Worthy, Hants) to the thegn Heahfyrth.
158	90^{rv}	***CS 473	854	Restitution to Winchester Cathedral of 3 hides at *Worthige* (Headbourne Worthy).
k 159	90^v–91	*CS 520	868	5 hides at *Worthige* (Martyr Worthy) to the thegn Hunsige.
k 160	91^{rv}	*CS 468	854	To the thegn Hunsige: exemption from secular dues of 3 hides at *Wordi* (part of Martyr Worthy).
161	91^v–92	**CS 389	825	5 hides at *Worthige* (Martyr Worthy) to Winchester Cathedral.
162	92–93^v	**CS 624	909	Confirmation of 50 hides at Whitechurch, Hants, to the *familia* at Winchester.
k 163	93^v–94	*CS 948	956	30 hides at *Ellendune* (land in Wroughton and Lydiard Millicent, Wilts.) to the thegn Ælfheah.
164	94–95	**CS 705	934	30 hides at *Enedforda* (Enford, Wilts.) 10 at Chilbolton, and 10 at Ashmansworth to Winchester Cathedral.

Charter No.	Folio No.	Edition	Date	Description
165	95ʳᵛ	**R xxv	934	English version of No. 164, without bounds.
k 166	95ᵛ–96	*W ix	968 × 972	Will of Ealdorman Ælfheah: *Ællændune* to the king. See No. 163.
167	96	*R cvi	1047 × 1053	Lease by Bishop Stigand and the *familia* at the Old Minster to Æthelmær: 1 hide at Sparsholt, Hants.
168	96ʳᵛ	*W viii	966 × 975	Will of Ælfgifu. (30 hides) at Princes Risborough, Bucks., to the Old Minster.
169	96ᵛ	*CS 618	900 × 908	Latin translation of No. 170.
170	96ᵛ–97	*CS 619	900 × 908	Lease (in O.E.) by the bishop of Winchester of 70 hides at Beddington, Surrey, to the king.
171	97–98	**CS 620–1	909	Renewal of beneficial hidation of Chilcomb, in return for confirmation by the bishop of Winchester to the king of leases of 100 hides at Downton and Ebbesborne, Wilts., and 70 in Beddington, Surrey. (ECW, pp. 244–8.)
172	98–99	*K 624	980	7 hides at Havant, Hants, to the Old Minster, subject to life interest of the fourth life under lease No. 173.
173	99–100	*CS 707	934	Lease for 4 lives to the thegn Wihtgar; 7 hides at Havant, Hants.
k 174	100ʳᵛ	*CS 979	956	5 hides at East Stoke in Hayling Island, Hants, to the thegn Æthelsige.
175	100ᵛ–101	*R cxiv	1053	The bishop of Winchester and the *familia* of the Old Minster to Wulfweard the White. Lease of 5 hides at Hayling Island (which had been left to Winchester by Queen Ælfgifu), with reversion to Winchester of this plus another 5 hides there.
k 176	101–102	*CS 742	939	17 hides at Droxford, Hants, to the king's sister Eadburgh.
k 177	102ʳᵛ	*CS 953	956	20 hides at Swanmore and part of Droxford to the lady Æthelhild.

Charter No.	Folio No.	Edition	Date	Description
178	102ᵛ–103	***CS 393	826	17 hides at Droxford to Winchester Cathedral.
k 179	103ʳᵛ	**CS 902	958	20 hides at *Æscesbyrig* (East Woolstone, Berks.) to the thegn Wulfric.
k 180	103ᵛ–104ᵛ	*CS 796	944	20 hides at *Æscesbyrig* (West Woolstone) to the thegn Wulfric.
k 181	104ᵛ–105	*CS 491	856	20 hides at *Æscesbyric* (West Woolstone) to the thegn Ealdred.
k 182	105ʳᵛ	*K 639	983	2½ hides at Westwood, Hants, to the thegn Ælfnoth.
k 183	105ᵛ–106ᵛ	*K 658	987	3 hides at Westwood and 3 yardlands at Farleigh Hungerford to the huntsman Leofwine.
k 184	106ᵛ–107ᵛ	*CS 758	940	12 hides at Exton, Hants, to the thegn Æthelgeard.
k 185	107ᵛ–108	*CS 959	956	15 hides at Bleadon, Som., to the thegn Ælfwold.
k 186	108ʳᵛ	*K 739	1023	7 hides at Hannington, Hants, to the thegn Leofwine.
k 187	108ᵛ–109	*CS 1042	958	20 hides at *Wudutune* (Wooton, Oxon.) to the thegn Æthelric.
k 188	109–110	*CS 673	990	15 hides at *Wudatun* (Wootton St Laurence, Hants) to the thegn Æthelweard.
k 189	110ʳᵛ	*CS 969	956	4 hides at *Wudetune* (unidentified) to the thegn Æthelwold.
k 190	110ᵛ–111	*CS 964	940	Lease of 4 hides at *Wudetune* (Wotton-under-Edge, Glos.) to the thegn Eadric.
191	111	†K 763	1042	1 hide at Coombe in East Meon, Hants, to the bishop of Winchester.
k 192	111ᵛ	**CS 508	866 × 867	6 hides at Buttermere, Wilts., to Ealdorman Wulfhere.
193	112ᵛ	*K 640	983	A fishery on the River Darent, Kent, to the bishop of Winchester.
194	112ᵛ	*CS 1054	960	10 hides at Itchen Stoke, Hants, to the bishop of Winchester, with reversion to the Old Minster.

Charter No.	Folio No.	Edition	Date	Description
195	113	*CS 180	749	5 hides at *Thruhham* (Park Farm, Beaulieu), 1 at *Eppelhyrste* (in Brockenhurst), and 1 at Whitley, all in Hants, to the church of Winchester.
196	113	*CS 565	879 × 899	50 hides at Chisledon, Wilts., and 60 at Hurstbourne Priors, Hants, to the bishop and *familia* of Winchester, in exchange for 100 hides at Cholsey, Berks., with appurtenant vills.
197	113ʳᵛ	*CS 544	877	The bishop of Winchester to the *familia*: 5 hides at Nursling, Hants.
198	113ᵛ	*CS 423	838	40 hides at Shalfleet, I.O.W., to the bishop of Winchester.
k 199	113ᵛ–114	*K 652	985	11 hides at Michelmersh, Hants, to Ælferd.
200	114	*K 622	979	5 hides at Long Sutton, Hants, to the Old Minster, to add to the 45 hides at Crondall.
201	114ᵛ	*CS 1068	961	5 hides at Avington, Hants, to the Old Minster.
202	114ᵛ	*CS 495	858	The bishop of Winchester to the king, with reversion to the church of Winchester: 60 hides at Farnham, Surrey.
203	114ᵛ–115	*K 783	1046	6 hides at Hoddington, Hants, to the bishop of Winchester.
k 204	115	*K 720	1012	A *prædium* in Winchester to Queen Ælfgifu.
205	115ᵛ	*K 750	1033	3 hides at Bishops Hull, Som., to the Old Minster.
206	115ᵛ	***CS 713	937	Beneficial hidation of Chilcomb, Hants.
207	115ᵛ	*ECW 128	979	Memorandum of restoration of Crondall, Hants, to Winchester Cathedral.

Charter No.	Folio No.	Edition	Date	Description
208	116	*CS 1307	973–4	45 hides at Crondall to the Old Minster.
209	116ʳᵛ	*K 753	1033	Renewal of privileges for the Old Minster.
210	116ᵛ–117	***H 113	N.D.	Record of an agreement between the New and Old Minsters (late insertion).
211	117	*ECW 180	N.D.	Boundary between Crondall and Elvetham (late insertion).
212	117	**CS 1313 (part)	975	Bounds of Bleadon, Som. (late insertion).
213	117	*Unpublished	12th c.	Bounds of *Wudetun* (unlocated). (Late insertion.)
214	117ᵛ	***CS 493	N.D.	Confirmation of beneficial hidation of Chilcomb.
k 215	118	†CS 734	939	15 hides at *Uferantun* (East Overton, Wilts.) to the nun Wulfswyth.
k 216	118ᵛ	*CS 875	949	4 hides at *Ofærtune* (Orton Waterville, Hunts.) to the thegn Frytheric.
217	118ᵛ–119	*CS 1316	975	Copy of No. 145.
k 218	119	**K 1284	984 × 988	Land at Wyke Regis, Weymouth, and Melcombe Regis, Dorset, to the thegn Atsere.

The Social and Political Problems of
the Early English Church

By ERIC JOHN

ONE of the most rewarding trends in recent historiography has been the growing realization amongst scholars of the importance of studying the history of the English Church not only in the minds and hearts of her members but in their social and political connections as well. This does not mean, and has not meant, the subordination of intellectual and spiritual factors to a merely economic interpretation. I am not suggesting we should substitute a study of incomes for a study of sanctity, merely that, as the rich *corpus* of recent work on the seventeenth century has shown, the two are not quite unconnected. It seems to me that no period in the history of the English Church invites this kind of treatment more than the beginning: but we have so far largely treated a process that must have had important social and political implications in terms of saints and saintlike conduct. To parody a famous remark of T. S. Eliot, faith strikes, sanctity occurs, conversion sets in: and so in a way it does. Yet it is obvious from the most superficial study of the period that the early saints were deeply involved in the social and political games of the 'England' of their day. It is only necessary to point to the extreme tact and ingenuity which Theodore of Tarsus needed when he tried to give the diocesan structure of the early Church a rational shape and greater stability than the shifting marches of the tribal kingdoms that then made up 'England'. If one approaches the problem from a different direction, it is obvious that a religion which required literacy in two languages from a people who did not have an alphabet of their own could flourish only if it had stable communities where letters could be taught and a native clergy trained. In *this* world this could be done only if someone were prepared to give these communities the scarcest and most precious of all the sources of power and wealth, land. Surely we cannot hold back from asking on what terms was this land given, at what price was it got?

Comparatively recently the basic foundations of the early English churchmen's world have been subject to a considerable revaluation. Questions that once seemed definitively answered have been re-opened, and if new definitive answers are still not exactly thick on the ground, it is obvious to all but the most prejudiced and least informed that something was very wrong with the old learning. Prominent in this search for new bearings in early English history has been Herbert Finberg. It is fitting then on an occasion such as this that an attempt should be made to raise tentatively in a kind of agenda of questions and approaches, some of the consequences of the new learning for the study of the beginnings of the Church.

It will be convenient as well as seemly to begin with people. The objects of the endeavours of the early missionaries seem to me to be less familiar, less like primitive versions of 'us', than they have done to most. They do not seem to have been very sure who they were themselves. Most early literary sources call them *Saxones*, or sometimes *Angli*, and do not attempt to differentiate between the two terms. Bede, of course, tried to separate *Angli* from *Saxones*: although he has persuaded the great majority of Anglo-Saxon scholars to follow him, in his day he failed to convince either his abbot or his bishop, his neighbour in Iona, his literary colleague in Malmesbury or, to judge by his practice, himself.[1] We may agree that these people had some sense of identity and we may as well call it English, but not without qualifications. They also had a very strong sense of their diversity and particularity. They were extremely vague about their Englishry and much more precise about being West Saxons and Mercians or Northumbrians, although even then there was room for bitter and protracted disputes about just who and what constituted Mercia or Northumbria.

These peoples, it seems to me, lacked that sense of identity amongst themselves, that clarity about who they were and what marked them off from strangers, which is a defining characteristic of real nations and true peoples. We ought not to study then the history of the early Church and its saints as though they formed part of the English nation and were aware that they did. This is a world in which the English nation is a very notional affair indeed, and the unity of the kingdoms that composed what Englishry there was was also precarious and contested. To put the point more particularly: how could a monk of Ripon or Lindisfarne not have loyalties to Deira and Bernicia, as well as to Northumbria and perhaps England? This is an obvious point, but it seems to me to have been too little regarded when looking at important problems of early Church history.

The kind of problems I have in mind primarily concern institutions and social structures: being historians and not sociologists, we can study these problems in depth as parts of processes which have middles and even ends—though origins are more obscure—that can be empirically investigated. In this case, what is more, most of the problems are focused by the career of a single individual, St Wilfrid. Now Wilfrid is few people's favourite saint. Pompous, proud, selfish, vainglorious, litigious, heedless of the welfare of the English and their Church, and in these days naturally triumphalist, is how he has seemed to a stream of distinguished scholars. It seems to me that if we go over Wilfrid's stormy career in the light of the caveats I have just entered, a rather different

[1] E. John, *Orbis Britanniae*, Leicester, 1966, pp. 4–5.

picture emerges, and one that, willynilly, affects current views on early English history in general.

Perhaps the oddest feature of Wilfrid's life is the radical disagreement of scholars on even the bare facts of his episcopal career. This disagreement is not due to paucity of evidence—or not primarily to this. We have a full and, by the standards of the time, good, biography of Wilfrid by one of his monks who knew him well, Eddius Stephanus. It seems likely that Eddius was brought to Northumbria by Wilfrid himself and that he visited Rome in his master's entourage,[1] and wrote soon after Wilfrid's death. In addition to this we have considerable information about him in Bede's *History* which uses, but does not acknowledge, Eddius' *Life*. Eddius' account of Wilfrid's early career is plausible enough— much more than many contemporary attempts at hagiography—up to a point. Wilfrid was unhappy at home, where an unsympathetic stepmother ruled, so he left for the Northumbrian court where he had influence with King Oswiu's Kentish queen. He was dependent on what she could do for him for a career and what she did was to send him to Lindisfarne to become a monk. After a while Wilfrid left on a 'pilgrimage' to Rome and on the way attracted the attention of the archbishop of Lyons and his brother. On his return he entered the archbishop's service, was tonsured, and might well have spent the rest of his life in Gaul if his patron had not been murdered. He himself narrowly escaped death and presumably had little alternative but to return to his native country. Here he was taken up by Alchfrith, the son of, and co-ruler with, King Oswiu of Northumbria,[2] and made abbot of his foundation at Ripon because he was ready to follow the Roman method of calculating Easter and abandon the Celtic custom followed at Lindisfarne and in the greater part of the British Isles. One

---

[1] *The Life of Bishop Wilfrid by Eddius Stephanus*, ed. B. Colgrave, Cambridge, 1927, c. x. I have cited Eddius throughout by reference to the chapters for the convenience of those using the other modern editions of Eddius. I have consulted the notes to Dr Moonen's edition, s'Hertogenbosch, 1946, and cited them as *Moonen*, followed by the page reference.

[2] R. L. Poole, *Studies in Chronology and History*, Oxford, 1934, p. 64, says Alchfrith held "a *provincia*, or under kingdom, in what we roughly describe as the West Riding of Yorkshire." This identification is vital to Dr Lane Poole's whole argument: it is therefore worth pointing out that no compelling evidence supports it and most of what little evidence there is, is against it. Florence of Worcester, i, p. 25, says Alchfrith succeeded Æthelwald, who we know certainly was king of Deira as a whole.—Bede, *Historia Ecclesiastica* [=HE], iii, c. 23. It is difficult to evaluate Florence's information at all precisely but what he says is reasonable enough. There is no other evidence that Dr Lane Poole's *provincia* had any regular existence, indeed it must have been made up of a mixture of the old kingdom of Elmet plus bits of Deira proper, which is a curious amalgam. From Bede and Eddius it is evident that Alchfrith's kingdom lay in southern Northumbria since his authority enabled him to establish an abbot of Ripon and grant him land *æt Stanford*. Dr Lane Poole, *op. cit.*, p. 72, identified this place as Stainforth on the Ribble, which is not obvious linguistically speaking and lies very far west. This is the only possible identification that will allow Dr Lane Poole's thesis to stand. Most scholars have taken the name to be Stamford, and Colgrave, *op. cit.*, p. 155, identifies it as Stamford Bridge, near York, following Smith, as does *Moonen*, p. 242. This is much the most plausible identification and it would make Alchfrith lord of York, and ruler of Deira, not just a hypothetical portion of it.

may note how little conventional piety Eddius uses to explain Wilfrid's entry into the religious life, and the frank acknowledgement that the need for a place in life and the effects of taking the wrong side in a political squabble played an important part in making Wilfrid first a monk and then an abbot. Wilfrid's career was, of course, made at the synod of Whitby when he was chief spokesman of the Roman party which won the day. He had been ordained priest, as a step towards becoming a bishop, by the Frankish bishop of the West Saxons, Agilberht, just before the synod.[1] The difficulties arise when we ask what happened next.

Eddius is not easy to understand here. The bishop of the Northumbrians at the time of Whitby, 664,[2] was called Colman, and is so described by Bede.[3] Eddius calls him *Eboracae civitatis episcopi metropolitani*:[4] it is in the highest degree unlikely that Colman was in any sense bishop of York, let alone 'metropolitan'. York lay in Deira, and the royal power in Northumbria in 664 was held by the Bernician, northern, portion of the country whose chief ecclesiastical centre was Lindisfarne, which was Colman's base as bishop. Deira, or some of it, enjoyed a certain independence under Alchfrith. It is not certain, or perhaps even probable, that Alchfrith was the son of Oswiu's then Queen, who was a member of the Deiran royal family, but she seems to have enjoyed some influence over him. He had become an enthusiastic follower of 'roman' ways, presumably under her influence. Now, as Plummer long ago pointed out,[5] Colman and his two predecessors cannot have been metropolitans as they had no suffragans; they used no territorial titles; and their bases were at Lindisfarne. It must follow, apparently, that Eddius is a barefaced liar who cannot be trusted in the simplest matters of fact. What is worse, the fabrication appears to continue immediately Eddius moves on to the next stage of his hero's career.

There is no doubt that after Oswiu had decided to abandon the tradition of Columba for that of Peter, Bishop Colman resigned his see and withdrew to Ireland. According to Eddius, Wilfrid was elected to the vacant see like John

[1] *Eddius*, c. x.

[2] I have followed Mr Kirby, *EHR.*, LXXVIII, 1963, pp. 519 *et seq.*, and the late Père Grosjean, *Analecta Bollandiana*, LXXVIII, 1960, pp. 233 *et seq.*, in dating the synod 664, not 663 as is sometimes done. I cannot follow Père Grosjean's interpretation either of Wilfrid's motives, or of his part in the Whitby affair. He writes: "N'est-il bien clair que Wilfrid a cru devoir mettre à profit la présence en Northumbrie de l'évêque Agilbert... Le calcul de Wilfrid était bon: l'évêque franc lui remit la direction des débats."—*op. cit.*, p. 250. I cannot see any scope for Wilfrid's *calcul*. There is no evidence that Wilfrid had, or could have had, anything to do with the decision to convoke the synod, which must have been taken, as was the decision that concluded it, by Oswiu and the Bernician court. Wilfrid was wholly committed to the 'roman' party long before the synod and he would not have become abbot of Ripon had this not been so. As the most senior Deiran cleric and the senior Northumbrian representative of the 'roman' observance, it was inevitable that he should play a prominent role without any calculation on his part.

[3] HE., iii, c. 25. [4] *Eddius*, c. x. [5] *Bedae Opera Historica*, Oxford, 1896, II, p. 117.

the Baptist and the Prophet Ezekiel.[1] It is implied but not explicitly stated that the see in question was the one vacated by Colman—what Eddius called the metropolitan see of York. It is certain that this is what Eddius meant to convey since he speaks a little later of Wilfrid returning from consecration in Gaul *ad sedem episcopalem Eboracae civitatis*.[2] Again Eddius cannot be right. Bede tells us that Colman's successor was a southern Irishman called Tuda; that is, the new bishop was a man sufficiently remote from current controversies, a convinced 'roman' and yet perfectly familiar with the usages of Celtic monasticism, and so ideal for that time and place.[3] Bede cannot have invented this and he goes on to explain that Tuda died soon after consecration. At this point he leaves the question of the Northumbrian episcopal succession for a long digression on the career of the monk Ecgberht which had ended only a short while before Bede was writing, more than half-a-century after the synod of Whitby. Bede then returns to the aftermath of Whitby, taking up his narrative as is his wont with the word *interea* which here as elsewhere is chronologically imprecise. He then tells us that Alchfrith sent Wilfrid to the kingdom of the Gauls to be consecrated bishop *eum sibi suisque*.[4]

What exactly did he mean? Eddius is quite unambiguous: Wilfrid was bishop of all the Northumbrians and his see was at York. But because of his omission of any mention of Tuda and his mistakes about the siting of the Northumbrian see and its canonical status he has found few scholars to agree with him. Most have preferred to follow Bede and ignore Eddius, but, as will be argued in a moment, Bede's account presents scarcely fewer problems than that of Eddius, not the least because of persistent ambiguities at the *cruces* in his narrative. As so often when faced with two conflicting accounts it is fatally easy to overlook the possibility that neither may be altogether candid. It seems to me that on close inspection a good case can be made out for Bede's being the more evasive of the two: that Eddius is doctrinaire rather than untruthful. It will be convenient, however, to follow tradition, take the sources separately, and concentrate first on the more reputable author, Bede.

Plummer, rejecting Eddius, supposed Bede to mean that Wilfrid was made bishop of Deira only, whilst Tuda was made bishop of Bernicia. When Tuda died, since Wilfrid had not returned from his Gaulish consecration, Oswiu made Chad bishop of all Northumbria with his seat at York.[5] In 669 Chad was replaced by Wilfrid who was at last bishop of York and Northumbria. The interpolation of Chad into the story is based on Bede again. Bede says that Wilfrid stayed away a long time in Gaul, so Oswiu imitated his son's example and sent Chad to the south of England to be consecrated *Eburacensis ecclesie*—

---

[1] *Eddius*, c. xi. Mr Mayr-Harting has pointed out the importance of Eddius' presentation of Wilfrid as an Old Testament prophet in a forthcoming book.

[2] *Eddius*, c. xii.   [3] HE., iii, c. 26.   [4] HE., iii, c. 28.   [5] *Bedae*, II, p. 323.

episcopus.[1] Then in 669 the new archbishop of Canterbury, Theodore of Tarsus, was sent to England by the Pope. One of his first acts was to point out that Chad had been irregularly consecrated. Chad immediately offered to resign his *episcopatum* if he had not received it rightly[2] but Theodore assured him that he had no wish to deprive him of his *episcopatus* and completed the consecration *catholice ratione*. Eddius' version is very different. He confirms that Wilfrid delayed his return and when he did arrive back in Northumbria Oswiu had intruded Chad into York. He blames this on the liturgical conservatives and says that Theodore deposed Chad as an intruder, restoring Wilfrid to what was rightfully his.

Plummer's version of all this will not do as it stands. He does not explain how Chad came to be consecrated bishop of York which lay in the heart of Deira, of which he supposed Wilfrid's patron was king, and yet was deposed, not for intrusion into another's see, but merely because of the irregularity of his orders.[3] One must go further than this and save Bede's candour by denying that Wilfrid was ever bishop of Deira and York before 669. Alchfrith and Wilfrid between them must have ruled only part of Deira, the country round Ripon and the West Riding. This step was taken by the late R. L. Poole in a paper that is still largely accepted as the definitive account of Wilfrid's career.[4] Some difficulties suggest themselves straight away. Why does not Bede, who knew of Eddius' false version of the events of 664–9, correct him, at least silently, by saying unambiguously what Wilfrid was made bishop of? It looks in more than one place as though Bede is going out of his way not to contradict Eddius whilst conveying a totally opposed version of the same facts. Bede differs from Eddius mainly in what he leaves out.[5]

To make things worse, Eddius was writing very little after 700 when many people were still alive who knew perfectly well the basic facts of Wilfrid's career. Indeed in view of the long and stormy effect that career had on Northumbrian politics it is probable that very few people did not know enough of

---

[1] HE., iii, c. 28.   [2] HE., iv, c. 2.

[3] According to Gregory the Great's *Responsa*, VI, HE., i, c. 27, Chad's consecration by a single bishop could be licit.

[4] *Studies*, pp. 56–81, followed by F. M. Stenton, *Anglo-Saxon England*, Oxford, 1967, pp. 124, 135. Levison, *Aus Rheinischer und Fränkischer Frühzeit*, Düsseldorf, 1948, p. 371, n. 2, seems to accept it. M. A. Carroll, *The Venerable Bede: His Spiritual Teachings*, Washington, 1946, p. 92, n. 179, gives a clear, slightly amended, summary of Dr Lane Poole's argument. The *Handbook of British Chronology* takes Eddius much more seriously. Mr J. Campbell, *Latin Historians*, ed. T. A. Dorey, London, 1967, rejects Dr Lane Poole's arguments altogether.

[5] D. J. Kirby, *BJRL.*, xlviii, 1966, p. 354, points out that: "Bede's knowledge of York history was very slight." It might on the other hand be that he preferred to keep a discreet silence on Deiran as distinct from general Northumbrian affairs as much as he could. Mr Kirby himself notes the curiously slight treatment of James the Deacon, p. 342, and explains this by a putative lack of a community to record his career, but he himself supplies some good reasons for supporting Nennius against Bede on the question of the baptism of Edwin in which James must have played some part on Bede's version, p. 352.

the facts to detect Eddius' lies at sight. It is very hard to believe that Eddius can have expected to deceive anyone by lies so barefaced as these and difficult to guess what his motives for telling them were. I do not think we can resolve these puzzles by merely looking at the words on the page, we must study them *in situ* and look a little at the kind of audience Bede and Eddius had in mind.

We know that Bede's audience was to be world-wide[1] and his fame second to none in English letters, whilst Eddius is read only by specialists and abused even by them. No doubt both our authors were writing to some degree with posterity in mind, but they can hardly have avoided seeing that posterity as much the same in its civility, its economic and social status grouping, as their own world.

Their world was very small and very upper-class. Bede's *History* ranges widely over the Britain of his day in both space and time. It has a multitude of characters but only three of them are revealed as not of the highest social class: the surely mythical Caedmon; an unnamed, mentally deranged tramp for whom Chad performed a miracle;[2] and a dumb, deformed pauper healed by John of Beverley.[3] For the rest it is a world of kings, queens, abbots and abbesses, monks and nuns, bishops and secular magnates, of the highest social standing. Bede was writing for, and was aware he was writing for, an élite who wanted to know about the doings of their own kind, which is hardly surprising since he knew perfectly well that the future of the Church he was writing about lay with just this class of person. One may cite his important and neglected general statement on the early days of the English nunneries.[4] Perhaps more significant because it is so trivial a point to get into a work like this, is Bede's remark about two of King Edwin's children who died in infancy. They have no importance whatever in Bede's narrative; none the less their fate is recorded with the note *et iuxta honorem vel regiis pueri vel innocentibus Christi congruum in ecclesia sepulti sunt.*[5] Bede, it will be remembered, has hardly more than this to say of James the Deacon. He would have found, to judge by his *History*, our obsession with the free peasant of Anglo-Saxon England very hard to understand.

Bede's audience then, and Eddius' too, was small, upper-class and in consequence necessarily involved in personal relationships with each other, as well as in social and political relationships. It was a world torn with feuds and tensions, public as well as private, if the two can be distinguished. This world had all the jealousies and spite of small, enclosed, and established élites. Bede himself was accused of heresy and forced to defend himself before his bishop, who happened to be Wilfrid, and very cross it made him.[6] He had learnt from Gildas

---

[1] There is even a translation in Japanese. [2] HE., iv, c. 3. [3] HE., v, c. 2.
[4] HE., iii, c. 8. The passage is discussed at length below. [5] HE., ii, c. 20.
[6] *Ep. ad Plegwine.*

apparently[1] the trick of presenting history as the story of the punishment of, and divine retribution for, the despisers of God's commands, and his intention is both to persuade and to warn the powerful amongst the English of the importance of fostering the Church. Page after page is devoted to the success of the faithful such as Oswald who accepted his victory over Cadwallon as proof of the efficacy of the Christian God;[2] the downfall of the wicked after initial success—again the obvious example is Cadwallon—looms large; and the rewards of sanctity are compared with the horrors of Hell. The vision of Hell and its horrors is an integral part of Bede's purpose. But he was only too aware of the limitations of supernatural sanctions in his world, and if his collection of moral *exempla* was to be acceptable to the Englishmen of his day it was not possible for him to say all he knew or reveal all he thought.

Mr Wallace-Hadrill has recently pointed out that Bede like Gregory of Tours "withheld dangerous material."[3] We need look no further than his preface with its hint of royal censorship. Or we may turn to the end of his *History* and what he says of Northumbrian monasticism. If one compares what he says there with what he wrote only months later from his death-bed to his bishop, the extent of his reticence is plain. Further Bede was not writing for Northumbria but for the English. A good deal of Bede's information and some of his incentive came from south of the Humber.[4] This part of England had once been tributary to the Northumbrian kings but was now subject to Æthelbald of Mercia, who is treated a good deal more gently by Bede than he was by St Boniface. Mercian susceptibilities were of some importance to Bede. Bearing all this in mind, I think we can see a little better what Bede was at in his dealings with Wilfrid.

The main difficulty in Dr Lane Poole's version of Wilfrid's career comes from what Bede says about Chad's tenure of the see of York. He saw clearly that if Bede's evidence is to be taken as complete and candid Chad cannot have been intruded into Wilfrid's see and therefore cannot have been deposed for that reason either. Bede seems to me to mean that Chad was consecrated to the see after Wilfrid had left to go to Gaul. He explains Chad's election by saying that after Wilfrid had left, Oswiu made Chad bishop of York *quo adhuc in transmarinis partibus propter ordinationem demorante* (Wilfrid). The *quo adhuc* surely

---

[1] J. M. Wallace-Hadrill, *Frühmittelalterliche Studien*, II, Berlin, 1968, p. 37. As Mr Wallace-Hadrill points out, one must allow Bede to have learnt this lesson from the Bible too. Eddius has a similar ideology which must be derived entirely from the Old Testament.

[2] HE., iii, c. 3.

[3] *Art. cit.*, p. 38. Mr J. C. Campbell, *art. cit.*, has an important discussion of this point, p. 177: "Had we to rely on the *Ecclesiastical History* for our knowledge of the Church in the first generation of the eighth century we should know little of it... There can be little doubt that Bede's failure to describe the conduct of those of his contemporaries of whom he disapproved was deliberate." Mr Campbell goes on to discuss Bede's treatment of Wilfrid in a section of the greatest interest.

[4] v. Bede's *Preface* to HE., pp. 5 *et seq.*

implies a causal relationship between Wilfrid's delay and Chad's election. Bede is implying that Wilfrid forfeited his see by his neglect of it, and since he gives no explanation of what caused Wilfrid's delay but a perfectly respectable reason for Chad's replacing him, he really avoids blaming either. If this is so then Bede as well as Eddius is telling us that Wilfrid was bishop of York—and the Northumbrians. This seems to fit into his chronological survey which Plummer appended to the *History* where Bede says s.a.664 *Ceadda ac Wilfrid Nordanhymbrorum ordinantur episcopi*.[1] When Bede, or anyone else, speaks of the see of the Northumbrians they cannot be shown to mean a part only of Northumbria. Nothing therefore in Bede's text requires us to think that Wilfrid and Chad were ever joint bishops or anything other than successive bishops of the whole see. It is also apparent that if Wilfrid delayed his return from Gaul he did not delay his consecration which took place the same year as Chad's, the same year as his election—this is confirmed by Eddius[2]—so Wilfrid was really quite speedy in securing consecration.

When we come to Bede's account of Chad's deposition we find him evasive in the extreme. He twice uses the word *episcopatus*. Chad on being challenged concerning the legality of his consecration immediately laid down his *episcopatus*, which might mean either his see or his episcopal dignity. Theodore replied that he ought not *eum episcopatum dimittere*[3] and completed his consecration *catholice ratione*. The obvious implication is that Chad's orders were defective on liturgical or canonical grounds[4] and the defects were supplied by the archbishop. It is therefore with some surprise that the attentive reader discovers Chad in the next chapter living in retirement at Lastingham and available for preferment as bishop of the Mercians. Bede has used the ambiguity of *episcopatus* to cover up the fact that Chad laid down both dignity and see and that Theodore restored only the rank. The reasons for this reticence seem obvious. By the time Bede wrote Chad was the ornament of the tradition of the chief Mercian see, Lichfield. Wilfrid, too, was always more highly regarded in Mercia than he was in Northumbria. Everything, including sense, in an eirenic work such as this, suggested a certain glossing over of the difficult beginnings of both Wilfrid's and Chad's careers. It is noticeable that Eddius, vigorous partisan as he is of his hero, is careful to avoid criticizing Chad personally for his intrusion. It follows that we cannot take Bede's *History* as a safe foundation for the chronology of Wilfrid's career as Dr Lane Poole did, especially if we intend to rely as much on Bede's silence as did Dr Lane Poole.

It also follows that Eddius cannot be as corrupt as his modern readers have

---

[1] HE., v, c. 24.   [2] *Eddius*, c. xii.   [3] HE., iv, c. 2.
[4] Chad was excluded from the probably mid-eighth-century verse martyrology that mentions all the bishops of York up to Wilfred ii.—H. Quentin, *Dictionnaire d'archéologie chrétienne et de liturgie*, II, pp. 642–4.

freely supposed. Can we then, accepting that neither of our sources is free to tell the whole truth and both have motives for suppressing inconvenient facts, make some sense of Wilfrid's career?

The first problem is the business about the metropolitan see of York. York had been a metropolitan see.[1] We know little of the history of the York area between the days of Roman Britain and those of Bede but we do know that the Northumbrians were confined to the coast until late in the sixth century. Elmet, the British kingdom lying in the Leeds area, was still unconquered in Æthelfrith's reign: its conquest was most probably achieved by Edwin, that is after the arrival of the Gregorian mission.[2] In view of the nearness of York to Elmet it would be unwise to assume too early a break in the York succession. Nor is it safe to underrate the possibility of the survival of traditions about York's former status. In Canterbury, which had been in English hands probably longer than any other part of Britain, it was still known that the old church given by Æthelberht to Augustine was formerly dedicated to St Martin.[3] It cannot then be ruled out that Eddius knew of York's original status.

Gregory the Great certainly did and proposed to create a province based on York for England north of the Humber. Paulinus had consequently placed his *cathedra* there and Eddius was likely to know both these facts. I should explain Eddius' deliberate ascription of a see and a status to Colman he never possessed by this knowledge. He probably knew York had once been a metropolitan see; he certainly knew that the Pope meant it to resume its status. So when writing a *Life* of the hero of the party of Peter, what better way of attesting his orthodoxy than to describe the see of the Northumbrians as the Pope said it should be?

It seems probable that Gregory's intention was known and discussed at Whitby. Bede tells us that Tuda succeeded Colman, and then Chad and Wilfred succeeded him: from what he says it is clear that the see of the Northumbrians has been moved from Lindisfarne to York but he gives no reasons and makes no comment. Bede says that Tuda was consecrated bishop of the Northumbrians[4] but does not say where his *cathedra* was placed. But he does speak of the election of an abbot of Lindisfarne in such a way that the election appears to be part of the arrangements necessitated by the departure of Colman. Later he tells us that from ancient times the abbot of Lindisfarne had been part

---

[1] *Eborius Episcopus de civitate Eboracensi provincia Britanniae*, attended the council of Arles in 314.—S. Frere, *Britannia*, London, 1967, p. 332. J. C. Mann, *Antiquity*, xxxv, 1961, pp. 316–20, showed that York was one of the four British metropolitan sees of the day.

[2] N. K. Chadwick, *Celt and Saxon*, Cambridge, 1963, p. 151.

[3] HE., i, c. 26. I am told by my archaeologist friends that it is not possible to identify the patron saints of churches in this period from inscriptions. Presumably then the knowledge of the patron of this church must have been preserved by oral tradition which seems to me interesting.

[4] HE., iii, c. 26.

of the bishop's *familia*[1]—this is an implicit denial that the bishop was subordinate to the abbot in the Celtic manner. This is certainly true from the time Lindisfarne became a bishop's seat again in 678, but for a generation before that Lindisfarne had been ruled by an abbot without a bishop. There is no evidence that before Whitby there had ever been an abbot at Lindisfarne other than its proper ruler, St Aidan, and his two successors as bishops of the Northumbrians. It seems most unlikely that after Whitby the appointment of an abbot as well as a bishop resident at Lindisfarne would have been made with all the schismatic overtones that arrangement had. I take it that Tuda either moved to York or meant to. At any rate there is no doubt that before the year was out the see had moved south. This meant that the bishop of the Northumbrian and Bernician king moved away from his court to York—and the potentially breakaway province of Deira. There is no doubt, then, that the move was made very soon after Whitby: there must have been a compelling reason, and I suggest that one of the consequences of the synod was an acceptance of Gregory's original wishes for the siting of the principal northern see.[2] With the exception of the omission of Tuda—and by the time Eddius wrote I doubt if he was of much interest to anyone except someone with a historian's sense of detail like Bede—Eddius gets things right, albeit in a pedantic and legalistic way.

Let us now turn to Wilfrid's stay in Gaul and its reasons. Eddius is scarcely less reticent about them than Bede. He ascribes Chad's intrusion to the remains of the party of Columba—he calls them, tendentiously, Quatrodecimans—but does not consider Chad to be of their number, and he says specifically that Wilfrid was ignorant of Chad's intrusion until his return.[3] Bede does not offer any explanation of Wilfrid's delay either and this is odd since such important and embarrassing consequences followed from it. Just what kind of reasons can Wilfrid have had? We know that it cannot have been his desire for an imposing consecration which he had secured before the year was out. It seems to me that the delay, like the synod of Whitby itself, is best explained by the perennial tensions of Northumbrian politics.

An anonymous reviewer in the *Times Literary Supplement* some years ago pointed out that Alchfrith's conversion to 'roman' ways added religious to the

---

[1] HE., v, c. 27.

[2] Another of Gregory's wishes seems relevant here since it can be shown to have been heeded before Bede recorded the document. HE., i, c. 27, contains the famous or notorious *Responsa*, cl. vi (which seems likely to be genuine) which requires that episcopal consecrations be arranged at a time when other bishops were at hand. Except in cases of dire necessity no consecration might take place without the witness of three or four bishops. Gregory suggests that visits by bishops from Gaul would make suitable occasions. This suggestion sounds very appropriate for its period and very unlike the work of a forger. Since on Bede's own admission there was only one fully licit bishop in England in 664 it is not surprising that Wilfrid should go to a Gaulish synod for consecration, especially if he knew of the papal demand, which I think he did. It is worth noting that Cuthbert was consecrated by Archbishop Theodore and six other bishops.—HE., iv, c. 28.

[3] *Eddius*, c. xiv.

existing political and dynastic tensions between Bernicia and Deira. Oswiu's conversion nipped this development in the bud, but it looks as though there was a price to be paid: obedience to papal commands and the removal of the Northumbrian *cathedra* to Deira. First a neutral bishop is elected but dies untimely and there is not much alternative to Alchfrith's brilliant young abbot, who had played so great a part at the synod. Plummer pointed out that it is evident from Bede's *History* that at some point Alchfrith rebelled against his father. Since Alchfrith disappears from history and Bede's pages after Whitby, he conjectured reasonably enough that this was when the rebellion occurred. Since this implies that the rebellion and its failure lay after Wilfrid's election and departure, it seems no very daring conjecture to explain Wilfrid's delay and Chad's intrusion as part of the aftermath of the rebellion. Oswiu could not at this point recall his see from York to Lindisfarne but at least he could see to it that he was served by a safe Bernician bishop instead of the client of his rebellious son.[1] I should think Eddius no less reticent here than Bede and I find his claim that Wilfrid was ignorant of Chad's election incredible. It seems much more likely that Wilfrid had heard bad news from Northumbria and he stayed in Gaul until he judged it safe to return. When he returned he was not without friends, and powerful ones. We are told that he acted as bishop on occasion for the Mercians[2] and it is plain that his relations with the rising dynasty of Mercia were already close. By 669 Oswiu was pretty well forced to accept Wilfrid unless he were prepared to add the Pope to his enemies, significantly just at a time when the Mercians were prepared to accept 'roman' Christianity.

In 678 Oswiu's son Ecgfrith rejected Wilfrid, ejected him from York, divided the see and neither he nor his successors ever completely restored Wilfrid again. Eddius says that the Queen turned Ecgfrith against Wilfrid because of his temporal possessions and the number of his monasteries. Archbishop Theodore was persuaded to act as accomplice in Wilfrid's disgrace and consecrated three bishops in what had once been the undivided see of the Northumbrians. Further Eddius claims they were unacceptable to Wilfrid as *aliunde inventos et non de subiectis illius parrochiae*.[3] This is scarcely illuminating, little more so than Bede who offers no explanation at all beyond the bare mention of a quarrel between Ecgfrith and Wilfrid.[4] In 678 the king of the Mercians was Æthelred, who was always Wilfrid's friend,[5] except when it was inexpedient

[1] *Bedae*, II, pp. 198–9.   [2] *Eddius*, c. xiv.

[3] *Ibid.*, c. xxiv. Dr Colgrave, p. 168, was puzzled by this passage and concluded that since the intruded bishops were all noted Northumbrian clerics Eddius was "amazingly inaccurate in his description of these men as being picked up elsewhere." I think he misunderstood what Eddius was trying to say. He tells us that three men not subject to Wilfrid's *parochia* were intruded into his *episcopatus*. If Eddius was using *parochia* in its Celtic sense of monastic connection, which must have been known to him, the sense is clear and accurate. The men were not Wilfrid's monks: they were clearly deliberately chosen to be uncongenial to Wilfrid.

[4] HE., iv, c. 12.   [5] *Eddius*, c. xlviii *inter alia*.

to offend Ecgfrith.[1] Some of the monasteries, whose number so offended Ecgfrith's queen, lay in Mercia and he died in one of them when on his way to obey a summons from Ceolred of Mercia who had promised "to order his whole life after my instruction."[2]

Now Wilfrid's lifetime and his tenure of power at York coincided with the ebbing of Northumbrian power south of the Humber and the rise of a new, Mercian hegemony in its stead, a process complete by the time Bede wrote his *History*. Oswiu certainly ruled all England as *brytenwealda* but this hegemony was seriously challenged on his death by Wulfhere of Mercia. His son Ecgfrith, Wilfrid's implacable opponent for most of his career, was temporarily successful in restoring Northumbrian hegemony,[3] and as a result reannexed Lindsey.[4] Wilfrid then, from the circumstances of his career, was little more *persona grata* with the Bernician dynasty than he was in Merovingian Gaul. It looks very much as though it was his identification with the cause of the party of *romanitas* together with his powerful Mercian connections, that made him both dubious to the Bernician dynasty and very difficult to get rid of altogether. It can scarcely be a coincidence, then, that Wilfrid's ejection in 678 occurred at a time when Northumbrian-Mercian relations were at breaking point and his fall was soon followed by the battle of Trent. Of this battle Sir Frank Stenton remarked: "The battle of Trent proved to be one of the decisive incidents in early English history, for Ecgfrith never again attempted to conquer any part of southern England, and his successors were kept from adventures in the south by the new dangers which threatened their northern border."[5] I would suggest that when tension was building up between Northumbria and Mercia, Wilfrid's Mercian connections became anathema to Ecgfrith who saw his power gradually waning before his southern rival, his bishop's friend. Certainly the break-up of Wilfrid's supra-tribal monastic connection was an important object of Northumbrian royal policy. It seems to me that it was his defence of this connection that accounts for Wilfrid's litigation at Rome much better than the division of his see. At any rate the synod that led Wilfrid to make his last voyage to Rome in 703 intended to force Wilfrid to allow Archbishop Beorhtwald of Canterbury to nominate new abbots and abbesses. Stress is laid in a *Northumbrian* synod on the demand that Wilfrid should surrender all his Mercian properties.[6] The king did not seek them for himself, nor did he, as Ecgfrith had done in 678, try to nominate new incumbents for the Northumbrian monasteries. Surely the point is that what mattered to the Northumbrian court, and what drove Wilfrid to Rome in protest, was the dissolution of this inter-tribal connection. It seems that Wilfrid was a little too English and too little Northumbrian for the northern establishment's liking.

[1] *Eddius*, c. xl.   [2] *Ibid.*, c. lxiv.   [3] *Ibid.*, c. xx.   [4] HE., iv, c. 12.
[5] *Anglo-Saxon England*, p. 85.   [6] *Eddius*, c. xlvii.

If I am right in this, Eddius is only a little less reticent than Bede in his reporting of Wilfrid's trials. Obviously Wilfrid cannot have been unaware of the importance of his Mercian connections both as a source of difficulty, and usually, as a source of strength and a defence. He can scarcely have avoided being something of a politician and making political calculations and some of his troubles he plainly asked for. The evidence, however, still suggests to me that Wilfrid had much higher aims than mere political success and that the welfare of the Church as he saw it was an important object of his policies. What is more, it seems to me that in broad outline he was quite right. To see the reasons for this we must leave the world of inter-tribal politics for the problems of contemporary social structure. We may as well begin with Wilfrid's part in the quarrels between 'romans' and Celts.

One has only to read through Bede to see how the Celts he knew, what we should call the Welsh roughly speaking, brought out the venom in a historian otherwise conspicuous for his tact and wide sympathies: Bede is much more anti-British than Eddius for instance. Ostensibly the issue that divided English and Celt was the proper mode of calculating Easter. This issue was at once important and trivial. As a matter of ritual and liturgical custom rather than a doctrinal heresy, we have, or ought to have, learnt from the social anthropologists how very important such matters are to primitive peoples. In pre-literate, or barely literate, societies, such a matter as the calculation of Easter can be also an expression of social identity. In spite of this, with certain exceptions, most of the Christian world did not rate the matter very highly. Bede himself says the difference only arose because of the isolation of the Celtic world from the rest of Christendom;[1] he did not say what caused the isolation. He has usually been followed in what seems a reasonable explanation, no one having produced a better one. It is evident that agreement about the keeping of Easter did not obtain in continental Europe.[2] Even in Ireland itself Dr Hughes has recently pointed out: "There is no evidence that the controversy, long-drawn out as it was, raised anything like the same bitterness in Ireland as it did in England."[3] It is obvious that the bitterness found in England was because the liturgical dispute had important social bearings.

In Northumbria the basic tension between Bernicia and Deira was annually paraded when one side of the court fasted for Palm Sunday whilst the other feasted for Easter Day: just as every Easter after Whitby was a basic confrontation of Briton and Saxon. In the south of Ireland where no secondary issues were involved liturgical revision and conformity seem to have been achieved fairly easily from renewed contacts with the Continent. Even that citadel of conservatism, Iona, conformed in Bede's lifetime, although it cannot have

[1] HE., iii, c. 4. [2] Mgr Ryan in *Essays presented to A. Gwynne.*
[3] K. Hughes, *The Church in Early Irish Society*, London, 1966, p. 108.

been palatable to its monks to be told how to calculate Easter by a province that stood for the most part *in statu pupillari* to the tradition of Columba. In point of fact it was only in the confrontation of Briton and Saxon that violence and bitterness marks the controversy and one wonders if the Welsh would have been the last to conform without the disincentive of Anglophobia? Now although the Easter question was clearly the main one discussed at Whitby and one that always occupied Bede's thoughts, it was not all that was at issue between Roman and Celt. It was these further questions that throw more light on Wilfrid's conduct. I am speaking of conflicting notions of the hierarchical structure of the Church, which seems to me more complicated on both the Celtic and Roman sides than it has seemed to others.

Continental Christianity had inherited the bias of imperial Rome towards *urbanitas*.[1] By the seventh century the idea that a bishop should have his *cathedra* in a town, and the way of looking at a diocese as though it were a type of imperial unit of local government, were so deep-rooted as to have survived a decline in town life to a point where *urbanitas* was nothing but a hindrance to decent church order.[2] In the ancient world towns supported schools and a general cultural life that could occasionally produce an Ambrose or an Augustine, as well as lesser men, for the Church. But early medieval Europe was a rural place where wealth and power were based on the domination of the land and its cultivators. The natural form of ecclesiastical structure for such a world was much more the monastery than the urban episcopal diocese. Gaulish monasticism, deriving as it did from an imitation of the life of the Egyptian monks, had inherited an eremitic bent. The disorders of the times often sent these monks flocking to towns for protection and this naturally increased the bishop's power over them. In any case ancient canon law gave monks, who were legally laymen, little protection against a hostile bishop, even if there had been any effective means of enforcing the law. It seems to me that the source of the obvious weakness of the Gaulish Church at this period lay in the way in which the episcopate was strong enough to control and limit the development of a native monasticism without being strong enough to guide the Church in general, and in being without many of the kind of bishops who might have sought to give this kind of guidance.

The Celtic world had the great advantage that it had no towns. It was, therefore, forced on conversion to find a type of ecclesiastical structure suited to its own needs. The solution was the tribal monastery, often, if not always, with a hereditary abbacy and one in which, although bishops would certainly be found for essential sacramental purposes, the ruler of the community was the

---

[1] E. Ewig, 'Kirche und Civitas in der Merowingerzeit', *Settimane di . . . Spoleto*, VII, 1960, pp. 45 *et seq.*

[2] M. Roblin, 'Cités ou Citadelles', *Revue des Etudes Anciennes*, LXXIII, 1951, pp. 301–11.

abbot. In some cases the abbot would himself be in episcopal orders and for many parts of Western Europe for some generations such a monastery would not have been easy to distinguish from a 'normal' episcopal *familia*: but in others, such as Iona, the abbot was not a bishop and such an arrangement would certainly have seemed unconventional if not scandalous to many. It does not seem to me sensible to speak as though the bureaucratic city-based episcopate were of the very essence of the Church and to use it as a model to apply to all periods and places. One cannot look at a blue-print of a social structure and judge it as good or bad, or one cannot do this sensibly. One must apply the test of function and results. If we do this it seems obvious that it was certain forms of Celtic monasticism that really mattered in the seventh century.

It must be obvious that the decisive task of the day was a missionary one, to convert the pagan, largely Germanic, peoples on the fringe of Christian Europe, and reform the decayed institutions of Gaul and elsewhere. By and large, the only organized groups of men who undertook missionary work on any scale were the Irish. In addition to this, without any tradition of literacy behind them or any residual Roman influence, they made some of their monasteries centres of learning that compared at least favourably with continental centres that could boast much longer traditions. If we take a single example, the obvious one, of St Columbanus, it is evident what one mission could do to reform a well-established but decadent Church.[1] Columbanus quarrelled with the Frankish bishops over the mode of reckoning Easter, of course, but in his letter to the Pope he is much more concerned that men as corrupt as these urban bishops should interfere with his monasteries. It is possible that Columbanus changed his method of calculating Easter before he died, and if he did not, his monks certainly did within a decade.[2]

Columbanus' idea of monasticism is worth looking at and easily accessible. It is evident from his *Regulae* that he had rejected the eremitical form of monasticism for a coenobitic rule subject to an authoritarian abbot. In this he was taking much the same 'eccentric' line as St Benedict had done a generation or so earlier. We now know that this kind of monasticism was much less common than used to be thought. Whether Columbanus himself knew Benedict's *Rule* may be doubted but it is not impossible since he greatly admired Gregory the Great's writings, as it may also be doubted if there were ever more than a handful of communities professing the *Rule* exclusively and completely before the tenth century.[3] But certainly the *Rule* is first found outside Monte Cassino in

[1] Courtois, *Settimano di. . . Spoleto*, IV, 1957; G. M. Walker, *Opera S. Columbani*, Dublin, 1957, intro.

[2] Walker, *op. cit.*, p. xxxiii.

[3] John, *Revue Bénédictine*, LXXV, 1965, pp. 212 *et seq.* Dom Hubert Dauphin, *Revue d'Histoire Ecclésiastique*, 1968, p. 1112, in a review of *Orbis Britanniae* does me the injustice of supposing me

company with Columbanus' *Regulae* and in houses of his connection.[1] I have spoken, as is customary, of Celtic monasticism, and certainly, as the activities of the tradition of Columba, as well others less famous, show the will to do missionary work and the ability to sustain it were not confined to Columbanus and his connection. None the less, in the importance of what was achieved Columbanus stands head and shoulders above the rest. It is, therefore, of some importance to ask, as Dr Hughes has asked, how typically Celtic was Columbanus,[2] and to see that for all we know he was not more typical than Benedict's Monte Cassino or Gregory the Great's little monastery in Rome. At any rate there were important and fruitful connections between all three.

It cannot be a coincidence that outside Celtic Christendom the only source of missionary activity was Gregory's Roman monastery from which Augustine and his companions were sent to Canterbury. Gregory was a thoroughly authoritarian abbot, filled with the spirit of Benedict's ideal abbot.[3] Tension between the monk, Gregory style, and the more traditional-minded clergy was felt in Rome itself, perhaps more strongly than elsewhere.[4] Even if Columbanus expressed himself strongly about the local episcopate, the monk-party in Rome agreed with him and, a few years after Columbanus' death, Gregory's true heir

ignorant of the text of Dom Guy Ferrari's book on *Early Roman Monasticism* because I cited it, and referred the readers to Professor D. Bullough's review in the *Journal of Ecclesiastical History*. I had, of course, consulted Dom Ferrari's book directly but wished to direct the reader to Professor Bullough's important comments on his conclusions. I was therefore aware that Dom Ferrari cited the traditional view of the basically Benedictine character of early English monasticism, with which I do not agree. I did not mention his remark because it seemed foolish to cite a book about Roman monasteries as an authority for a cliché about English monasticism, and churlish to chide it on a matter of peripheral concern for the subject of the book. Dom Dauphin appears to argue that, because one of the most ancient manuscripts of the *Rule* is of English provenance, this proves Benedictine monasticism existed in England before the tenth century. This scarcely follows in the era of the *regula mixta*. Benedict Biscop adopted an eclectic ruled based on his experience of the way of life in seventeen different monasteries.—*Bedae Opera*, I, p. 374. Wilfrid certainly introduced the *Rule* into Northumbria and, if Dom Hallinger is correct, probably into England.—*Eddius*, c. xiv and cf. c. xlvii. But it cannot have been followed fully in his monasteries in view of what Eddius tells us about the way Wilfrid controlled the abbatial succession and the nature of his will.

[1] John, *art. cit.*, p. 218.   [2] *Op. cit.*, p. 59.

[3] Etienne Delaruelle, 'L'Eglise Romain et ses Relations avec l'Eglise Franque', *Setimmane di. . . Spoleto*, VII, 1960, p. 161: "Cette époque n'est pas celle des *Dictatus Papae* et l'on sait déjà que ce pape n'est pas un canoniste, mais un pasteur et un moine; il ordonne, mais à la manière de l'abbé dans la Règle de saint Benoît: *Ausculta fili*."

[4] The extremely unpleasant story of the death of Gregory's immediate successor, Sabinian, in the Whitby *Life* of Gregory is probably an echo of this controversy. Sabinian replaced monks appointed by Gregory with secular clergy.—Duchesne, *Liber Pontificalis*, i, p. 315, n. 6, and cf. the epitaph *loc. cit.* The next pope, Boniface IV, was a disciple of Gregory and a lover of monks but he was succeeded by Deusdedit who once again deposed monks and restored the secular clergy. The most important pro-monastic pope after Gregory was Honorius I (625–38). He founded a monastery; was admired by the Columbanian monk Jonas, and gave the first charter of exemption from episcopal authority to a community of monks, Columbanus' foundation at Bobbio; cf. his obituary in *LP* and Duchesne's notes. It would be interesting to know if the savagery of the reaction to Honorius' doctrinal indiscretions had anything to do with these Roman politics.

in more ways than one, Honorius I, granted Bobbio the first charter of exemption from episcopal control in history. In this way the monks were by implication recognized as part of the clergy, a policy which, if the Augustinian mission is anything to go by, Gregory the Great fully shared. The importance of the charter of exemption for the future of the Church and the achievement of an authentic Benedictine monasticism cannot be more than mentioned here. Columbanus' monks returned the compliment. The cult of Peter, which in early Merovingian Gaul had been very much an 'also ran' behind that of Martin and Denis, the local saints, was promoted by them to the status of principal Gaulish cult, whose most exalted clients were, of course, the Pippinides.[1] The importance of the cult of Peter in early medieval papalism has long been known.

I am suggesting that the conventional antitheses by which we judge this period, or at least English historians do, either contrasting Celtic and continental Christianity or opposing Celtic individualism to Roman organization, will not altogether do. We need to look at certain kinds of monasticism, less rare perhaps in the Celtic world, but not demonstrably common even there. We need to oppose these more or less coenobitic monasteries to that *damnosa hereditas* of imperial Rome, the traditional diocese, which had long outlived the social structure that was its *raison d'être*.[2]

From its geographical as from its social situation, the infant English Church was placed in the middle of all this, and it is by no means easy to see just what the consequences of Whitby were where it mattered, in ecclesiastical organization. The removal of the see of the Northumbrians from Lindisfarne suggests that there were consequences and that these were important. It also suggests that the pull of urban tradition was strong, and, if what I have written above has any force, the removal was not obviously a reform. We must here face an important question about contemporary English society: were there in fact any towns? The older learning discounted the possibility. We have been told for a long time that the Anglo-Saxons hated town life and ignored or abandoned the

---

[1] Delaruelle, *art. cit.*, pp. 163 *et seq.*

[2] A good deal of confusion on this point is due to the fact that work done on English diocesan organization is concerned for the most part with the twelfth and later centuries. It is instructive to compare some of the detailed studies of the diocese of the high middle ages, say C. R. Cheney, *English Synodalia*, taken in conjunction with the same author's Ford Lectures, *From Becket to Langton*; or F. Barlow, *Durham Jurisdictional Peculiars*, with what Bede and Eddius have to say about the nature of the episcopal office. We may notice their assumption, especially clear in the key text, Bede's letter to Ecgberht, that the bishop baptizes and confirms his entire flock. It scarcely seems that there was any trace of a true parochial organization in England before the tenth-century reformation when the evidence is clear. On the Continent St Boniface's reform legislation for the Frankish Church is relevant. He even found it necessary to order the subjection of the clergy to their diocesan bishop; cf. Herr Ewig's brilliant essay in H. Jedin and J. Dolan, *Handbook of Church History*, III, London, 1969, pp. 13–14. Parishes were, after all, what the dioceses of the high middle ages were all about.

Romano-British foundations they found here; the trouble with this learning is that contemporaries did not talk like this at all. In his exposition of the Gospel of Mark, Bede writes: "Ut cum forte villam aut oppidum, aut alium quemlibet locum in quo sit domus orationis Deo consecrata, intramus."[1] In his *History* he says St Alban was martyred *iuxta civitatem Verolamium*,[2] which could be an antique reminiscence, but he describes Paulinus' first convert as *praefectus* of the city of Lincoln, which could not.[3] He speaks of Oswald's royal city,[4] as well as giving a description of London which points undeniably to a thriving urban community. All these references seem to point to a number of towns as going communities of some kind.[5]

Certainly if the early English had not towns they showed remarkable foresight in choosing the sites of important future urban centres in which to put their bishops. Winchester was not the first West Saxon see, but its foundation dates from the first generation of West Saxon Christianity. The foundation decree speaks of a see *in Wentanam civitatem*.[6] It was plainly an urban centre of some importance by 1066,[7] and in the light of this Mr Biddle's excavation reports are of special interest.[8] It looks very much as though there was continuous occupation of Canterbury.[9] Worcester was the seat of a bishop before 700 and literary evidence exists to show it was an urban centre of sorts not more than a century later. Professor Finberg has some interesting observations on Gloucester, Bath, and Cirencester in this connection.[10] Perhaps the most interesting of these early examples is a real *exceptio quae probat regulam*, the primitive West Saxon see of Dorchester. No one would expect on the traditional learning to find continuity with Roman Britain here, but there is some interesting evidence.

Bede says Birinus the apostle of Wessex was given *civitatem quae vocatur Dorcic* for his see.[11] It is really a very odd choice as a centre of the West Saxon see and hardly surprising that Winchester was quickly found more suitable. After all even in the tenth century Dorchester lay on the marches of Wessex proper, and, to judge by its attachment to Ramsey, was deemed to belong to the *scir* of the ealdormen of East Anglia, not Wessex. Something of the expla-

---

[1] Migne, *Patrologia Latina*, xcii, 243 B.   [2] HE., i, c. 7.   [3] HE., ii, c. 16.
[4] HE., iii, c. 12.
[5] *Eddius*, c. xxxvi *et seq.*, speaks of Osfrith *praefectus . . . quae praeerat Inbroninis urbi regis* (Moonen, p. 367, discusses the identification of this place and tentatively chooses Broomridge in Northumberland; Colgrave remains agnostic). Osfrith was given charge of Wilfrid and the passage suggests that Broomridge, if that is where it was, was some kind of centre of government and contained at least what Colgrave called dungeons. The anonymous *Life* of Cuthbert, ed. Colgrave, Cambridge, 1940, pp. 116, 122, speaks as though Carlisle were still inhabited. Bede's *Life*, Colgrave, *op. cit.*, p. 243, is specially interesting on this.
[6] Haddan and Stubbs, *Councils*, III, pp. 126–7.   [7] Harmer, *Writs*, no. 111 and commentary.
[8] *Antiquaries Journal* in progress.
[9] *Civitas Capitals*, ed. J. S. Wacher, Leicester, 1966, p. 91.
[10] *Gloucestershire Studies*, Leicester, 1957, pp. 58 *et seq.*   [11] HE., iii, c. 7.

nation of this odd choice is suggested by the existence of a town there in Roman British times as a late inscription reveals.[1] Professor Frere, moreover, thinks Dorchester was occupied rather than destroyed by the invaders.[2] It would be unwise then to dismiss too easily the familiarity of the contemporary sources with the *civitas*; but it is incredible that they can have been of sufficient size to support an efficient diocesan organization of either the classical or the properly medieval type.

However one looks at it, the vitality of the English Church depended on its monasteries: the diocese, especially where associated with these decayed urban remains, is not likely to have been of much real value. Now the young English Church was particularly fortunate in that it was well-placed to draw on the experience of the Celtic and Gaulish monasticism, already beginning to influence each other. The sources of influence of Irish monasticism on the new English Christians need no demonstration, the Frankish sources are less familiar.[3] Bede himself tells us[4] of the daughter of a king of Kent who went to a convent in Brie, adding that since there were so few convents in England many nuns from Britain went to Gaul. He points out that girls, it is implied of high birth, went especially to Brie, Chelles, and Andelys. This is supported by casual references in saints' lives. There is such a reference in the most ancient *Life* of St Gertrude. St Mildred, who later became abbess of Minster in the isle of Thanet, went to Chelles and we know from the *Life* of an abbess of Chelles that more than one English king asked her for teachers to be sent. Professor Finberg has suggested that the first abbess of Wenlock in Shropshire, a Frankish nun called Liobsynde, came to England as the result of such an invitation.[5]

[1] R. Wright, *RIB.*, no. 235, which mentions a *beneficiarius consularis* apparently established there. I take it that this is the evidence behind Frere, *Britannia*, p. 195. It is just worth noting that Professor A. H. M. Jones, *The Later Roman Empire*, Oxford, 1964, II, p. 595, points out that *beneficiarii* belonged to a class that "sometimes rose to be bishops." The inscription is, of course, pagan. I am indebted to my colleague Dr G. B. Jones for drawing my attention to this inscription.

[2] *Britannia*, p. 377. He also assumes that Romano-British towns none the less died out "later."— *Civitas Capitals*, pp. 87 *et seq.* It is easy to imagine that some or even all British towns would succumb to the English invasions but as it is clear that some did not and were occupied, it seems to me that a good deal more evidence than Professor Frere adduces is necessary to allow one to dismiss all continuity of urban life from the scene.

[3] For some of what follows I am indebted to a personal communication from the late Père Grosjean. I alone am responsible for the interpretations put upon the evidence.

[4] *HE.*, iii, c. 8. It should be remembered that Frankish and Irish influences were not mutually exclusive. There were Irish monks and more than one Irish *paruchia* in Francia.—Grosjean, *Analecta Bollandiana*, LXXXV, 1957, pp. 373 *et seq.*; Hughes, *op. cit.*, cap. 9.

[5] *The Early Charters of the West Midlands*, Leicester, 1961, pp. 208–9. For St Gertrude, see Grosjean, *art. cit.*, pp. 388 *et seq.*; for Chelles, see *Vitae Bertilae*, ed. Levison, *Monumenta Germaniae Historica, s.r. Merovingicarum*, VI, p. 106. An East Anglian princess, Æthelburg, was abbess of Farmoûtier-en-Brie.—F. M. Stenton in *The Anglo-Saxons*, ed. P. Clemoes, London, 1959, pp. 44 *et seq.* Hereswith, sister of St Hilda and one-time wife of an East Anglian king, became a nun at Chelles.—Stenton, *op. cit.*, p. 46. Hilda herself intended to go to Francia at one time.—Cf. Grosjean,

All this must have had an effect on English church life. It cannot be a co-incidence that the double monastery, so popular in early England, is found earlier in Gaul but not in Ireland. It will be noticed that our evidence points to the influence of a group of monasteries lying in that part of Gaul most closely connected with the kindred of the rising Pippinides: this can hardly be un-connected with the close associations of the Anglo-Saxon monk-missionaries of the next generation with the Carolingians. But it cannot be denied that it was English monasteries, all-male communities influenced by the Celtic world like Jarrow or Malmesbury, rather than mixed communities influenced by the Frankish, that counted: the urban diocesan episcopal *familia* has little to show.[1] Alcuin alone must say much for York but there is not much else. Canterbury under Theodore was, of course, very important but was it the cathedral or the monastery? The fact that early kings of Kent and archbishops of Canterbury were buried in the monastery is surely significant. In the light of all this St Wilfrid's litigation takes on a slightly different aspect.

It would follow that the universal criticism heaped on his head for resisting the division of the Northumbrian see into three is misplaced, as is the assump-tion that Archbishop Theodore assisted King Ecgfrith in a matter pertaining to the good order of the Church and nothing more. When dioceses were split in the early Middle Ages or the boundaries of provinces changed, politics were never far away. One might cite the history of the see of Magdeburg in Ottonian times; the history of north-west France, especially the see of Dol, throughout the period; and, coming nearer home, the inglorious history of the province of Lichfield in the next century. In so far as these new dioceses fed on monas-teries,[2] they must have done as much harm as good.

If we turn to Wilfrid's litigation it is obvious that it was his vast monastic connection that mattered to him and drove him to Rome, not the division of the diocese. In his first plea before the Pope, Wilfrid seems prepared from the beginning of the lawsuit to accept the division of the diocese.[3] He tells the Pope: "if again it has been decided to appoint bishops in the same see over which I have been ruling . . . let only such be preferred with whom I can serve God in unity." This is Wilfrid's initial plea, and it is to be noticed that before the suit has opened he concedes the principle of the divided diocese: what he is claiming in effect is the right to chose his colleagues. He goes further and says he is willing to accept an increase in the number of the northern bishops, not

Anal. Boll., LXXVIII, 1960, p. 368; cf. also E. Ewig, 'Milo et eiusmodi similes', *Sankt Bonifatius*, Fulda, 1954, p. 418 and n. 31. I do not think this list is exhaustive.

[1] Cf. the late Dr Colgrave's interesting remarks on the limitations of Whitby as an intellectual centre.—*Celt and Saxon*, p. 130.

[2] *Rev. Bén.*, LXXV, 1965, p. 227. One of Archbishop Theodore's earliest canons sought to protect monasteries from bishops.—HE., iv, c. 5.

[3] *Eddius*, c. xxx.

only if the Pope decrees so, but if Archbishop Theodore and his fellow bishops think it expedient. In effect the Pope gave him nominal restoration, but in fact only the right to choose his colleagues.[1] Not surprisingly in view of the Mercian orientation of Wilfrid's *familia*, this was never obeyed. In view of the provocative choice of bishop—and it is often overlooked that Wilfrid was not offered colleagues, but first ejected and then presented with three men to take his place all chosen as likely to be unwelcome to him[2]—his persistence in opposition is intelligible. Wilfrid's last plea was largely undertaken in defence of his monastic connection.[3]

Obviously with Wilfrid's Mercian connections it is hardly surprising that the Northumbrian court should regard him with suspicion: it may be, however, that Wilfrid was not motivated by political considerations, or not primarily. I should judge his political involvement as no more than the consequences of his attempt to be a truly Catholic bishop.

Wilfrid's connection was a great one and his power was mainly shown by either acting as titular abbot himself or getting the abbot or abbess to make over the monastery's property to him personally.[4] It must be noted that Columbanus had just such a connection which was maintained, as Wilfrid's was not, for some time after his death; so did every monastic reformer of note until the triumph of Cluny made them unnecessary. What these connections were aimed against was the intrusion of the family into the monastery. The main problem was the choice of abbot or abbess. It is obvious that from the first the family sought to intervene in the monastery and turn the abbatial office at least

---

[1] *Eddius*, c. xxxii.

[2] One of them was closely associated with Chad's intrusion into York; another was Eata, who had been ejected from Ripon to make way for Wilfrid; a third was closely associated with Whitby, a house hostile to Wilfrid.—*Eddius*, c. liv. The first two can be seen as inclining towards liturgical conservatism, if one wishes, but not the third. Whitby was closely associated with the immediate family of Edwin and the 'southerners', and therefore with the 'roman' party. It is here that the first *Life* of Gregory was written. See Colgrave on the *Life* in *Celt and Saxon*. Mr Wallace-Hadrill, EHR., April 1969, has some suggestive remarks about the purpose behind this *Life* in his review of Dr Colgrave's edition which confirm the 'roman' rather than the Celtic orientation of the house. Yet St Hilda and her community opposed Wilfrid. What all three new bishops had in common was a probable antipathy to the Mercians.

[3] *Eddius*, c. li, shows that Wilfrid wanted only protection for his *parochia* and their lands; he is prepared to let what may happen to York so long as he can keep his monasteries of Hexham and Ripon. The usual opinion that Wilfrid's main object in litigating in Rome was to preserve his diocese intact seems very unjust to him. Although Aldhelm's remarks about the Welsh refusing to so much as eat with English Christians has almost reached the status of something every schoolboy may be supposed to know, *Eddius*, c. xlix, is less familiar. Part of this last attempt to break up Wilfrid's connection was directed against Wilfrid's monks at Ripon, and presumably elsewhere. They were excommunicated. If one of their priests or abbots ate with a layman and blessed the food, it was to be cast away "as if offered to idols." Vessels which they had touched had to be washed before anyone else did. It is impossible that Eddius can have invented this; it happened only a little while before he wrote.

[4] *Ibid.*, c. xxi.

into a family fief. This was apparently the case even in Irish monasticism, as the history of Iona shows. Even Bede took hereditary succession of this kind for granted when he relates a miracle performed by St John of Beverley for an abbess, healing her sick daughter whom she intended to succeed her.[1] The early history of Gloucester abbey shows it to have been in the same case,[2] and the Withington dispute shows the system at its worst.[3] Even Wilfrid expected a kinsman, though an experienced monk, to succeed him at Ripon,[4] and several more instances are noted by Plummer.[5] There were attempts to evade or mitigate this system. Bede's own abbot sought a papal privilege to prevent a kinsman succeeding him,[6] and was successful at least for a time. But it was Wilfrid who made the most sustained attempt to circumvent the system by his vast connection on the lines of the Celtic *paruchiae* which had been successful elsewhere. By the end of Wilfrid's life it must have been obvious that political conditions meant an end to the connection and in his will, in which he considered himself competent to chose his successor at Ripon, he left a third of his property to his abbots and abbesses "so that they may be able to purchase the friendship of kings and bishops."[7]

The need for monks to bribe their bishop speaks volumes for the nature of early English episcopacy, and it must throw light on Wilfrid's long fight against so many of his brother bishops. I have already pointed to the obvious resemblances between Wilfrid's and Columbanus' lives and their monastic policies. It is relevant to point also to the generation following Wilfrid. In England Bede's strictures on the family monasteries of his old age and his broad hints about the quality of the Northumbrian episcopate in his letter to Bishop Ecgberht go some way to bear out Wilfrid's conduct. Bede dates the serious decline of the Northumbrian Church to a point in effect very near the time of Wilfrid's death.[8] Wilfrid's true successors must be sought on the Con-

---

[1] HE., v, c. 3.   [2] *Orbis Britanniae*, pp. 83–8.   [3] *Ibid.*, p. 85.   [4] *Eddius*, c. lxiii.
[5] *Bedae*, II, p. 262.   [6] *Ibid.*, I, p. 393.   [7] *Eddius*, c. lxiii.
[8] In his letter to Ecgberht and his dating of the rise of the fraudulent monasteries. There may be a little more to be said for these communities than Bede allows. The evidence suggests that the pagan English were polygynous and continued to be so for some time after the conversion. There is direct evidence that the pagan Germans whom St Boniface sought to convert—who seem to have been regarded as rather similar sorts of people to the 'Anglo-Saxons'—were polygynous, since Gregory II allowed them to contract bigamous marriages under certain conditions.—S. *Bonifatii et Lulli Epistolae*, ed. Tangl, Berlin, 1955, no. 26. The decisive evidence seems to me, however, inferential. It appears to have been a widespread Germanic custom for sons to marry surviving stepmothers.— D. Whitelock, *The Beginnings of English Society*, London, 1952, p. 150. It is known to have happened twice in Anglo-Saxon history when Æthelberht's son and, in the ninth century, King Ælfred's brother and the daughter of Charles the Bald were involved. This appears to be a clear case of one of the customs which social anthropologists call the levirate and widow inheritance. It is not possible in this case to distinguish which since there was no issue of either marriage, and the criteria for distinguishing which custom obtained is whether the biological father was regarded as the true father of children of this marriage (i.e. widow inheritance) or whether the dead husband was deemed the true father (i.e. the levirate). Since this custom was mentioned by Gregory the Great—or whoever

tinent,[1] notably his disciple Willibrord. Willibrord and Boniface seem to have disliked many of their contemporary bishops much as Wilfrid did his,[2] and to have sought similar remedies, breeding their own bishops in their monasteries.

At this distance just how secular-minded a man Wilfrid was cannot be known with certainty. But judged against the standards of his day—standards, that is, embodied in the lives and careers of what all would concede were the best churchmen of their day, Gregory the Great, Columbanus, and so on—Wilfrid does seem to belong in this company. Like them he could not always keep clear of politics and they like him have some dubious episodes to explain away. At any rate Wilfrid seems a truly representative 'English' churchman of his day in a way that no one else was. The great champion of Rome and Peter, he never got much change out of Peter's vicar, who perhaps hardly understood his very Celtic policies. His missionary zeal, his belief in authoritarian communities, under the authority of St Benedict's *Rule*, all place him amongst a small group of dedicated monks,[3] who whatever their origins, Irish, Roman, English, had a

wrote the *Responsa*—without any further discussion of the problems of paternity to which the levirate must have given rise, I should think it safer to suppose that the Anglo-Saxons practised widow-inheritance. Like the levirate, it is in all known cases invariably accompanied by polygyny. My colleague Professor Worsley points out to me that both my instances are royal, and in primitive societies it does not follow that royal customs are necessarily practised by commoners too. But the discussion of the issue in the *Responsa* and its incorporation in Bede suggests to me that it was a common custom. Professor Worsely also points out that to an overwhelming majority of primitive tribes, this custom would be as detestable as it was to Gregory the Great; the Anglo-Saxons were very savage indeed. It does not follow that because a society admits polygyny many or most men have more than one wife. In most surviving polygynous societies most men are monogamous. Demographic reasons make it possible for a limited degree of polygyny to be possible even in societies with a roughly equal number of men and women. In Anglo-Saxon society the probable degree of violence, especially in the North, must have accentuated the number of young widows. We cannot of course estimate the degree to which polygyny was practised, but at least it is possible that men of high status groups, to which Bede's family abbots plainly belonged, who were prepared to live a monogamous life, tempered with religious offices of some kind, may have felt themselves to have undergone a *conversatio morum* more intense than Bede allowed. Some searching questions about Anglo-Saxon kinship structure, and some important doubts about the existence of the Germanists' putative tightly organized families, are raised by Dr Baric, 'Kinship in Anglo-Saxon Society', *British Journal of Sociology*, IX, pp. 3–4. I owe a good deal here to discussions with Dr Baric and Professor Max Gluckmann.

[1] Levison, *England and the Continent in the Eighth Century*, Oxford, 1946, pp. 50 *et seq*.

[2] Ewig, *Sankt Bonifatius*, pp. 412–40, for an idea of what diocesan politics on the Continent were like in the next generation after Wilfrid's death. From Bede's letter there were certain similarities between the Northumbrian bishops of the time and those like Milo of Trier, whom Willibrord and Boniface seem to have disliked because they came from families where "herrschte eine religiös-kirchliche Gesinnung, die aber nicht von der art Bonifatius war" nor perhaps of Wilfrid or Bede either.

[3] At the council of 703 Wilfrid defended himself and his long career; what he thought he had done well is not without interest. He makes no reference whatever to his episcopal career. He is proud of having extirpated Celtic heresies but for the rest his pride is in his monastic achievements. He taught the Northumbrians the right tonsure; the use of double antiphons in primitive fashion; the introduction of the *Rule*. This passage deserves more notice in assessments of Wilfrid's motives than it has been given.

vision of a Church very different from the one they actually lived in and did a remarkable amount to bring it about.[1]

---

[1] Since the above paper was written *Christianity in Britain*, ed. M. W. Barley and R. P. C. Hanson, Leicester, 1968, has appeared. Several of the papers it contains are relevant to my subject. I was also unable to consult until too late Mr J. Campbell's important introduction to his edited translation of Bede's *History*, New York, 1968, which has some interesting remarks on Wilfrid.

The Economic Problems of the See of York: Decline and Recovery in the Sixteenth Century

By CLAIRE CROSS

A LEGEND has long persisted that the temporalities of the see of York suffered disastrously at the time of the Reformation through spoliation by the crown. Unembellished evidence confirms that in the decade between 1536 and 1546 Archbishops Edward Lee and Robert Holgate surrendered to Henry VIII a very large part of their ancient episcopal lands and that vast northern estates, which the archbishops of York had possessed since long before the Conquest, passed permanently into royal ownership. Yet some early York historians have been reluctant to admit that the crown granted to the see ecclesiastical revenues, chiefly arising from the recently dissolved monasteries, in at least partial recompense for the lands the two successive archbishops had renounced. Undoubtedly during the middle years of the sixteenth century the see of York underwent a period of serious economic disruption but it seems that the archbishops did not have to face a lasting catastrophic fall in their income. Indeed, by 1600 the archbishop of York received an income from temporalities nominally equal to the income his predecessor had enjoyed in 1536. What had changed, and this had long-term consequences both religious and social for the subsequent history of the see, was the source of this revenue.

The first historians of York, James Torre, who wrote his immensely detailed collection on the church in York towards the end of the seventeenth century, and Archbishop John Sharp, who commissioned a reconstruction of the pre-Reformation lands of the see soon after he entered upon his archiepiscopal responsibilities in 1691, from either prudence or considered judgement, did not dwell upon the Henrician impoverishment of the see.[1] Torre meticulously described the manors which Archbishop Lee in 1543 and Archbishop Holgate in 1545 had granted to the crown but refrained (as was his custom) from commenting on the transaction, apart from observing that Holgate "exchanged with the king many of his archiepiscopal lands for other rich parsonages appropriated to the dissolved monasteries."[2] There was no remark at all on the valuable account of "the present estates of the archbishops of York with some

---

[1] J. M. Biggins, *Historians of York*, St Anthony's Hall Publications, No. 10, 1956. Torre's two manuscript volumes are in the Minster Library, York.

[2] York Minster Library, Torre, MS. Minster volume, pp. 473, 350–436.

account of their origins" compiled for Archbishop Sharp in 1700.[1] No such reticence curbed later historians. Browne Willis in 1727 wrote largely about the "sacrilegious alienations" begun by Lee in 1543. He reserved, however, his most severe censures for Holgate because of his neglect of the see which "within a month after his translation [January 1544] he greatly impoverished, by passing away to the king and his heirs . . . thirteen manors in Northumberland, forty in Yorkshire, six in Nottinghamshire, and eight in Gloucestershire; in lieu of which he obtained . . . thirty-three impropriations and advowsons, late parcels of abbey lands. . . And though, by these unworthy measures he had heaped and amassed a great deal of wealth, beyond what any other bishop in England was master of, yet it did not prosper with him: for in Edward VI reign he met with his troubles. . ." Having used for his evidence a sixteenth-century manuscript collected by Archbishop Sharp, Willis concluded: "this see being thus pillaged and garbled in Henry VIII's reign, King Edward VI had no room to plunder, nor was here any alienation extorted in Queen Elizabeth's reign. . ."[2] Francis Drake, York's great eighteenth-century historian, took over Browne Willis's opinions as he took over much of his history of the Minster, and repeated the allegations against Edward Lee and Robert Holgate for their improper surrender of archiepiscopal lands to the crown.[3] And so the legend developed. Like most legends it contains a modicum of truth.

When they came to try to describe in detail the extent and the value of the ancient episcopal lands of the see of York, Torre and Sharp discovered that no pre-Reformation receiver-general's accounts (or indeed any detailed accounts) had survived in York. Under these circumstances Torre, confined to York, contented himself with the piecemeal information he could extract from the dean and chapter archives, particularly from the dean and chapter lease books. Sharp took the matter further and had a search made of the Public Records in London. The Henrician survey of the lands of the see seems already to have been missing, but he did find a manuscript in the First Fruits Office which gave a complete description and valuation of the pre-Reformation lands of the see in 1534.[4]

Little new material for reconstructing the ancient archiepiscopal lands has been found since the investigations of Archbishop Sharp. Information in York itself is sparse in the extreme; indeed, the very memory of the pre-Reformation estates seems largely to have disappeared. There exists, however, in the Public Record Office a valor of all the possessions of Edward Lee made at the visitation of the province by Richard Leyton and Thomas Legh on 12 January 1535[6] and

[1] The Church Commissioners' records deposited in the Borthwick Institute, York (to which reference is made by kind permission of the Archivist), CC Ab.2.6. [67789].
[2] Browne Willis, *A Survey of the Cathedrals of York, Durham, Carlisle...*, I, 1727, pp. 27, 44–5, 19.
[3] F. Drake, *Eboracum*, 1736, p. 452.   [4] Browne Willis, *Survey*, I, p. 18.

this provides a detailed description of archiepiscopal lands immediately before their general disruption.[1] By 1536 it is clear that the lands of the see of York were administered in nine distinct units, most of them of very ancient formation: in Northumberland the archbishop held the regality of Hexhamshire; in Yorkshire the lordship of Ripon, the barony of Sherburn, the lordship of Otley, and the lordship of Beverley; in Nottinghamshire the lordships of Scrooby and Southwell; and lastly, outside the northern province, the barony of Churchdown in Gloucestershire, and the lordship of Battersea in Surrey.

The regality of Hexhamshire was both one of the most ancient and one of the most valuable possessions of the see of York. In 674 Queen Etheldrid is said to have given it out of her dower to Archbishop Wilfrid in order to endow the archbishopric of York. The regality consisted of the thirteen manors of Hexham, Errington, Wall, Acomb, Hallington, Keepwick, Greenridge, Keenley, East Allen, Catton, Ninebanks, West Allen, and Newlands. Archbishop Melton in 1319 considered that Hexhamshire alone produced a third of the revenues of the archbishopric. Later in the fourteenth century the value of the regality fell sharply because of Scottish raids, but during the latter part of the fifteenth century the income derived from the Northumberland property slowly recovered.[2] Henry VIII's visitors valued the regality of Hexhamshire at a clear annual value of £196 19s. 4¾d.[3]

In Yorkshire the lordship of Beverley in the East Riding brought in the highest revenues in the early sixteenth century. Like the regality of Hexhamshire it had come to the see long before the Conquest: Torre maintained that King Athelstan had given it to the archbishopric.[4] It included the manors of Kingston upon Hull, Patrington, Tharlthorpe, Frismarsh, Hall Garth, Elloughton, Wetwang, Wilton, Bishop Wilton, Beverley, Skidby, and Bishop Burton. This collection of manors, most of them grouped around Hull but three, Wetwang, Wilton, and Bishop Wilton, in the north part of the East Riding, much nearer to York, was considered in 1536 to produce £462 5s. 10d. free of all encumbrances.[5]

Two other Yorkshire lordships, the barony of Sherburn, and the lordship of Ripon, approached the lordship of Beverley in value. The barony of Sherburn included property in York itself and the manors of Bishopthorpe, Cawood, Wistow, Sherburn, and Bishopslathes. Although by the sixteenth century the barony was apparently administered as a single unit its component manors, unlike those in the regality of Hexhamshire or the lordship of Beverley, seem to

---

[1] Public Record Office, SC 11/766. This document does not seem to have been used previously by northern historians. It was not published by the Record Commissioners in vol. v of the *Valor Ecclesiasticus* where there is no account of the temporalities of the see of York.

[2] A. B. Hinds, *History of Northumberland*, III, pt I, Hexhamshire, 1896, pp. 20–66.

[3] P.R.O., SC 11/766.   [4] Minster Library, Torre, MS. Minster vol., pp. 350–3.

[5] P.R.O., SC 11/766.

have been acquired over a much longer period of time. According to Torre, Athelstan had given the manors of Sherburn, Cawood, and Wistow (and probably Bishopslathes) to the see, but it was not until some centuries later that Archbishop Walter de Grey in 1241 bought the manor of Bishopthorpe near York and attached it to the lordship.[1] Leyton and Legh in 1536 considered that the barony of Sherburn brought in the clear annual value of £329 9s. 3½d. The same visitors valued the lordship of Ripon at a clear annual total of £262 15s. 9½d.[2] Archbishop Sharp thought the see had acquired the entire lordship through the gift of Athelstan. It consisted of the manors of Ripon, Sharrow, Stainley, Ripon Holme, Coltsgate Hill, Penny Croft, Castle Dyke, Whitcliff, Thorp, Monkton, Thornton, Nidderdale, and Bishopside, all close to Ripon and straddling the borders of the West and North Ridings. The lordship of Otley completed the pre-Reformation estates of the see of York in Yorkshire. Otley, a single manor, had yet again come to the see through the generosity of King Athelstan. In 1536 it was estimated to bring in the clear annual sum of £70 15s. 7d.[3]

Outside Yorkshire, but still within the northern province, the see of York owned two important estates in Nottinghamshire, the lordship of Scrooby and the lordship of Southwell. The lordship of Scrooby was composed of six manors: Scrooby itself, Laneham, Askham, Sutton, Northsoke, and Ranskill and was valued in 1536 at a clear £167 11s. 4¾d. a year. Sharp recorded that King Edward granted the lordship of Southwell to the see in 958. By 1536, although made up of various dependent manors, Southwell was being administered as one consolidated unit in a way that the Scrooby lordship apparently was not; the royal visitors valued Southwell lordship at a clear £147 19s. 10d. a year.[4]

The two other estates which the archbishop of York possessed in the south of England just before the Reformation lay very far from the centre of the archiepiscopal see. The more ancient, the barony of Churchdown in Gloucestershire, had belonged to St Peter's Abbey, Gloucester, before the Conquest and seems to have been acquired by the see of York on the translation of Bishop Ealdred of Worcester to York in 1061, although the abbey did not finally cede the barony to York till 1157.[5] It consisted of the eight manors of Churchdown, Hucklecote, Norton, Shurdington, Whitcomb, North Cerney, Compton Abdale, and Oddington. Isolated in the west of England and hundreds of miles from the nearest other archiepiscopal lordship, the barony of Churchdown must always have presented problems of administration for the archbishop's

---

[1] Minster Library, Torre, MS. Minster vol., pp. 350–63. See also Sharp's description of the ancient lands of the see.—Borthwick, CC Ab.2.6. [67789].

[2] P.R.O., SC 11/766.   [3] Borthwick, CC Ab.2.6. [67789]; P.R.O., SC 11/766.

[4] P.R.O., SC 11/766; Borthwick, CC Ab.2.6. [67789].

[5] V.C.H. Gloucestershire, VI, 1965, pp. 89, 93–4.

receiver-general. Nevertheless, it was a possession well worth retaining, being valued in 1536 at a clear £186 18s. o¼d. a year. In contrast with the barony of Churchdown, the lordship of Battersea in Surrey had been deliberately acquired by Archbishop Laurence Booth in the reign of Edward IV and had obviously been bought because of its convenient situation near to London. Compared with the other eight pre-Reformation lordships of the see of York its clear annual value was trivial; it produced in 1536 a mere £14 18s. 1d. a year.[1]

Since no receiver-general's accounts exist we can never know the income the archbishops of York derived one year with another from their ancient estates immediately before the Reformation. There were, however, apparently two separate valuations made by government officials in the 1530's which because of the circumstances behind their compilation can be assumed to be reasonably realistic. In 1534 the see of York was valued at £2,035 3s. 7d. for the purpose of assessing the First Fruits owing to the crown.[2] In the valor of 1536 Leyton and Legh estimated the see of York to be worth a little more than this. They calculated the total clear annual value of the see in spiritualities and temporalities to be £2,195 0s. 4¾d. Excluding the revenue from spiritualities the clear annual income from the nine temporal lordships of the see in 1536 seems to have been £1,839 13s. 2¾d.[3] Probably in good years, before Henry VIII assumed the headship of the English church, the archbishop's officials could have hoped to have received around £2,000 from the York temporalities, approximately £1,000 a year less than that which the *Valor Ecclesiasticus* indicates the archbishop of Canterbury enjoyed.[4] The archbishopric of York consequently can be considered to have been a rich see before the Reformation, but it was much less rich than the bishopric of Winchester, valued even in 1559 at £3,700, or the bishopric of Durham, assessed at £2,821 1s. 5d. in 1534.[5]

In 1542 the series of events began which, in the space of two years, transformed the whole economic basis of the see of York. The dissolution of the monasteries and the consequent acquisition of former monastic lands by the crown seem to have encouraged certain royal officials to move on to the next logical step, the acquisition or partial acquisition of episcopal lands by the crown. One radical went so far as to suggest that Henry VIII should confiscate all episcopal lands and that the English episcopate should become a purely salaried body; he thought 2,000 marks a year would suffice for the archbishop of Canterbury, £1,000 a year for the archbishop of York, and that these sums should come

[1] P.R.O., SC 11/766.

[2] Browne Willis, *Survey*, I, p. 18. Willis maintained he had taken this figure from a manuscript collected by Archbishop Sharp. This is the valuation of the see of York used by Dr Hill.—C. Hill, *Economic Problems of the Church*, 1956, p. 26.

[3] P.R.O., SC 11/766.

[4] Canterbury was valued at £3,005 18s 8¾d.—*Valor Ecclesiasticus*, I, p. 7.

[5] Hill, *Economic Problems*, p. 26; Browne Willis, *Survey*, I, p. 227.

partly from spiritualities, partly from a central government court.[1] This was a proposal centuries ahead of its time; even Tudor government officials clung to the idea that bishops, like kings, should live off their own estates, but some certainly thought that these estates could well be pruned and the overplus given to the king. They devised plans to require bishops to surrender episcopal manors to the crown and to accept in exchange scattered parcels of monastic lands and other revenues which had recently come to the crown. As Strype commented: "This way of exchanging lands was much used in those times: wherein the princes commonly made good bargains for themselves, and ill ones for the bishoprics."[2]

The archiepiscopal see of Canterbury first attracted the crown's attention. Between 1536 and 1547 Cranmer entered into no less than eight transactions whereby he surrendered ancient archiepiscopal manors to the crown, and Henry VIII or his executors granted him numerous monastic properties in exchange.[3] The turn of the northern see came in 1542. Edward Lee had been made archbishop of York in 1531, perhaps because of his activity in canvassing support on the Continent for the royal divorce. Despite the circumstances of his appointment, he had long been suspected to be a conservative, opposed alike to the royal supremacy and to the new learning and, therefore, had little chance of withstanding the royal will.[4] By an indenture of 12 November 1542 Lee 'sold' to the king the four ancient archiepiscopal manors of Beverley, Skidby, and Bishop Burton in Yorkshire (part of the lordship of Beverley) and the manor of Southwell in Nottinghamshire. He received in return, as the indenture of 19 February 1543 sets out, £71 2s. 10d. in cash and fourteen separate assignments of lands and advowsons. Most of this new property had formerly belonged to Yorkshire monasteries. The crown granted Lee the site of the priory of Marton, and its lands in Marton and Sutton-in-the-Forest in Yorkshire, and the site of the priory of Molesby and its lands, and also lands which had been held by Newburgh priory. The archbishop also acquired Yorkshire land which had once belonged to the Charterhouse of Mount Grace, and the manors of Sutton-under-Whitestone-Cliff, and Kilburn in Yorkshire, and several granges, all of which had been among the possessions of Byland Abbey, together with granges which had belonged to Rievaulx, and lands and a manor which the Knights of St John of Jerusalem had held in Yorkshire. In addition

---

[1] British Museum, Cotton MS. Cleopatra E. IV, fols. 207–8. This document has been edited by L. Stone.—'Political Programme of Thomas Cromwell', *Bulletin of the Institute of Historical Research*, XXIV, pp. 9–11. But for an attribution to Thomas Gibson not Cromwell, see G. R. Elton, 'Parliamentary Drafts, 1529–40', *B.I.H.R.*, XXV, pp. 125–30.

[2] J. Strype, *Cranmer*, I, Oxford, 1812, p. 404.

[3] F. R. H. Du Boulay, 'Archbishop Cranmer and the Canterbury Temporalities', *Eng. Hist. Rev.*, LXVII, pp. 19–36.

[4] *Dictionary of National Biography*, XXXII, pp. 347–9 under 'Edward Lee'.

the archbishop received the advowsons of twelve Yorkshire churches and of one church in Nottinghamshire.[1]

All this constituted a straight exchange of archiepiscopal manors for former monastic lands, but the indenture contained one curious provision. As well as the parcels of former monastic land Lee also received the manor of Topcliffe with its very extensive appurtenances in the surrounding Yorkshire villages. This property had never had any connection with a religious house, but had formed part of the estates of the earls of Northumberland which Henry, sixth earl of Northumberland, had left to Henry VIII by will in 1537.[2] The Topcliffe lordship, a valuable consolidated estate, was quite unlike the other relatively small assignments of monastic property and the crown apparently very soon regretted having alienated it to an ecclesiastic.

If the exchange of lands between Edward Lee and the crown seems complicated, it is as nothing compared to the exceedingly intricate exchange to which his successor had to agree. Lee died in September 1544; in January 1545 the king appointed Robert Holgate, who had previously been the non-resident bishop of Llandaff and, since 1538, president of the council in the north, archbishop of York.[3] The price of Holgate's elevation was a mammoth alienation of ancient archiepiscopal lands which Browne Willis and Drake could never forgive. Six weeks after his induction as archbishop on 14 March 1545 Holgate surrendered to the crown the entire barony of Hexhamshire in Northumberland, the barony of Churchdown in Gloucestershire, the manor of Sherburn and Bishopslathes (part of the barony of Sherburn), the whole of the lordship of Ripon, the remainder of the lordship of Beverley which Lee had not exchanged, the lordship of Scrooby in Nottinghamshire, and the Percy lordship of Topcliffe which the see had only been given two years previously.[4] By this one transaction the archbishopric lost some fifty-two ancient manors and this total does not include the newly acquired Percy estates. Of the ancient possessions of the see only the manors of Bishopthorpe, Cawood, and Wistow (part of the barony of Sherburn), and the manor of Otley remained.

The property which the crown granted the archbishop made scant pretence to be an equal exchange. In return for his archiepiscopal manors Holgate received some thirty-nine rectories which had formerly been appropriated to Yorkshire monastic houses. These rectories lay almost entirely in Yorkshire (two were in north Lincolnshire) and had once been in the possession of the monasteries and abbeys of Gisburn, Marton, Newburgh, Monk Bretton, St Oswalds, Pontefract, St Mary's, York, Whitby, Kirkham, Malton, Meux, and

[1] P.R.O., C 66/717. Summarized in *Letters and Papers of Henry VIII*, xviii, i, no. 226 (66).
[2] *V.C.H. The North Riding*, ii, pp. 70–7.
[3] A. G. Dickens, *Robert Holgate, Archbishop of York and President of the King's Council in the North*, St Anthony's Hall Publications, no. 8, 1955.
[4] P.R.O., C 66/750. Summarized in *Letters and Papers*, xx, i, no. 465 (39).

the Knights of St John of Jerusalem. The right to receive tithes and other income came to the see with the impropriate rectories, and in addition the archbishop of York now held the presentation to at least thirty-three vicarages, whereas before the Reformation his direct ecclesiastical patronage had not been extensive. As Professor Dickens has recently remarked these "very substantial grants of tithes, patronages, and revenues which [the archbishops then received] materially increased their power over their clergy and the whole ecclesiastical system of the North."[1] For the purposes of revenue, quite apart from this increase in patronage, the rectories in the exchange deed were said to bring in the clear annual sum of £505 0s. 6¼d. The archbishop held the lands and impropriations by a knight's fee and paid the crown an annual rent of £203 17s. 5d.[2]

Contemporaries, royal officials no less than the archbishop's own servants, recognized that by these two exchanges the revenues of the see of York had been considerably diminished, although the extent of the reduction even at this period may have been exaggerated. The year after Robert Holgate's exchange with the crown the king in an indenture of 22 October 1546 agreed in the future to accept £1,000 from every successive archbishop as the full payment of First Fruits,[3] which is a little less than half the First Fruits demanded by the crown before the York exchanges had begun.[4] In addition Henry released Holgate entirely from paying First Fruits of £1,831 13s. 3¼d. for his see of York in consideration of the fact that his lands had been much diminished by his gift to the crown of 14 March 1545.[5]

This gift, or rather double gift, made by Lee and Holgate to the crown of the regality of Hexhamshire, part of the barony of Sherburn, the lordship of Beverley, the barony of Churchdown, the lordship of Ripon, the lordship of Scrooby, and the lordship of Southwell involved the surrender of lands which on the valuation of 1536 brought in the total clear annual revenue of £1,563 8s. 3¼d., a very large sum indeed for the archbishop to have lost.[6] Against this loss, however, must be set the lands and impropriations the crown granted to the see. The manors of Kilburn and Sutton-under-Whitestone-Cliff together with their appurtenances which Henry VIII had given to Lee in 1543 were valued at £57 4s. and £103 10s. a year respectively in 1597, the date of the earliest surviving receiver-general's account. Then the rectories of the Great Collection (as the mass of the rectories of the exchange of 1545 soon came to be known) together with the Cleveland rectories, the Holderness rectories, the West Riding rectories, the wealthy rectory of Doncaster accounted

---

[1] Dickens, *op. cit.*, p. 19.   [2] P.R.O., C 66/750.
[3] P.R.O., C 66/795. *Letters and Papers*, XXI, 2, no. 332 (63).
[4] Browne Willis, *Survey*, I, p. 18.
[5] *Letters and Papers, Addenda*, I (2), no. 1737.   [6] P.R.O., SC 11/766.

for separately, and the two Lincolnshire rectories in 1597 raised a total annual income of £779 2s.[1] Thus in 1597 the impropriations together with the new manors the see had received permanently from the crown produced an income of £939 16s. Because of the price rise this sum is probably somewhat in excess of the gross sum the archbishop received immediately after the exchanges had gone through and it does not take into account the annual rent of £203 17s. 5d. at first charged upon the impropriations. When these two points are allowed for it seems reasonably accurate to conclude that through the two exchanges with the crown Lee and Holgate had in combination at this stage forfeited something like half the pre-Reformation annual income of the see.[2]

Had the revenues of the see of York remained at the low ebb of 1546 then Browne Willis would have been justified in censuring Holgate for his sacrilegious alienations, but the death of Henry VIII in practice marked the end of the threat to the remaining possessions of the northern archbishopric. For some sees the reign of Edward VI brought further exchanges and a consequent loss of revenue. In 1547 the new bishop of Lincoln, for example, was required not only to make a disadvantageous exchange of lands with the crown but also to grant manors to Edward duke of Somerset.[3] Through these alienations the revenue of the bishopric of Lincoln was more than halved. Dr Hembry has described in detail how the see of Bath and Wells owned twenty-four manors in 1548 and how it had lost all but seven by the time of Somerset's fall. In 1551 Edward VI's council persuaded Ponet at Winchester to give up the endowments of his rich see for an annual income of 2,000 marks, and Hooper at Gloucester in 1552 had to enter into a similar bargain.[4] For York, however, Edward VI's reign brought a period of peace if not of prosperity. Robert Holgate remained undisturbed in his possession of the see and of its surviving income, troubled only by matrimonial difficulties: his wife, whom he married in 1549, was alleged to have been precontracted to another.[5] The case, however, ultimately went in Holgate's favour and in 1553 he and his wife jointly purchased the former archiepiscopal manor of Scrooby which he intended after their deaths should be restored to the see.[6] For Holgate the accession of Mary meant immediate disaster; in October 1553 he was sent to the Tower and in the following March deprived of his archbishopric for marriage; but it proved, nevertheless, to be a memorable time in the history of the revenues of the see.

In 1555 Mary nominated Nicholas Heath to be the next archbishop of York and the Pope confirmed his election. To the Catholic Mary and the Catholic

[1] Borthwick, CC Ab.6.1. [67791].   [2] See the tables at the end of this article.
[3] R. E. Cole, *Chapter Acts of the Cathedral Church of St Mary of Lincoln, 1547–1559*, Lincoln Record Society, 15, 1920, pp. vii–ix.
[4] P. M. Hembry, *The Bishops of Bath and Wells, 1540–1640*, 1967, pp. 105–53.
[5] *D.N.B.*, XXVII, pp. 128–30, under 'Robert Holgate'.
[6] *C.P.R. Edward VI*, v, pp. 298–9.

Heath the see of York owes a debt which subsequent Protestant archbishops have never been able adequately to acknowledge. Within a few months of Heath's translation to York, Mary released him and his successors from the payment of the annual rents amounting to £258 7s. which had been charged upon various lands and rectories given by the crown to the see at the time of the first and second Henrician exchanges. Mary also granted Heath Suffolk Place in Southwark, once the property of Charles, late duke of Suffolk, in compensation for York Place which had come into the hands of the crown, though the archbishop sold this property soon after.[1]

Far more important, however, than the release from annual rent charges was the restitution to the see of three of its pre-Reformation lordships. Through the generosity of the queen and the energy of Heath, aided by Cardinal Pole, the archbishopric regained the lordship of Ripon in Yorkshire, and the lordships of Southwell and Scrooby in Nottinghamshire. By an indenture of 20 February 1557 which recited how "the revenues of the archbishop of York are much diminished by the grant and surrender of divers lordships formerly belonging thereto made by Robert, late archbishop; and divers lands which formerly belonged to the archbishopric to the yearly value of £1,200 and beyond are in the hands of the crown" Mary granted the lordship of Scrooby and its attendant manors and the lordship of Southwell back to the see.[2]

This restoration of the Nottinghamshire lordships may have been a little less munificent than on first sight it appears. The crown had retained the lordship of Scrooby in its own hands and one of the many grants Edward VI had made to John, duke of Northumberland, had been the office of keeper of the manor and park of Scrooby.[3] Then, in May 1553, scarcely more than a month before he died, Edward VI had permitted Archbishop Holgate and Barbara his wife to buy back the manor of Scrooby and lands in Ranskill for the sum of £630 7s. 6d.[4] As has been mentioned earlier Holgate had intended to restore this manor to the see after the deaths of himself and his wife, so morally, if not legally, in 1557 Scrooby could already be considered to have been returned to the see. The remaining manors of Laneham, Askham, Sutton, and North Soke had not been included in Holgate's purchase, but Mary in this grant of 20 February 1557 restored these estates also to the archbishopric.

No prior transaction had taken place to qualify Mary's generosity in returning the manor of Southwell to the see. In the fourteen years which passed between the surrender of Southwell to the crown in 1543 and its restoration by Mary, Southwell had undergone a series of changes in ownership which directly reflect the political instability of those years. Henry VIII had retained the manor and placed a succession of keepers over the house and parks of

---

[1] *C.P.R. Mary*, III, pp. 187–8; *ibid.*, III, p. 439.   [2] *Ibid.*, pp. 264–5.
[3] *C.P.R. Edward VI*, IV, p. 344.   [4] *Ibid.*, v, pp. 298–9.

Southwell;[1] his son in 1550 granted the manor to John, then earl of Warwick and later duke of Northumberland.[2] A year later Warwick alienated the manor to John Beaumont, Master of the Rolls, but his enjoyment of the manor can only have been brief for in May 1552 Beaumont was forced to surrender his property and goods to the crown for a gross abuse of his judicial office.[3] The next grant of the manor brought its new owner even less profit: only days before he died Edward made the manor over to Sir Henry Sidney: this grant was subsequently cancelled on the Patent Roll with a note that Sidney surrendered the manor of Southwell to Mary on 17 October 1553.[4] Although Mary allowed several leases to be made of lands in the manor of Southwell, the estate had no more owners before it passed back to the archbishop of York in 1557.[5]

The valuable lordship of Ripon had a far less eventful history after Holgate had exchanged it with the crown. In 1545 the crown immediately annexed it to the duchy of Lancaster, and it remained under the administration of the duchy until Mary restored it to the archbishopric.[6] The three lordships of Ripon, Scrooby, and Southwell on the 1536 valuation brought in an annual revenue of £578 7s. 0¼d. Mary had indeed dealt very well with the see. One of her last acts had been to confirm to Archbishop Heath and his successors as archbishops of York all the rectories and vicarages granted in the Henrician exchanges, but now held by the archbishop in frank almoign and no longer by knight service, an unseemly form of fee for a churchman.[7] After his study of the lands of the archbishopric, Torre with justice concluded "in truth, the see of York owes to Queen Mary and this archbishop more than a third part of its present revenues."[8]

On the accession of Elizabeth, another Protestant sovereign, the newly restored lands of the archbishopric again seemed likely to fall prey to an impecunious monarch. The first parliament of Elizabeth passed an act which allowed the queen during the vacancy of a see to exchange episcopal manors and other lands for impropriations and other ecclesiastical revenues still in royal possession, and the bishops elect tried in vain to persuade the queen for the greater good of the church to forego or at least to limit the profits to herself from such exchanges.[9] In fact a few days after she had received the remonstrance of the bishops the queen instructed the Barons of the Exchequer to

[1] *Letters and Papers*, XIX (1), p. 646; *Ibid.*, XXI (1), no. 199 (59).

[2] *C.P.R. Edward VI*, III, pp. 71–4; *Ibid.*, IV, pp. 61–2.

[3] *D.N.B.*, II, pp. 57–8 under 'John Beaumont'.   [4] *C.P.R. Edward VI*, V, pp. 60-2.

[5] *C.P.R. Mary*, I, p. 291; *Ibid.*, III, p. 47. *C.P.R. Philip and Mary*, IV, p. 117.

[6] *Letters and Papers*, XX (2), no. 850 (21). There is no mention of the regrant of the lordship of Ripon in the calendars of Patent Rolls for the reign of Mary, but it is quite certain the lordship was restored at this period. The archbishops were drawing revenues from Ripon again by the reign of Elizabeth.— Borthwick, CC Ab.6.1. [67791].

[7] *C.P.R. Philip and Mary*, IV, p. 420; *C.P.R. Mary*, III, pp. 187–8.

[8] Browne Willis, *Survey*, I, p. 46.

[9] J. Bruce and T. T. Perowne, eds., *Correspondence of Matthew Parker*, Parker Society, Cambridge, 1853, no. lxviii.

proceed with an exchange of lands of the sees of Canterbury, London, Ely, Hereford, and Chichester, and, ominously for the northern sees, then to investigate a "like exchange with the rest of the bishoprics that be richly endowed, as York, Winchester, Durham, Bath, Sarum, Norwich, and Worcester."[1] By 1559 York could well again be considered to be richly endowed but, in spite of the threats, the lands of the see escaped any further changes at this time.

As Elizabeth's reign progressed influential laymen, rather than the queen herself, presented a greater danger to the integrity of the lands of the see. Leicester, never averse to improving his own fortunes at the expense of the church, tried unsuccessfully to wrest Southwell from the archbishopric in 1587.[2] Archbishop Sandys, who must have been a formidable adversary even for Leicester to encounter, thwarted his attempt, as he also did a proposal to lease or otherwise part with York House in London. "These be marvellous times," Sandys complained to Burghley, "The ministers of the word, the messengers of Christ, are become *contemptibiles omni populo*, and are esteemed *tanquam excrementa mundi*. This was foreshowed, and in our time performed. It may be feared God hath some great work in hand. For this ignominy is done unto himself."[3] Yet Sandys for all his indignation succeeded only in postponing and not preventing the ultimate surrender of York House. The last exchange of lands of the see of York, a very minor exchange when compared with the two Henrician exchanges, took place in 1622 when Archbishop Toby Matthew agreed to surrender York House to the crown in return for the Yorkshire manors of Brighton, Sancton, Acomb, and Beckhay Grange.[4]

With this one exception of York House the lands of the see of York proved to have reached a state of equilibrium by the beginning of Elizabeth's reign; the archbishops managed to retain lands which had never been alienated in the Henrician exchanges together with the lands restored by Mary, but the other ancient lands which they had lost, they lost permanently. The history of these former archiepiscopal properties deserves to be mentioned if only because it mirrors in a small span the great secularization of church lands which the sixteenth century witnessed. The regality of Hexhamshire, surrendered by Holgate to the crown in 1545, remained in royal possession throughout the rest of the sixteenth century, and its thirteen constituent manors continued to be treated as one unit. Sir John Forster, warden of the Middle Marches and the dominant landowner in the area, administered the regality on behalf of the crown. A survey of 1608 gave the rental of the regality of Hexhamshire as £191 14s. 1¼d., a slight decrease upon the valuation made by the Henrician commissioners in 1536. With the union of the crowns of England and Scotland

---

[1] *Parker Correspondence*, no. lxix.   [2] J. Strype, *Annals of the Reformation*, III, 1728, p. 461.
[3] *Ibid.*, III, pp. 550–1.   [4] Borthwick, CC Ab.2.6. [67789].

in 1603 the significance of the regality as a border zone disappeared and hence also its particular political importance to the crown. In 1632 Charles I agreed to sell the whole regality to Sir John Fenwick who had married one of Sir John Forster's daughters.[1]

The barony of Churchdown in Gloucestershire, which the crown also gained from the see of York in 1545, resembled the regality of Hexhamshire in that it too continued to be administered as a single unit. The crown, however, retained the barony for a far shorter time: on 1 June 1552 Edward VI granted the barony together with its manors of Churchdown, Hucklecote, Norton, Shurdington, Witcomb, North Cerney, Compton Abdale, and Oddington to Sir Thomas Chamberlain, and during Elizabeth's reign Chamberlain received two confirmations of his absolute possession of the property together with a release of rent charges.[2]

The ancient episcopal manor of Sherburn-in-Elmet in Yorkshire (and possibly also the subsidiary manor of Bishopslathes which may have been subsumed within the head manor of Sherburn) found its way equally quickly into lay hands. For the payment of £1,554 18s. 4d. on 9 June 1549 Edward VI granted the manor, its lands, and liberties to Richard Tyrrell and Ambrose Wolley. Fifteen years later, in January 1564, Richard Tyrrell and Grace his wife obtained a licence from the crown to alienate this chief manor of the barony of Sherburn to William Hungate and, although the archbishops did succeed in establishing their claim to certain parks in the vicinity of Sherburn which they maintained had never formed part of the manor, the manor of Sherburn itself was never reunited to the now truncated archiepiscopal barony of Sherburn.[3]

Of all the four lordships, or parts of lordships, which the archbishopric lost through the Henrician exchanges, the lordship of Beverley seems to have suffered the greatest fragmentation. The crown did not even receive this lordship of twelve manors as one unit, for the manors of Beverley, Skidby, and Bishop Burton came to the crown in 1543, but the remainder of the lordship only two years later. In 1552 Edward VI, in an exchange of lands on this occasion with a layman, granted John duke of Northumberland the three manors of Beverley, Skidby, and Bishop Burton in return for certain lands of the duke.[4] On the execution of Northumberland these manors reverted to the crown, but Elizabeth made a new grant of the manors of Beverley and Skidby, which his father had once held, to Lord Robert Dudley in 1561.[5] Leicester, however, only kept Beverley and Skidby for five years and then exchanged them with Eliza-

[1] A. B. Hinds, *History of Northumberland*, III, pt I, Hexhamshire, pp. 20–66; *Letters and Papers*, XX (1), no. 465 (54); *C.P.R. Elizabeth*, IV, no. 1384.

[2] *C.P.R. Edward VI*, IV, 357; *C.P.R. Elizabeth*, I, p. 305; *Ibid.*, III, no. 2147.

[3] *Letters and Papers*, XXI, (1), no. 1248; *C.P.R. Edward VI*, II, p. 342; *C.P.R. Elizabeth*, III, no. 256.

[4] *C.P.R. Edward VI*, IV, pp. 117–18.   [5] *C.P.R. Elizabeth*, II, pp. 189–91.

beth for other crown lands nearer to the centre of his estates in Warwickshire.[1] Other manors and lands which had formerly been part of the lordship of Beverley were retained by the crown in the earlier years of the reign of Elizabeth and leased to laymen; in 1563 Christopher Estofte, a member of the council in the north, obtained a thirty years' lease of the manor of Bishop Burton and lands in Bishop Burton and Wilton; two years later the queen granted Thomas Appleyard a twenty-one years' lease of the demesne lands of the manor of Bishop Wilton; in 1568 William Kirkeby had a similar lease of lands in Elloughton, and in 1569 Christopher Hatton leased demesne lands in Patrington from the crown for thirty years.[2] Of all these manors which had made up the lordship of Beverley the only manor the crown appears to have alienated before 1572 is the manor of Kingston on Hull, the reversion of which Mary made over to Sir Henry Gate in 1557.[3] None of these manors, however diverse their individual histories, ever returned to the church but all were permanently secularized.

No historians have questioned the fact that the see of York lost many lands in the sixteenth century of great economic and historical value; but whether the archbishopric also sustained a lasting substantial decrease in its income is a matter much more open to dispute. In his seminal book on the economic problems of the English church between 1583 and 1640, Dr Hill made the important point that, harried though they may have been by avaricious laymen, late Elizabethan bishops "were still rich and powerful enough to be envied and criticized. Canterbury, Winchester, and Ely were all worth more than £2,000 a year; York, Durham, Salisbury, London were all over £1,000."[4] The Elizabethan archbishops of York certainly enjoyed an income well over £1,000; indeed, their annual income exceeded £1,000 by far more than some seventeenth- and eighteenth-century apologists for the church have been prepared to admit. Unfortunately, no receivers' accounts for the see of York survive before the very end of the sixteenth century, but an approximate assessment of the income of the see can be made with reasonable accuracy for the beginning of Elizabeth's reign to include the revenues restored to the see by Mary. The ancient lands of the see which the archbishop had retained under Henry VIII, part of the barony of Sherburn, the lordship of Otley, and the manor of Battersea together produced £280 11s. 3½d. annually on the 1536 valuation. Then, on the basis of the same valuation, the ancient lands restored by Mary, the lord-

[1] *C.P.R. Elizabeth*, III, no. 2567.

[2] *Ibid.*, II, p. 508; *Ibid.*, III, no. 1942; *Ibid.*, IV, no. 1927; *Ibid.*, IV, no. 2575.

[3] *C.P.R. Mary*, III, p. 448.

[4] C. Hill, *The Economic Problems of the Church*, p. 39. Dr Hill here had in mind the net annual income received by the archbishops and bishops, whereas throughout this article I am more concerned with the income produced by the archiepiscopal lands rather than with the net income the archbishop actually enjoyed.

ship of Ripon, the lordship of Scrooby, and the lordship of Southwell, brought
in a further £578 7s. o¼d. The income of the new lands and impropriations
cannot be calculated with the same precision since 1597 valuations have to be
used, but the two new manors of Kilburn and Sutton-under-Whitestone-Cliff
and their appurtenances may already have produced £160 14s. a year while the
rectories of the Great Collection and other impropriations and tithes in Yorkshire may perhaps have been worth the 1597 sum of £779 2s. a year. Therefore
the see could well have received a total income from temporalities in 1560 of
£1,798 14s. 3¾d. In 1536 before any of the exchanges had taken place the
Henrician visitors had stated that the clear annual value of the temporalities of
the see amounted to £1,839 13s. 2¾d. Apparently in 1560 the see of York was
within some forty pounds of the identical annual income at which it had been
valued before all the tumultuous changes of the latter years of the reign of
Henry VIII.[1]

It could plausibly be argued that these reconstructed figures for 1560 hide a
number of hidden charges, that, for example, the archbishop may well have
been indebted to the crown for First Fruits and tenths, and that the remaining
archiepiscopal lands may have been leased to laymen for long terms at disadvantageous rents. Grindal, to name only one Elizabethan archbishop of
York, maintained that his clear annual income taking one year with another
did not exceed £1,300; but by this acknowledgement he also implied that his
gross income was in excess, presumably considerably in excess, of this figure.[2]
There can be no positive answer to such objections for the early years of
Elizabeth's reign but the series of receivers' accounts which begin in 1597 can
provide some sort of retrospective check. In 1597 the archbishop of York had a
total annual income of £1,889 16s. 6d. In 1601 his income fell a little to
£1,805 13s. 6d.; the following year it fell further to £1,794 16s. 8¾d.; in 1605
it declined even more to £1,783 os. 8½d. Then in 1609 came a notable rise to
£2,057. There are then no receivers' accounts until 1627 in which year the
archbishop received a very similar sum of £2,027 6s. o¾d. The average income
for the five years around the turn of the sixteenth century was approximately
£1,866 2s. 9d., and of this the average sum brought in by the exchange impropriations alone came to £797 12s.[3]

These bald figures do not take into account the income in kind which the
archbishop still enjoyed "for his better means of maintenance and hospitality."
In 1638 he received 144 quarters of wheat from the rectories of Hutton-on-
Derwent, Nafferton, Skipsea, and Haxey and also 389 quarters of barley, 37

---

[1] All these figures are based on P.R.O., SC 11/766, the 1536 valuation, and on Borthwick, CC
Ab.6.1. [67791], the 1597 valuation.

[2] W. Nicholson, ed., *Remains of Edmund Grindal*, Parker Society, Cambridge, 1843, p. 354. I owe
this reference to the kindness of Dr Hill.

[3] These figures are taken from the following accounts: Borthwick, CC Ab.6.1–6. [67791–67796].

quarters of oats, and 21 quarters of pease. The tenants of Cawood, Wistow, Sutton-under-Whitestone-Cliff, Kilburn, Hutton-on-Derwent, and Nafferton provided 253 hens, 36 capons, 24 geese, 10 swine, and 1,000 eggs. Nor did the archbishop's servants fail to exact a tithe from the sea. His tenants at Whitby and Lythe dispatched to Bishopthorpe annually 400 salt fish, 5,000 herrings, and six horse loads of wet fish.[1]

The fragmentary Parliamentary valuations and prices named in the subsequent sales of the lands of the see give yet further evidence of the wealth of the see of York in the seventeenth century. The York archiepiscopal lands apparently raised a grand total of £63,786 7s. 1¾d. which would suggest a notional annual income from rents nearer to £3,000 than to £2,000.[2] At the Restoration all the former archiepiscopal lands returned to the see and when, forty years later, Archbishop Sharp at the beginning of his archiepiscopate "took early and extraordinary pains to qualify himself for so weighty a charge as he had undertaken by inquiring into . . . the present estates and possessions of the archbishopric of York" he found that his income was £2,519 16s. 2d.[3] This sum did not include the provisions in kind from certain rectories so that his total income in 1700 was in the region of at least £2,800. The archbishop carefully noted that a third of his income came from rents which were not capable of improvement. His eighteenth-century successors had no hesitation in raising the rents of the larger part of the lands of the see which could be improved.[4] Taking a general view of the income of the archbishopric of York between 1536 and 1700, it is difficult not to conclude, as Professor Du Boulay concluded for the see of Canterbury, that in the long run the crown dealt with the see relatively gently.[5] The archbishops of Canterbury and York, even if this was no longer true of all their episcopal brethren, could still be counted princes of the church.

Yet while over the span of the century the Henrician exchanges together with the Marian restorations do not seem to have caused a notable decrease in the archbishop's income it cannot be denied that the exchanges did bring about a marked change in the economic basis of his revenue. In 1536 the archbishop received a negligible part of his income from impropriations; after the second exchange, which brought the 'Great Collection' of rectories to the see, between a third and a half of the whole archiepiscopal income came from this one source. In 1559 the Elizabethan bishops elect had felt some scruples, when they protested against the queen's scheme to proceed with the further ex-

[1] Borthwick, CC Ab.2.1. [67799].
[2] *Ibid.*, CC Ab.8.4. [67555]; Browne Willis, *Survey*, I, pp. 21–6.
[3] T. Newcome, *Life of John Sharpe D.D.*, I, 1825, pp. 134–6.
[4] Borthwick, CC Ab.2.6. [67789].
[5] F. R. H. Du Boulay, 'Archbishop Cranmer and the Canterbury Temporalities', *Eng. Hist. Rev.*, LXVIII, pp. 19–36.

changes of episcopal lands in return for crown impropriations, lest provision of an adequate living might not be made for the incumbents of impropriated benefices.[1] The archbishop of York, for one, after 1546 owed his wealth in no small measure to the relative privation of some thirty-three vicars of livings of which he was now rector. Archbishop Sandys saw the mote in his opponents' eye, but ignored the beam in his own. In a sermon he preached on the evil effects of impropriations he maintained that the common people in the country areas "pine away and perish for want of this saving food: they are much decayed for want of prophecy." "But why doth the country want preachers?" he continued. "The people pay tithes of that they have; therefore there must needs be sufficient to maintain them. If things were well ordered, this sequel were good. But the chiefest benefices were by the Pope long since impropriated unto monks which devoured the fruits, and gave a silly stipend unto a poor Sir John to say mass; and as they left it, so we find it still. Where livings were not impropriated by the Pope, there they are for the most part so handled, that patrons maintain themselves with those tithes which the people give, and ministers have that which the patrons leave."[2] "Thus," commented Strype, "did the zealous archbishop represent publicly these wrongs to the discouragement of the ministry; and which he himself had felt and struggled with."[3] He held back, however, from explaining to his readers that Sandys benefited from impropriations as much as any great lay impropriator.

Whereas Sandys attacked only lay impropriators and passed in silence over impropriators who were churchmen, at least one of his successors in the see does seem to have felt that rich prelates of church had a duty to help the lower clergy who scraped an inadequate living from an impropriate benefice. His biographer described how, when Sharp became archbishop of York, he devised a new rule for himself which did not come "within the ordinary and stated duties of his office" by reserving the prebends in his gift for the clergy beneficed in his diocese or retained in his family. "He made it his unalterable practice always to elect them out of such as lived in his diocese, and had recommended themselves by doing their duties in their respective parochial cures. By which means no cathedral in England was better attended by clergy, and the service more regularly performed than at York; or the ministers of small livings in any diocese more encouraged to attend their charge; because this good bishop would reward their diligence by such compensations, more especially those in York city, on whose conduct the world had a more especial eye; hoping his example would influence his successors to take the like course."[4] Yet how much

---

[1] Bruce and Perowne, *Parker Correspondence*, no. lxviii.
[2] J. Ayre, ed., *Sermons of Edwin Sandys*, Parker Society, Cambridge, 1842, pp. 154-5.
[3] J. Strype, *Annals of the Reformation*, III, 1728, p. 556.
[4] T. Newcome, *Life of John Sharpe D.D.*, I, pp. 117-19.

more would Sharp have helped his poor clergy if, instead of selecting the deserving among them for Minster prebends, he had permanently enlarged their livings by restoring to them the impropriations he held, archiepiscopal impropriations which by 1700 annually exceeded £1,000 in value.[1] But this would have amounted to a virtual social revolution within the church, raising up the clerical poor, bringing down the ecclesiastical princes, till they approached a common mediocrity of income; and the religious leaders of the reign of Queen Anne were no more capable of contemplating such an innovation than Elizabeth's churchmen had been.

The myth that the archbishops of York in the sixteenth century endured grievous spoliation at the hands of the crown which eighteenth-century historians have perpetuated should be recognized for what it is, a pious deception. The archbishops, indeed, lost very many ancient manors which had belonged to the see from time immemorial, and a considerable part of these manors was lost permanently; but they received from the crown lands and, above all, impropriations in exchange. By at least 1600 the archbishop of York received an income nominally as substantial as that enjoyed by his predecessor immediately before the Reformation, an income moreover which continued to appreciate considerably throughout the seventeenth and eighteenth centuries. Those who in the long run bore the cost of the two exchanges of land Henry VIII had made with the see of York were not the archbishops of York but members of that much abused ecclesiastical estate, the incumbents of livings now impropriated to the archbishopric.

[1] Borthwick, CC Ab.2.6. [67789].

TABLE I

THE ANCIENT ARCHIEPISCOPAL LANDS OF THE SEE OF YORK

County	Lordship	1536 Valuation (P.R.O., SC 11/766) £ s. d.			1597 Valuation (Borthwick, CC Ab.6.1) £ s. d.			1700 Valuation (Borthwick, CC Ab.2.6) £ s. d.			Fate after the Reformation
Northumberland	Regality of Hexhamshire Manors of Hexham, Errington, Wall, Acomb, Hallington, Keepwick, Greenridge, Keenley, East Allen, Catton, Ninebanks, West Allen, Newlands	196	19	4¾	—			—			Alienated at the 1545 exchange, then remained with the crown till 1632 when it was sold.
Yorkshire	Lordship of Ripon Manors of Ripon, Sharrow, Stainley, Ripon Holm, Coltsgate Hill, Penny Croft, Castle Dyke, Whitcliff, Thorpe, Monkton, Thornton, Nidderdale, Bishopside	262	15	9½	266	12	8½	303	5	4	Alienated at the 1545 exchange and annexed to the Duchy of Lancaster. Restored to see by Mary.
,,	Barony of Sherburn (total valuation 1536 £329 9s. 3½d.)										
	Palace and tenements in city of York	7	2	0	6	19	3	10	4	8	Remained with see.
	Manor of Bishopthorpe	23	15	3½	21	1	7	20	1	8	Remained with see.
	Manor of Cawood	77	5	2	71	15	7	215	14	9	Remained with see.
	Manor of Wistow	75	15	7	77	9	10	118	16	7½	Remained with see.
	Land in Sherburn	10	19	7	—			70	0	0	Remained with see.
	Manor of Sherburn	83	51	4 [sic]	—			—			Alienated at 1545 exchange. 1549 sold by crown to Richard Tyrrell. 1564 sold by Tyrrell to Wm. Hungate.
	Manor of Bishopslathes	53	6	8	—			—			Alienated at 1545 exchange.
,,	Lordship of Otley	70	15	7	76	6	11	77	5	5	Remained with see.
,,	Lordship of Beverley Manors of Kingston on Hull, Patrington, Tharlthorpe, Frismarsh, Hall Garth, Elloughton, Wetwang, Wilton, Bishop Wilton, Beverley, Skidby, Bishop Burton	462	5	10	—			—			Alienated at 1543 and 1545 exchanges. In 1572 still in crown hands except for Kingston on Hull which had been granted to Sir Henry Gates.
Nottinghamshire	Lordship of Scrooby Manors of Scrooby, Laneham, Askham, Sutton, Northsoke, Ranskill	167	11	4¾	181	9	1½	183	5	4	Alienated at 1545 exchange, but restored by Mary.
,,	Lordship of Southwell	147	19	10	114	17	2¾	225	15	1	Alienated at 1543 exchange, but restored by Mary.
Gloucestershire	Barony of Churchdown Manors of Churchdown, Hucklecote, Norton, Shurdington, Witcomb, North Cerney, Compton Abdale, Oddington.	186	18	0¼	—			—			Alienated at 1545 exchange. In 1552 granted by the crown to Sir Thomas Chamberlain.
Surrey	Lordship of Battersea and Wandsworth	14	18	1	68	16	8½	58	18	7½	Remained with see.

TABLE II

VALUE OF ARCHIEPISCOPAL LANDS PERMANENTLY LOST TO THE SEE (1536 valuation: P.R.O., SC 11/766)	£	s.	d.
Regality of Hexhamshire	196	19	4¾
Part of Barony of Sherburn			
Manor of Sherburn	83	51	4
Manor of Bishopslathes	53	6	8
Lordship of Beverley	462	5	10
Barony of Churchdown	186	18	0¼
	985	1	3

VALUE OF MANORS GRANTED TO THE SEE IN EXCHANGE FOR ANCIENT LANDS (1597 valuation: Borthwick, CC Ab.6.1)	£	s.	d.
Manor of Kilburn	57	4	0
Manor of Sutton-under-Whitestone-Cliff	103	10	0
	160	14	0

VALUE OF IMPROPRIATIONS GRANTED TO THE SEE IN EXCHANGE FOR ANCIENT LANDS (1597 valuation: Borthwick, CC Ab.6.1)	£	s.	d.
Rectories in the Great Collection	457	10	8
Cleveland rectories	122	1	10
Holderness rectories	84	18	6
West Riding rectories	76	10	10
Doncaster rectory	34	13	6
Oweston rectory		66	8
	779	2	0

	£	s.	d.
	985	1	3
	939	16	0

VALUE OF ARCHIEPISCOPAL LANDS TEMPORARILY LOST TO THE SEE IN 1543 AND 1545 BUT RESTORED BY MARY (1536 valuation: P.R.O., SC 11/766)	£	s.	d.
Lordship of Ripon	262	15	9½
Lordship of Scrooby	167	11	4¾
Lordship of Southwell	147	19	10
	578	7	0¼

Total income of the see in 1536 (excluding spiritualities) £1,839 13s. 2¾d. (P.R.O., SC 11/766)

Total income of the see in 1597 (excluding spiritualities) £1,889 16s. 6d. (Borthwick, CC Ab.6.1)

Economic and Social Change in the Forest of Arden, 1530–1649

By V. H. T. SKIPP

I

IN her survey of farming regions for *The Agrarian History of England and Wales, 1500–1640*,[1] Dr Joan Thirsk remarks that no study of Arden Warwickshire has yet been made for the period concerned: the present essay is an attempt to fill this gap. Some reference will be made to Rowington, a parish of 3,217 acres lying 7 miles SSE. of Solihull.[2] Otherwise attention is concentrated on a compact block of five parishes—Elmdon (1,127 acres), Sheldon (2,500 acres), Bickenhill (3,771 acres), Yardley (7,590 acres), and Solihull (11,296 acres)—which lie close to the ancient heart of the forest, in territory representing the fringe of pre-Conquest agrarian development.[3]

The primary settlement pattern consisted of small hamlets, some originating as Saxon vills, others as colonies founded in the post-Domesday period. By the time detailed documentation becomes available each hamlet is associated with an area of open- or common-field land, as also is the planted borough of Solihull, founded from the Domesday Ulverlei (Olton) in the late twelfth century.[4]

The Warwick–Birmingham road, however, marks the limit of nucleated settlement and of common-field agriculture in northern Arden. South of this, extensive areas of Yardley and Solihull were cleared by private enterprise in the twelfth and thirteenth centuries, and so came to be characterized by private

[1] p. 97.

[2] I am indebted to Mrs J. A. Woodall for making the Rowington material available.

[3] The initial researches into these parishes were carried out by a series of Birmingham University extra-mural classes under the author's direction, as follows: Sheldon, 1957–60 (see V. H. T. Skipp, *Discovering Sheldon*, 1960); Bickenhill, 1960–3 (see V. H. T. Skipp and R. P. Hastings, *Discovering Bickenhill*, 1963); Elmdon, 1960; Yardley, 1960–7 (see V. H. T. Skipp, *Medieval Yardley*, 1970); Solihull, 1960–7.

The collation of parochial data is being undertaken by a further extra-mural class, which has been meeting at Solihull, under the author and Dr D. E. Gray, since 1967. Statistics in the present article which are derived from probate inventories are mainly the work of Mr H. Austin, Mr T. England, Mr R. A. McMillan, and Mr A. J. Stubbs. Population statistics have been produced by Miss A. D. Harris, with the help of Mr G. Harris, Miss K. Proctor, Miss E. Sherwood, and Mrs M. Stephenson. Others who have rendered substantial help include Mr G. L. Bishop, Mr E. B. Lascelles, Mr E. Owen, Mrs B. Shackley, Mrs E. M. Varley, Mrs K. Weller, Mrs J. A. Woodall, Mr G. J. Wright.

[4] In this article it is proposed to use the term 'common field'. B. K. Roberts (in 'A Study of Medieval Colonization in the Forest of Arden, Warwickshire', A.H.R., 16, p. 102) points out that "it is difficult to prove that all four necessary conditions" required by Dr Thirsk's definition of 'common field' "were present in the Middle Ages," but adds "The author is of the view that they were. . ." This is the present writer's position, arrived at quite independently. In any case, several of the field systems can be shown to have fulfilled Dr Thirsk's conditions subsequently.

assarts in severalty. This meant that these two parishes had a greater proportion of enclosed land than the others; and, since severalties were held on free tenure, they also had a much higher proportion of freeholders.[1]

Keuper marl, a heavy reddish clay, is the basic soil of the area, but overlying this at many points are glacial deposits of sand, gravel, and mixed drift. The founders of the hamlets, both in pre- and post-Conquest times, showed preference for the lighter soils, making their clearances either on small isolated drift patches, as at Mackadown (Sheldon) and Marston Culy; or on the edges of larger ones, as at Hill Bickenhill, Longdon, and Greet. In general, therefore, common-field land utilized relatively shallow drift areas, while severalties were situated either on marl, or else on the larger expanses of drift. The most barren glacial stretches, however, such as Yardley Wood, Solihull Wood, and Bickenhill Heath, served exclusively as waste.

Many of the common-field hamlets developed independent manorial structures. The small parish of Bickenhill eventually comprised seven manors: Church Bickenhill, Middle Bickenhill, Hill Bickenhill, Wavers Marston, Marston Culy, Lyndon, and Kineton. In other cases a series of hamlets was contained within the same manor and parish, as at Yardley, which, apart from the parent settlement, encompassed Lea, Tenchlee (later Acock's Green), and Greet. Longdon was unusual in that it had divided loyalties: although in Solihull parish, from about 1270 onwards it was attached to the neighbouring manor of Knowle.

As might be expected the peak of medieval agrarian and demographic development occurred in the late thirteenth century, when the population density at Yardley was in the region of 1 person to 10 acres.[2] Though the fourteenth-century contraction must have been sharp enough, there are reasons for thinking that the 'depression' of the later middle ages was less harmful and prolonged than it is reputed to have been elsewhere. Certainly, by 1524 local populations had recovered to something approaching their 1300 level, with an estimated 1 person to 12 or 13 acres.[3]

But if Tudor numbers were not so very different from those of the late thirteenth century, there was a marked contrast in social structure. In the early middle ages peasant wealth seems to have been fairly evenly distributed. At Yardley in 1275 only 3·7 per cent of the taxpayers had been assessed on

[1] In early fourteenth-century Yardley free tenants probably outnumbered customary by 2:1; at Solihull, with its burgage tenures, the proportion was even higher. By 1632 there were only 5 copyhold and 9 leasehold tenures in the latter manor, as against 75 free tenancies.

[2] This figure is based on the subsidy roll for *c.* 1275 (*Worcestershire Historical Society*, I, 1893), but allowance has been made for exemptions and evasions. It was assumed that the average household numbered 5 persons.

[3] Based on the 1524 subsidy rolls for Bickenhill, Solihull (P.R.O. E 179/192/139), and Yardley (Birmingham Reference Library 392220, III, fol. 182).

movable goods worth more than twice the average amount, and these leading peasants paid only 9 per cent of the total tax. By 1524 8·6 per cent had a personal estate above the twice average mark, and they contributed 25·6 per cent of the parish quota. At Solihull in the same year Rycharde Gryswolds paid £2 (on land), which represented 26 per cent of the sum levied; 10 out of the 129 remaining taxpayers found a further 25 per cent between them. Such families were by no means of great wealth, but they probably exercised considerable social influence: the more so since local manors generally lacked a resident squire. At one time several fees had been in royal hands or attached to a great baronial estate, but from the reign of Elizabeth there was a tendency for them to be acquired by nearby knightly families, who often let the demesnes to local yeomen or gentry.[1]

Instances of piecemeal consolidation and enclosure of common-field selions are found from the late fourteenth century. Nevertheless, *c.* 1550 about 11 per cent of the land was still common field, and 1·5 per cent common meadow; common pasture accounted for perhaps 9 per cent. As already suggested, though, there were significant variations from parish to parish (TABLE I); and even more, between individual manors.[2]

II

Much of the discussion which follows derives from the analysis of 217 probate inventories made between 1530 and 1649.[3] For the purpose of assessing agrarian developments these were divided into four categories, according to the value of the farm—i.e., crops and stock—as follows: (1) above twice the average farm value, (2) between average and twice average, (3) between half average and average, (4) below half average.[4] (Smallholders adjudged to farm less than 5 acres were excluded.)

In the mid-sixteenth century the agrarian economy of Arden was predominantly pastoral, the main emphasis being on cattle. Seventy farmers who died between 1530 and 1569 left 989 head of cattle between them, a mean of 14·1

[1] During the late sixteenth century Sheldon and Marston Culy passed to the Digbys of Coleshill; Church, Hill, and Middle Bickenhills to the Fishers of Great Packington; and Lyndon to the Devereuxs of Castle Bromwich. Solihull was with the Throckmortons of Coughton throughout the sixteenth century, but in 1629 was conveyed to Sir Richard Grevis of Moseley, who in the same year also purchased Yardley.

[2] Sixteenth-century Kineton, as far as is known, had no common-field land, while at Church Bickenhill the proportion was as high as 64 per cent. Church Bickenhill, on the other hand, was virtually devoid of common pasture, though its inhabitants had the ancient right of grazing their "horsses, beasse, Cattell and sheepe" on "Bicknell heathe", which was located in Hill Bickenhill and Wavers Marston.—Skipp and Hastings, *op. cit.*, p. 22.

[3] These consist of 81 Yardley inventories, 10 Rowington (Diocesan Record Office, Worcester); 25 Bickenhill, 50 Sheldon, 51 Solihull (Joint Record Office, Lichfield).

[4] Although the analyses which follow are by 40-year periods, average values were worked out on a 20-year basis, i.e., 1530–49, 1550–69, etc. A mid-point average $\frac{\text{Mean} + \text{Median}}{2}$ was used.

TABLE I

ESTIMATED SEVERALTY AND COMMON LAND, *c.* 1550

Parish	Common field		Common meadow		Common waste		Severalty land
	Estimated acreage	% of parish	Estimated acreage	% of parish	Estimated acreage	% of parish	% of parish*
Bickenhill (3,771 acres)	1,380	36·6	195	5·2	520	13·8	40·0
Elmdon (1,127 acres)			Not known				
Sheldon (2,500 acres)	640	25·6	80	3·2	150	6·0	61·0
Solihull (11,296 acres)	300	2·7	40	0·4	640	5·6	87·0
Yardley (7,590 acres)	500	6·7	80	1·0	950	12·5	75·0

* An allowance of about 5 per cent has been made for roads, watercourses, etc.

each. Big farmers averaged 33·0, substantial 17·0, middling husbandmen 10·9, and lesser husbandmen 4·0 (TABLE II). The larger parishes, with their higher proportion of land in severalty, tended to support more cattle. Over the period 1530–1649, forty-three Sheldon and Bickenhill farmers averaged 10·7 cattle; eighty-three at Solihull and Yardley averaged 13·6.

It is usually said that Arden was concentrating mainly on meat production at this time,[1] but in these parishes the keeping of kine and the breeding of calves seem to have been no less important. Oxen are encountered on only nineteen of the seventy farms and were kept chiefly for draught purposes. Five farmers carried 8–10, six 2–5, while eight had teams (?) of 6. Steers were being fattened for beef on two of the big farms: Richard Brokes of Solihull (1547) had 15 steers, as well as 6 oxen. But usually they occur in small numbers on holdings lacking oxen, and so presumably served at the plough in their stead.

Eight of the nine big farmers, thirteen of the nineteen substantial, and fifteen of the twenty-nine middling husbandmen had mixed (beast/kine) herds. However, in all three categories kine outnumbered beasts by almost 2 to 1 (TABLE II). Five substantial and four middling farmers had kine, calves, and sometimes heifers, plus draught animals. One substantial and four middling husbandmen kept kine, heifers, and/or calves exclusively, as did all but two of the thirteen lesser husbandmen.

[1] *The Agrarian History of England and Wales*, ed. Joan Thirsk, IV, 1967, p. 94.

Actual evidence for dairying is relatively slight. One man has a "deyhouse," two a "Mylkehowse." Although there are ample "loomys," "payls," "kymnels," etc., "mylke panns" and "mylkpotts" receive only isolated references. Four inventories list "a churne," and three (butter) "stenns." Nine of the seventy peasants have "Whytmeate," "Cheysses," or "hard cheses," ranging in value from 1od. to 23s. 1od., and seven others left "chesfatts," a "chese presse," or "cheese cratche."

TABLE II

MEAN AVERAGE NUMBER OF LIVESTOCK PER FARM, 1530–1649

	Oxen	Steers	Beasts*	Bulls	Calves	Heifers	Kine	All Cattle	Horses	Sheep	Swine
(a) 1530–69											
Large farms (above twice average) 9	5·6	2·2	6·7	0·2	5·1	1·1	12·1	33·0	4·7	17·6	5·3
Substantial farms (between average and twice average) 19	2·3	0·8	3·3	0·3	3·3	1·1	5·8	17·0	2·7	14·6	5·4
Middling farms (between half average and average) 29	0·7	0·8	2·1	—	2·0	1·0	4·4	10·9	2·4	7·4	4·1
Small farms (below half average) 13	—	0·2	0·2	—	0·7	0·5	2·5	4·0	0·5	1·7	1·4
All farms 70	1·6	0·9	2·6	0·1	2·5	0·9	5·5	14·1	2·5	9·6	4·1
(b) 1570–1609											
All farms 34	0·4	0·3	1·8	0·2	2·1	1·3	4·5	10·4	1·7	11·6	2·8
(c) 1610–49											
All farms 68	0·6	0·2	1·2	0·1	1·5	1·0	4·0	8·6	1·6	11·4	1·5

* Including bullocks, twinters, and yearling beasts.

Winter herds (October–March) were smaller than their summer counterparts by 35·5 per cent. Numbers of kine, heifers, and calves are 26·2 per cent lower; of oxen, steers, beasts 45·6 per cent less. Seven of the ten peasants whose estates were appraised between October and December had hay, the mean value being 22s. 4d.—an inventory of 1557 reckons hay at 3s. 4d. per load. Between January and March six out of ten had supplies and their average remained as high as 19s. 5d. In ten out of eleven April inventories, on the other hand, stocks were exhausted.

Though big farmers sometimes kept large numbers of sheep,[1] in this sample only two flocks exceeded 40 (48, 46). Rich farmers averaged 17·6 sheep and lambs, substantial 14·6, middling husbandmen 7·4, and lesser husbandmen 1·7. Pigs were less numerous than might have been expected, ranging from a mean of 5·3 on large farms to 1·4 on small; the corresponding averages for horses were 4·7 and 0·5.

Using the twenty-two summer inventories which give details of growing crops, as well as livestock, it is possible to form some idea of what might be called the 'model' farm economy (TABLE III).

TABLE III

MODEL FARM ECONOMY, 1530–1649

(based on summer inventories)

	1530–69 22 inventories	1570–1609 13 inventories	1610–49 19 inventories
Mean acreage of winter corn per farm	3·2	1·5	3·3
,, ,, ,, spring corn per farm	2·8	1·8	5·5
,, ,, ,, unspecified corn per farm	0·5	2·7	2·4
Mean sown acreage per farm	6·6	6·0	11·2
Estimated fallow acreage per farm	3·3	3·0	5·6
Mean total arable acreage per farm	9·9	9·0	16·8
Mean number of cattle per farm	18·1	14·3	12·2
,, ,, ,, horses per farm	2·5	1·6	2·0
,, ,, ,, sheep per farm	10·6	15·0	20·6
,, ,, ,, pigs per farm	5·1	4·9	2·3
Estimated grass acreage per farm	22·7	18·9	18·3
Estimated mean total acreage per farm	32·6	27·9	35·1

The average number of cattle on these farms is 18·1, of horses 2·5, of sheep 10·6. It is difficult to know what acreage to allow per head of livestock. But, bearing in mind fallow grazing and common pasture rights, and also the fact that the forest acre was equivalent to about 1·5 statute acres, we shall probably not be far wrong if we reckon cattle and horses at one acre of enclosed land each, and sheep at five to the acre.[2] Our 'model' holding would then have about 23

---

[1] Two Rowington farmers (not included in this analysis) had particularly large flocks. John Jenetts, gentleman (1559) had 280 sheep, as well as 108 cattle; Roger Oldnale (1563) 640 sheep and 45 cattle.

[2] At Solihull in 1789 all types of land were apparently still being reckoned in forest acres. The tithe survey of that year totals 7,323 acres. If we multiply this figure by 1·5 we arrive at 10,985 acres,

acres of grass, against which the arable allocation works out at about 10 acres—
i.e., 6·6 acres sown, plus an assumed 3·3 fallow. So the mean farm of this
sample is 33 acres, of which rather under a third was arable, and over two-
thirds pasture and meadow.

TABLE IV gives a breakdown of estimated farm sizes—on the same conjec-
tural reckoning. Taking the period 1530–1649 as a whole, over a third of the
holdings fall into the half to one virgate range, while another third were between 30 and 79 acres. Tenures larger than this were uncommon. The Knowle
survey of 1605[1], and the Rowington survey of 1606,[2] have a higher proportion
of 5–14 acre holdings, but otherwise broadly confirm the inventory findings.

TABLE IV

ESTIMATED FARM SIZES, 1530–1649

	Farm size in acres					Mean farm size in acres
	5–14	15–29	30–49	50–79	80+	
1530–69 (22 summer inventories)	3	8	7	3	1	32·6
1570–1609 (13 summer inventories)	3	6	3	—	1	27·9
1610–49 (19 summer inventories)	4	7	3	4	1	35·1
Totals 1530–1649 (54 summer inventories)	10	21	13	7	3	32·3
Knowle survey, 1605 (74 holdings)	27	31	5	5	6	29·0
Rowington survey, 1606 (63 holdings)	19	18	14	10	2	—

The majority of farmers sowed winter and spring crops on a roughly fifty-
fifty basis. For the former, three pinned their faith exclusively in wheat (10
acres); seven cultivated "rye and wheat" (37½ acres); two muncorn (4 acres);

which—allowing for 400–500 acres of common waste—is very close to the modern reckoning of
11,296 statute acres.
    The ratio "5 sheep : 1 horse or cow" is suggested by the 1740 Bylaws of Sheldon (Parish Chest),
where stinting is on the basis of "One Horse or Mare for a Day work of Land, One Cow for a Day
Work, or ffive sheep for a Day Work."
    [1] P.R.O., LR 2. 228. 548. Transcribed by Mr G. L. Bishop.
    [2] P.R.O., LR 2. 228. 577. Transcribed by Mrs J. A. Woodall and Mr G. L. Bishop.

twelve preferred rye on its own (36½ acres).[1] As "Lent tilth" eight cultivated oats (19 acres); one barley (½ acre); one "barley and oats" (2 acres). The rest favoured a combination of corn and peas, three growing "oats and peas" (16 acres); one "barley, oats, and peas" (3 acres); one "oats, peas, and drage" (12 acres).[2]

Although there are exceptions—John Blacknall (1533) of common-field Sheldon had 30 acres of arable—most farmers were producing corn on a purely subsistence basis. Indeed, thirteen out of the seventy (19 per cent) appear to have eschewed arable cultivation altogether. One winter and three summer inventories of large or substantial farmers lack sown arable; while one substantial, four middling, and four lesser husbandmen have no corn, either growing or garnered.

III

The period so far discussed coincides with Leland's journey through Arden and confirms his report of it, about 1540, as being "muche enclosyd, plentifull of gres, but no great plenty of corne."[3] By the end of the seventeenth century Camden's continuator, Edmund Gibson, is presenting a very different picture: "the Inhabitants," he says, "have turn'd so much of Wood- and Heath-land into Tillage and Pasture, that they produce corn, cattle, cheese, and butter enough, not only for their own use, but also to furnish other Counties; whereas, within the memory of man, they were supply'd with Corn, &c. from the *Feldon*." Indeed, according to Gibson, "the great progress the *Woodlanders* have made in Agriculture" meant that the "County began to want Pasture."[4]

By means of the inventories it is possible to trace something of the chronology and manner of this progress. During the period 1570-1609 cattle are rather less numerous than before, the average dropping from 18·1 to 14·3 on summer farms (TABLE III), and from 14·1 to 10·4 over all inventories (TABLE II). To some extent this must be due to the fact that rich farmers are inadequately represented in this small sample of thirty-four. However, that can hardly be the whole explanation, for sheep are more numerous, the mean rising from 10·6 to 15·0 in summer inventories, and from 9·6 to 11·6 generally. It should also be noted that the big drop as far as cattle are concerned is with oxen, steers, and beasts: from 5·1 over all inventories in the 1530-69 period to 2·5 in the period 1570-1609. Against this, the numbers of kine, heifers, and calves decline only marginally, from 8·9 to 7·9. Moreover, evidence of dairying is increasing. Dairy utensils, including "pottes for butter" and "cream pottes," are

---

[1] Seven winter inventories are used in this sample, as well as the 22 summer ones. However, 5 inventories simply speak of (winter) corn.

[2] In 6 instances the crop is unnamed, while 1 farmer grew only winter corn.

[3] *The Itinerary of John Leland in or about the Years 1535-1543*, ed. L. T. Smith, 1964, II, p. 47.

[4] *Camden's Britannia, Newly Translated into English: with large Additions & Improvements*, ed. Edmund Gibson, 1695, p. 510.

now frequently encountered; and every other peasant is involved in cheese-making. But, despite such adjustments, Gibson's radical agrarian change does not apparently belong to the reign of Elizabeth: for the proportion of sown arable to estimated grass remains virtually the same as before (24:76, as against 23:77—TABLE V (*a*)); as does the ratio of crop to stock values (TABLE V (*b*)).

TABLE V

ARABLE/PASTURE AND CROP/STOCK RATIOS, 1530–1649

	(*a*) Ratio of sown arable to estimated pasture in summer inventories		(*b*) Ratio of crop to stock values—all inventories	
	Number of inventories	*Arable/Pasture ratio*	*Number of inventories*	*Crop/Stock ratio*
1530–69	22	23:77	70	17:83
1570–1609	13	24:76	34	18:82
1610–49	19	38:62	65*	31:69

* The discrepancy between the number of inventories used here and in TABLE II is due to the fact that in three instances crop and stock values cannot be clearly established.

During the next forty years, 1610–49, the trend towards fewer cattle and more sheep continues (TABLES II and III). So does the growth of dairying. One out of every six farmsteads (11:68) by this time has a dairy or milkhouse; forty-one of the sixty-eight inventories list cheeses, and fourteen others cheese-making equipment. Luke Rider of Solihull (1630) has "Cheese in the house . . . £10;" Robert Harrison of Sheldon (1645) "one hundred weight of cheese." In twelve additional cases the "small," "greate," or "softe" cheeses (sometimes coupled with butter) are valued at £1 or over. Warwickshire already looks well on the way to becoming one of Defoe's three principal cheese-producing counties.[1]

But an even more significant development of this early Stuart period is the sudden advance of cereal production. Over the previous eighty years crops had accounted for only 17 or 18 per cent of the total farm produce; now there is a rise to 31 per cent. Similarly, the proportion of sown arable goes up sharply from 24 to 38 per cent (TABLE V).

Our 'model' summer farm, 1610–49, has an estimated 18·3 acres under grass. Against this, 11·2 acres are sown with crops. Allowing one-third for fallow as before, this suggests an average arable area of almost 17 acres per farm.

[1] Daniel Defoe, *A Tour through England and Wales*, Everyman edn, 1959, II, p. 131.

Supplementary indications of the swing to arable are not wanting. In the period 1530–69, 32 per cent of the fully inventoried farmsteads had barns. By the 1610–49 period the corresponding figure was 76 per cent. Numbers of ploughs, harrows, carts, and wains also increased appreciably (TABLE VI).

TABLE VI

AVERAGE NUMBER OF PLOUGHS, HARROWS, CARTS, AND WAINS, 1530–1649

	Number of (summer) inventories	Mean average per inventory		
		Ploughs	Harrows	Carts & Wains
1530–69	22	0·2	0·7	0·5
1610–49	19	0·8	1·1	1·9

Much of the additional arable was used for spring corn. At 3·3, the mean winter-corn acreage is virtually identical with that for the mid-Tudor period (TABLE III). Some of the unspecified corn (2·4 acres per farm) may have been winter-sown, but hardly enough to challenge the ascendancy of declared 'Lenten tilth' at 5·5 acres.[1]

Rye was still the chief winter crop, being cultivated by four farmers (33¾ acres); while five opted for "rye and wheat" (15 acres).[2] Oats, too, persisted as the principal spring grain (29½ acres), though barley (21½ acres) was in greater prominence than in earlier samples. Peas claimed 13 acres, "barley & oats" 12, flax and hemp 2¾.[3]

TABLE VII shows that the mounting interest in arable cultivation was shared by all categories of farmer, from the 60–100 acre man, down to the lesser husbandman with 10–15 acres. At the same time, it is the big farmer who is most strongly committed to the new trend, his crop value advancing from 16·8 per cent of the appraised farm produce to 37·4 per cent, as compared with the small peasant's movement from 14·2 to 23·3 per cent.

Perhaps the wealthy Solihull severalty farmer, Robert Palmer, who died in June 1649, best epitomizes 'the wind of change'. His farm must have comprised about 80 acres. Apart from one mare and the plough-team of six oxen (£39), he had a moderate-sized herd of "eight Cowes and one Bull," "five two year old heifers," "six weaning calves," valued collectively at £48. The farmstead had a "day house," equipped with "a Churne," "a skimmer," "a cheese presse;" and a chamber in the house contained "Certaine cheese" worth about £2. Palmer's

---

[1] In any case, 11 winter inventories produce a corn average of only 3·7 acres.

[2] Of the 30 winter and summer inventories available for this sample, 21 refer only to (winter) corn.

[3] One inventory lists "barley, oats and peas" (10 acres); two "oats and peas" (9 acres); one "barley and peas" (½ acre); 6½ acres were unspecified.

other livestock consisted of "Tenne sheepe and six lambs" (£5 5s.), "one store Swine and A gilt with piggs" (£2 6s. 8d.). Bearing in mind common grazing rights, it is likely that he would have needed about 30 acres of grass. His growing corn occupied 34 acres: namely, "eight dayes works of wheate and Ry" (£18), "eight dayes worke of Barley" (£10 13s. 4d.), "sixteene dayes work of oats and

TABLE VII

MEAN AVERAGE CROP AND STOCK VALUES, 1530–69 AND 1610–49

	Number of inventories	Crop Value £ s. d.	% of farm produce	Stock Value £ s. d.	% of farm produce	Crop + Stock Value £ s. d.
(a) 1530–69						
Large farms	9	11 1 10	16·8	57 8 3	83·8	68 10 1
Substantial farms	19	3 0 9	16·4	15 11 7	83·6	18 12 4
Middling farms	29	1 5 10	12·0	9 7 10	88·0	10 13 8
Small farms	13	13 6	14·2	4 1 6	85·8	4 15 0
All farms	70	2 17 9	15·2	16 2 8	84·8	19 0 5
(b) 1610–49						
Large farms	9	39 2 2	37·4	65 8 4	62·6	104 10 6
Substantial farms	18	15 1 1	27·6	39 9 1	72·4	54 10 2
Middling farms	13	6 6 8	25·5	18 9 6	74·5	24 16 2
Small farms	25	2 6 3	23·3	7 12 0	76·7	9 18 3
All farms	65	13 10 1	31·2	29 15 1	68·8	43 5 2

two dayes work of pease" (£21 6s. 8d.). Including "Corne in the Barne un-thresht" from the previous year (£6 6s. 8d.), the total crop value comes to £56 6s. 8d. This has to be compared with the £39 invested in draught animals, and £55 12s. in other livestock. "In the fold yarde" Palmer had "One weane body two payre of wheeles two payre of Tumbrill Draughts two Tumbrill Skirts two plowes one great harrow two little harrows and yokes and Tewes and all other tooles belonging to Husbandry" valued at £5.

IV

Apart from reporting the fact of agrarian change in seventeenth-century Arden, Edmund Gibson provides valuable contemporary clues as to how it was accomplished. In the first place, he says "the Iron-works in the Counties round, destroy'd such prodigious quantities of wood, that they quickly lay the Country a little open, and by degrees made room for the plough."[1]

During the period 1570–1609 eighteen out of seventy inventories record

[1] Gibson, op. cit., p. 510.

substantial timber, either "on the ground" or "about the house," the value adding up to £101. At Knowle in 1605 there were 7,000 oaks and 100 ash trees "growing in the woods of the demesne and in the waste of the . . . manor," of which 2,000 oaks were reserved "for timbering." Roger Bestwick was renting the right to "All the Lopps and Shreds of Oak . . . in Knoll Common . . . and other waste land," though there was a proviso that he should replace trees "that shall die through lopping." John Cope, Esq., however, had "thrown to the ground forty better oaks," and Fulk Grevill had cut down others, "by what right" the jurors did not know. John Hugford in the same year had 300 oak trees on his farm, including 6 which had been cut for timber. There were also 8 (felled?) ash trees, plus 152 cartloads of firewood.[1] Rychard Prettyes of Solihull (1571) left "the tymber in Norton Wood" £2; "hewen tymber" £9; "sawed tymber" £1 6s. 8d.; and "Fyer wood" £6 14s. 4d.

Such men may, or may not, have been sending their "Fyer wood" to "the Iron-works in the Counties round." In any case, local metal-workers, cowpers, carpenters, wheelwrights, tanners, and tile-makers must have consumed considerable quantities of timber. Thomas Lynescombe, Tylemaker of Yardley (1598), had "Wood & tymber att the house & in the grounds," £5 16s. 8d.; and Thomas Walton (1554) "At Nether Tylehowse . . . wood & kyddes" 50s. 0d., and "At ye over tile howse . . . woodes" 26s. 8d.

It is perhaps significant that by the period 1610–49 the value of timber in sixty-eight inventories has fallen to under £40. Moreover, this is the time when "Coles" begin to supplement firewood, at least for domestic purposes.[2] In 1632, when asked about woods in Solihull manor, the jurors reply: "Woods they find, but to a very small valew."[3]

However, if the country was being laid "a little open," this process was not accompanied by any dramatic extension of the cultivated area. Part of Bickenhill Heath was enclosed in 1612 (see page 97), and in 1605 a Knowle farmer held "five closes called le Waste."[4] Eleven people are known to have established small encroachments on the Solihull commons between 1612 and 1632, varying in size from a quarter to one acre.[5] But in the latter year, ten others were fined 6d. and ordered to "throw open their enclosure before Michaelmas on pain of 10s."[6] The fact that Arden had seen intensive colonization in the thirteenth century, and relatively little long-term contraction thereafter, meant that un-

[1] Knowle survey, 1605, *loc. cit.*
[2] The decline in the number of pigs, from a mean of 4·1 (1530–69) to 1·5 (1610–49) may be another pointer, suggesting as it does a reduction in the supply of pannage. On the other hand, one would have expected the advance of dairying to counteract this, for whey could be fed to the pigs.
[3] Survey of the Manor of Solihull, 1632.—Warwick Record Office, Greswold of Malvern Deeds (uncatalogued), Box 24.
[4] Knowle survey, 1605, *loc. cit.*   [5] Solihull survey, 1632, *loc. cit.*
[6] Court Roll, 6 April 1632.—British Museum, Additional Rolls 17772.

appropriated land was less plentiful than in other woodland areas where early development had been inhibited by forest law. By the seventeenth century, indeed, common pasture was in sufficiently short supply to be stinted at Solihull, Yardley, and Rowington—and pretty certainly at Bickenhill, Elmdon, and Sheldon—though not at Knowle.

The second reason Gibson suggests for Arden's progress is "the assistance of *Marle*." In fact, marling had been consistently practised here from early medieval times, even continuing during the fifteenth century, when it is often said to have passed out of vogue:[1] four Solihull peasants were fined in 1421 because they "dug clay from the soil of the Lord King."[2] All the same, references to marling are particularly numerous during early Stuart times. By now freeholders of Solihull, though not cottagers, were entitled to excavate marl on the lord's waste, provided "they shall either raile or hedge the . . . pitt sufficiently for the safeguard of cattell." In 1631 we hear of such "a marle pit lately digged upon the common." Three years later "John Thorne, Richard Powell, and John Withies dug marl in the common way," while others "dug clay . . . on the way next to Garretts Green, and George Slowe received it, making contempt of court by receiving the marl, & thus the common way was destroyed." In 1667 Richard Bache of Solihull had "One load of Lyme and earth meaned together to lay on for barley."

Apart from tree-clearance and marling, Gibson speaks of "other useful contrivances;" and there can be little doubt that foremost among these was the development of convertible or 'up-and-down' husbandry: whereby, to quote from the well-known 1649 survey of the neighbouring manor of Hampton-in-Arden, it was "a usual course with the inhabitants to plow their ground which they doe call pasture for twoe or three yeares together, and then to lett it lye for pasture fifteene or twenty yeares and then plowe it againe, and this they doe with a greate parte of their pasture ground."[3]

Early seventeenth-century deeds frequently speak of what was presumably 'up-and-down' land as "a close of arable or pasture," the first noted examples of this usage occurring in the early 1600's. Similarly, there are many instances of the division of closes into parts, so that the new temporary tillages could be rotated. At Yardley in 1603 we hear of "two Closes . . . now in three partes divided adjoining together . . . whereof the one ys called hilbury fyelde and the other known as Longe burryfyelds;" and in 1641 of "one other Close of pasture called Nether Hurst now in two parts divided."[4] The Knowle survey (1605) mentions "Two closes of pasture now divided into three, near Bentley Heath;"

---

[1] Sir William Ashley, *The Bread of Our Forefathers*, 1928, p. 138.

[2] British Museum, Additional Rolls 17759–88. Other quotations from the Solihull court rolls in this paragraph derive from the same source.

[3] Birmingham Reference Library, 511984.   [4] *Ibid.*, 371529; 427783.

the Solihull survey (1632) "a parcel of land . . . late William Collmores . . . now into two parts divided," "Broome Close now into two partes divided," etc. At Church Bickenhill in 1649 "one close of pasture ground called the Castle Hills" was "devided into seaven parts, whereof some parte thereof is att present plowed, it being the usuall course thereabouts soe to doe."[1]

Convertible husbandry in its fully developed form involved not only the ploughing up of pasture, but the laying down of arable to temporary leys. Although such a procedure was far from impossible on the common fields, enclosed arable was obviously more amenable to it. This—plus the general zeal for improvement—may in large measure account for the period's unusually intensive enclosure activity.

At Bickenhill in 1614 a tripartite indenture was made between Sir Clement and Sir Robert ffysher; Thomas Wall, yeoman; and Hugh Large, husbandman. The parties, we learn from the preamble, "by agreement between them have lately . . . enclosed divers of theire landes and groundes lying within the Common ffyeldes of Hill and Myddle Bicknell . . . by layinge theire landes there convenyentlye together and inclosinge thereof in severall." The purpose of the indenture was to confirm and legalize this exchange. In all, the area involved was probably about 300 acres, the Fisher's allotment including "parte of . . . Bicknell heathe nowe layed or sett out by stakes postes and rayles."[2] By 1677, 137 out of 322 acres belonging to the Fisher and Cousens families in the common fields of Church Bickenhill were enclosed.[3] Although direct information is lacking, considerable areas of Wavers Marston and Elmdon are suspected of passing into severalty during the late sixteenth and the first half of the seventeenth century, the movement perhaps reaching its peak between 1620 and 1660.[4] At Sheldon part of the field called Monland had become "one separate close called Little Monland" by 1601, and in 1661 we hear of "the severall ffeild called great Monlande."[5]

Less evidence of enclosure is forthcoming from the larger parishes, with their smaller proportion of common field; but even here a certain amount can be discovered. At Yardley in 1642 William Marston has "fourteen lands . . . lately inclosed and lying together . . . in the common field called Heynefield." But there is still "one land or selion of the customary land of John Flynt . . . lying amongst them." In order to complete his severalty Marston is prepared to grant "two other lands or selions within the said field called Heynefield . . . for and in lieu of the said selion of John Flynt lying among the said fourteen lands."[6]

---

[1] *Ibid.*, 511984.   [2] Skipp and Hastings, *op. cit.*, 1963, pp. 23–4.   [3] *Ibid.*, p. 25.
[4] *Ibid.*, pp. 52–3. This conclusion is based on the comparison of fieldnames with the first and last appearance of matching surnames in the parish registers.
[5] Skipp, *Discovering Sheldon*, 1960, p. 18.
[6] Deeds of Pinfold Farm, Yardley.—In the householder's possession.

Much of the irregularity between tenant holdings in different fields, which Gray noted in the Jacobean terriers of Arden,[1] was undoubtedly due to the practice of gradual consolidation. At Church Bickenhill William Brook in 1677 had 7 acres of arable in Water Sheepe field, 4½ acres in Little field, but none at all in the third field, Troughmore. Thomas Hanch had 7 acres in Troughmore, only 5 butts (1 acre) in Water Sheepe, and no land in Little field.[2]

With such methods predominating, it need not be assumed that seventeenth-century enclosure involved a great deal of engrossing. Although a question-mark must hang over Elmdon and Wavers Marston, elsewhere the first clear evidence for the amalgamation of tenancies is not found until the 1670's.[3]

V

The widespread adoption of convertible husbandry, with its ploughing up of immemorial pastures, must go a long way by itself towards explaining the increased arable acreages found in inventories. But, aside from their partiality for this more efficient method of cultivation, farmers may also have been tempted to extend their arable by the relative profitability of cereal production over livestock husbandry at this time.

Work on cattle and crop values shows that Arden prices moved roughly in accord with national index figures. The average value of one acre of sown arable in the period 1530–59 was 6s. 1d.; by the period 1620–49 this had increased to £1 2s. 8d. Between 1530 and 1549 cattle and oxen averaged 10s. 6d.; between 1630 and 1649, £2 0s. 1½d. This means that corn and cattle prices advanced at approximately the same rate (373:382). However, we know that nationally the prices of meat and dairy produce did not keep abreast of livestock values; in fact, they little more than doubled between the mid-sixteenth and the mid-seventeenth centuries.[4] Assuming the same locally, the marketing of corn should have been to the husbandman's advantage. It may also be reasonably surmised that the district's expanding population (see below) would have created a growing demand for cereals, particularly since the Feldon was producing less than formerly.

Little is available regarding the disposal of produce. Gibson speaks of the furnishing of "other Counties," while in the early eighteenth century Defoe reports that Warwickshire men regularly sent their cheeses to London, Hull, and to "Sturbridge Fair" at Cambridge.[5] Locally, Birmingham—already by 1640 a manufacturing town of over 5,000—was probably the main outlet.

[1] H. L. Gray, *English Field Systems*, p. 86.   [2] Skipp and Hastings, *op. cit.*, p. 26.
[3] *Ibid.*, pp. 27–8.
[4] *The Agrarian History of England and Wales*, ed. Joan Thirsk, IV, p. 603.
[5] Defoe, *op. cit.*, pp. 131, 141.

Solihull itself, despite an ancient market charter, may be discounted. The jurors of 1632 reported "that there is & hath been time out of mind, they beleeve, a faire kept every yeare ye first day of August, being Lammas day, and they have heard that there is or ought to be a Market kept every Wednesday weekly in ye Borough of Solihull aforesaid, but ye same is now little frequented."

The shift from a predominantly grass economy to one based on "keeping the land in grass and corn alternately" proved to be a permanent change of direction in Arden agriculture. The ratio of sown arable to estimated pasture in ten summer inventories for the period 1680–1709 is 40:60. At Solihull in 1789 32·6 per cent of the land (2,390 acres) was carrying arable crops; 11·4 per cent (831 acres) lay fallow. Seeds and seed clover accounted for 13·4 per cent (981 acres); mowing grass and mowing clover for 23·9 per cent (1,752 acres). Permanent pasture (1,369 acres) stood at 18·7 per cent.[1] In his 1794 report to the Board of Agriculture, John Wedge describes the area as "mostly in tillage."[2]

VI

For the purpose of assessing social developments inventories were sorted into new categories based on (1) the net estate, and (2) the total value of all goods and chattels.[3] It was also decided to introduce a fifth economic grade—below quarter average—a grade which was unnecessary before, because of the exclusion of smallholders and the landless. TABLE VIII sets out the numbers in the various wealth groups period by period, arranging them as far as possible in accordance with occupation and status.

The terms 'yeoman' and 'husbandman' are rarely found in inventories until Stuart times. By then both terms occur in all economic groups, including below quarter average; though, except for two husbandmen and one yeoman, these last lack their farm, their household, or both, and are therefore presumed to have died in retirement. Such people aside, 6 of the 18 practising yeomen have estates worth more than twice average, and 8 come into the between average and twice-average category. Husbandmen, as one would expect, tend to be one notch down, with 5 out of 10 in the second economic group. Of the

---

[1] Tithe survey of Solihull, 1789, Birmingham Reference Library, 433099.

[2] W. Marshall, *The Review and Abstract of the County Reports to the Board of Agriculture*, IV, 1815, p. 284.

[3] In the statistical work on social status, wealth categories were based on the net estate. For house size, value of furnishings, etc., it was decided to base calculations on the total of goods and chattels. This last indicates the *actual* standard of living of the person concerned; whereas the net estate tells us only the degree to which that standard was, or was not, justified. William Hill, yeoman, of Yardley (1611), had goods and chattels worth £53 17s. 6d., but owed debts of £76 6s. 0d. Technically he was bankrupt; nevertheless he was living in a six-roomed house and enjoying standards of comfort which were appropriate to his yeoman status.

TABLE VIII

OCCUPATION AND STATUS BY WEALTH CATEGORIES, 1530–1649

Columns *I–V* represent the following wealth categories: *I* above twice the net average estate; *II* between average and twice average; *III* between half average and average; *IV* between quarter and half average; *V* below quarter average. A mid-point average was used.

Status and/or Occupation	1530–69					1570–1609					1610–49				
	I	*II*	*III*	*IV*	*V*	*I*	*II*	*III*	*IV*	*V*	*I*	*II*	*III*	*IV*	*V*
Parson, without farm	1	1													
Priest/chaplain, without farm	1		1											1	
Parson, with farm											2				
Gentleman, without farm											1				
Gentleman, with farm	1	1_1	1			1					1				
Yeoman farmer	1		1								6_{21}	8_1	2_1	1	1^1
Yeoman, retired							1								2
Husbandman farmer							1	2_1			1_1	5_1	1	1	2^1
Husbandman, retired							1							1_1	3
Farmer (no status given)	7	13_1	21	10		1	6_1	4	6		2_1	5	3_1	3	1^1
Male, retired (no status given)							1_1	1			1		1_1	1	
Widow farmer		2	3	1			2	1	1		1_1	1_1	3_1	2	
Widow, without farm							1					1_1			1
Farmer-craftsman	2	4	1	1		2	3	3	1^1		2_2	4	3	4_1	1^1
Craftsman, without farm			1	2				1						3	2^{17}
Smallholder (no status given)								2_2	4					1	
Labourer, with smallholding								1						3	1
Labourer, without land															2
Spinster														1	1
Category totals— net estate	13	21	29	14	—	4	16	15	12	—	17	24	13	22	17
Category totals— goods and chattels	13	19	31	14	—	4	14	15	14	—	9	27	15	29	13

Inferior figures denote the number of instances in which the goods and chattels estate (i.e., the net estate after discounting debts and/or leases) is one wealth category lower than the net estate. Inferior *italic* figures denote the number of cases where the goods and chattels estate is two categories lower; inferior **bold** figures the number of cases where the goods and chattels estate is three categories lower.

Superior figures indicate the number of instances where the goods and chattels estate is one, two (*italic*), or three (**bold**) categories higher than the net estate.

6 labourers named in the 1610–49 period, 3 had estates below half-average, and 3 below a quarter average. Craftsmen were of two distinct kinds. Those without land generally had below average estates. Farmer-craftsmen, by contrast, feature prominently in the above average groups.

Looked at from the point of view of wealth, we may say that the above average class consisted of gentlemen, parsons, prosperous yeomen, and prosperous farmer-craftsmen. The average to twice average group was dominated by substantial yeomen, substantial farmer-craftsmen, and prosperous husbandmen; the below average by poorer yeomen, middling husbandmen, middling farmer-craftsmen, together with the better-off specialist craftsmen. Finally, in the below half and below quarter average categories we find lesser husbandmen, smallholders, most of the landless craftsmen, labourers, and retired people of various kinds.

In the agrarian sphere the period 1570–1609 was considered to be one of relatively little change. On the social front it brought important developments, and in particular the first phase of the 'housing revolution'.[1] For the forty years 1530–69 the average house size among inventories which give the necessary details was 4·9 rooms (TABLE IX). However, almost two-thirds of the inventoried houses are left undescribed, and the bulk of these must have been of 1, 2, or 3 rooms. Means based on the lower and upper reckonings are provided in the table, but if for the purposes of discussion we take the middle figure, then the estimated house size for the early Tudor period works out at 3·0 rooms. The corresponding mean for the next forty years, 1570–1609, is 4·6, representing an increase of 1·6 rooms. The period 1610–49, which may be taken as roughly coinciding with Phase 2 of the housing revolution, brought a further increase of 1·4, to give an average house size by mid-Stuart times of 6·0 rooms.[2]

Phase 1 of the 'rebuilding' was characterized mainly by ground-floor expansion, peasants adding a kitchen, a second bed-chamber, or, where means permitted, both.[3] Fieldwork reveals a significant scatter of more important houses that were newly built, or extensively enlarged, during this period—e.g., Solihull's Hillfield Hall and Witley Farm; Yardley's Blakesley Hall and Swanshurst Farm. But, as far as inventories are concerned, it is not until Phase 2 that we

[1] See M. W. Barley, *The English Farmhouse and Cottage*, 1961. Barley dates the first phase of the housing revolution 1575–1615; the second phase 1615–1642.

[2] Inventories of lodgers, and those which clearly refer to only part of a house, have been excluded from the analyses. All service rooms which have chambers over them in some inventories, and are known therefore often to have been part of the house (e.g., dairy, milkhouse, boulting house, backhouse, shop, tavern) were included in the figures, but not purely agricultural or industrial premises (e.g., barn, cowhouse, mill, tilehouse, etc.).

[3] At this time some of the kitchens were separate buildings, rather than an integral part of the house: in the 1605 Knowle survey James Geires's farmstead is described as "One dwelling house of three bays, one barn of three bays, one kitchen of one bay."

TABLE IX

AVERAGE HOUSE SIZE BY WEALTH CATEGORIES, 1530–1649

Wealth categories are here based on the mid-point average of goods and chattels as follows: *I* above twice average; *II* between average and twice average; *III* between half average and average; *IV* between quarter and half average; *V* below quarter average.

	1530–69					All categories	1570–1609					All categories	1610–49					All categories
	I	*II*	*III*	*IV*	*V*		*I*	*II*	*III*	*IV*	*V*		*I*	*II*	*III*	*IV*	*V*	
Number of inventories specifying rooms	9	6	7	3	–	25	4	11	8	10	–	33	9	26	11	17	6	69
Mean average number of rooms in above	7·0	4·6	3·1	3·0	–	4·9	8·8	6·9	4·1	3·7	–	5·5	11·0	6·5	7·7	5·2	4·0	6·7
Number of inventories not specifying rooms (excluding those of apparent lodgers)	4	13	23	9	–	49	–	3	4	3	–	10	–	1	2	5	4	12
Average house size assuming undescribed houses to have been of: one room	5·2	2·2	1·5	1·5	–	2·3	8·8	5·6	3·1	3·1	–	4·4	11·0	6·3	6·7	4·2	2·8	5·9
two rooms	5·5	2·9	2·3	2·3	–	3·0	8·8	5·8	3·4	3·3	–	4·6	11·0	6·3	6·8	4·5	3·2	6·0
three rooms	5·8	3·5	3·0	3·0	–	3·6	8·8	6·1	3·7	3·5	–	4·8	11·0	6·4	7·0	4·7	3·6	6·1

find the widespread chambering over of halls, parlours, etc.; or, alternatively, the erection of a new two-storied house.[1]

TABLE IX suggests that all wealth categories, at least down to the below half average, improved their accommodation more or less equally, each about doubling its house size over the eighty years concerned.[2]

Meanwhile, parallel advances were occurring in domestic comfort. When investments in hard and soft furniture, kitchen and tableware, are added up, we find that the average for the 1530–69 period is £6 17s. 4d., representing 20·5 per cent of the value of all goods and chatells (TABLE X). By Elizabethan times the mean has risen to £10 10s. 4d. (30·2 per cent); and in the early Stuart period it stands at £17 4s. 9d.[3] (26·9 per cent).

Again, the less prosperous peasants showed improvements which were comparable with those obtained by their richer neighbours. As between the first and last periods, the value of household goods in the homes of the wealthy and substantial increased by 289 per cent and 275 per cent respectively; the furnishings of middling and lesser peasants increased by 310 and 247[4] per cent.

VII

Though the chief explanation for the sharp climb in estate values between 1530 and 1649 (TABLE XII) must be the declining value of money, the housing and furnishing revolutions provide indisputable evidence of greater peasant wealth; as do the increasing numbers of inventories specifying ready cash, and debts due to, or from, the testator (TABLE XI).

It will be noted, moreover, that changes in the agrarian structure came much too late to be in any way responsible. Not only is this implied by TABLE XII; it is confirmed by the fact that Phase 1 of the housing revolution preceded the agricultural changes, while Phase 2 accompanied them.

In Arden, as elsewhere, the crucial consideration in accounting for this sudden spurt of prosperity must be the pronounced gap which opened out during the mid-sixteenth century between the peasant's relatively stable outgoings, on the one hand, and the ever-rising prices he could command for his surplus farm produce, on the other.

Particularly fortunate in this respect were the forest's innumerable freeholders. At Solihull in 1632 the chief rents of seventy-five free tenants—including all the big severalty farmers—add up to only £14 16s. 10d.—the value of a

---

[1] The Knowle survey of 1605 specifies 6 out of 158 houses as being "newly built", while in the Rowington survey of 1606 only 1 out of 80 houses is so described.

[2] By the 1610-49 period named gentlemen and parsons (4) average 13 rooms per house; named yeomen (20) 7·7 rooms; named farmer-craftsmen (14) 7·5 rooms; named husbandmen (10) 3·3 rooms.

[3] This figure excludes estates below quarter average, which do not occur in the preceding periods. The corresponding figure in TABLE X, however, is that for all inventories.

[4] Again, this figure ignores estates below quarter average.

plough-team. At Knowle in 1605, 937 acres of specified freehold land yielded an average of 1·8d. per acre. Charles Waringe, gent., held "one Capital Messuage called Burye Hall . . . and certain lands in Longdon End" amounting to 225 acres for a rent of 8s. 11d.; plus lands called Williamsons (68½ acres) for a further 12½d.[1]

TABLE X

MEAN AVERAGE VALUE OF FURNITURE, GOLD & SILVER, AND APPAREL, BY WEALTH CATEGORIES, 1530–1649

Wealth categories * are based on the mid-point average of goods and chattels as follows: Column *I* above twice average; *II* average to twice average; *III* half average to average; *IV* quarter average to half average; *V* below quarter average; *VI* all categories. Amounts to nearest shilling.

		I	II	III	IV	V	VI
Number of inventories	1530–69	13	19	30	12	—	74
	1570–1609	4	12	14	13	—	43
	1610–49	9	27	12	22	10	80
		£ s.	£ s.	£ s.	£ s.	£ s.	£ s.
Hard furniture	1530–69	1 18	0 14	0 9	0 5	—	0 15
	1570–1609	4 15	1 18	1 3	0 13	—	1 6
	1610–49	9 13	3 15	2 19	1 8	0 17	3 6
Soft furniture	1530–69	8 12	3 3	2 7	1 10	—	3 10
	1570–1609	14 2	8 10	3 12	2 8	—	5 10
	1610–49	22 17	8 3	6 18	3 10	1 17	7 11
Kitchen and tableware	1530–69	5 18	2 7	1 18	1 4	—	2 12
	1570–1609	14 3	4 3	2 12	1 11	—	3 14
	1610–49	12 16	5 5	4 14	2 8	1 4	4 15
All furniture	1530–69	16 8	6 4	4 14	2 19	—	6 17
	1570–1609	33 0	14 11	7 7	4 12	—	10 10
	1610–49	45 6	17 3	14 11	7 6	3 18	15 12
Gold & silver	1530–69	1 14	2 1	—	—	—	0 16
	1570–1609	3 5	0 3	0 7	0 4	—	0 10
	1610–49	1 13	0 4	—	—	—	5 1
Apparel	1530–69	2 7	0 18	0 18	0 10	—	1 1
	1570–1609	3 13	1 4	1 2	0 13	—	1 4
	1610–49	5 9	1 15	2 1	1 3	0 16	1 18

    * Discrepancies between the 'Category totals—goods and chattels' given in TABLE VIII and the number of inventories used here are due to the fact that in some instances the value of items cannot be accurately established.

    [1] Reliefs at Yardley and Solihull were half the chief rent. Between a third and a half of Yardley's freeholds were non-heriotable, the others yielding "the best goods or Cattells;" at Solihull heriot was the best weapon.

TABLE XI

MEAN AVERAGE OF READY CASH, DEBTS, AND LEASE VALUES, 1530–1649

Averages have been calculated on the total number of inventories used for each period.

Period	1530–69	1570–1609	1610–49
Number of inventories	74	43	80
READY CASH Number of inventories specifying cash Percentage Mean average amount (to nearest shilling)	9 12·2% £1 2s.	4 9·3% £0 11s.	24 30·0% £2 6s.
DEBTS DUE TO TESTATOR Number of inventories specifying debts due Percentage Mean average amount (to nearest shilling)	4 5·4% £0 6s.	13 30·2% £3 17s.	24 30·0% £5 19s.
DEBTS OWED BY TESTATOR Number of inventories specifying debts owed by testator Percentage Mean average amount (to nearest shilling)	8 10·9% £1 15s.	4 9·3% £0 18s.	11 13·8% £2 18s.
LEASES Number of inventories specifying leases Percentage Mean average amount (to nearest shilling)	3 4·1% £0 6s.	8 18·6% £1 8s.	18 22·5% £5 18s.

TABLE XII

AVERAGE NET PERSONAL ESTATE VALUES, 1530–1649

Period	Number of inventories	Mean average £ s. d.	Median average £ s. d.	Mid-point average £ s. d.	1530–69 mid-point average adjusted to Phelps Brown Index* £ s. d.
1530–49	23	17 5 1	13 4 10	15 5 0	15 5 0
1550–69	54	33 11 0	22 16 0	28 3 6	22 8 0
1570–89	27	34 10 2	31 9 4	32 19 9	28 5 0
1590–1609	20	49 11 8	35 4 6	42 8 1	38 7 0
1610–29	51	58 14 0	29 11 8	44 2 10	46 5 0
1630–49	42	69 7 0	52 8 1	60 17 7	54 7 0

* E. M. Carus-Wilson, ed., *Essays in Economic History*, ii, 1966, p. 195.

Rather higher sums were often due from customary tenants. The Knowle survey particularizes 1,127 acres of copyhold land. About 30 per cent of this (332 acres) was rented at from 1d. to 3¾d. per acre; 47 per cent (533 acres) at between 4d. and 7¾d.; 22 per cent (247 acres) between 8d. and 1s. 3d.; and 1 per cent (15 acres) at over 1s. 3d. But at a time when the sown acre was valued at £1 2s., even the top rate of 3s. 7½d. must have offered reasonable prospects.

At Knowle in 1635 entry fines had recently been increased: "It was the Ancient Custom of this Manor to admit an Heir for one Penny and a purchaser was admitted paying one Years Chief Rent for a fine, but now the Lords . . . take a year and a half's Rent upon the Admittance of an Heir, and 2 Years Rent upon the admittance of a Purchaser." Heriot (due only from tenants dying seized) was "the best Horse Ox or Cow . . . Otherwise the best Good or Chattell."[1] The Yardley copyholder (in 1609) owed a similar heriot, but paid "noe Fyne for his admittance."[2]

Leasehold tenure was becoming increasingly common in late Tudor and early Stuart times. Only three out of seventy-four inventories (4·1 per cent) dated 1530–1569 specify unexpired leases, their total value amounting to £22 10s. (TABLE XI). In the 1570–1609 period eight out of forty-three inventories (18·6 per cent) list them, and the sum involved increases to £60 10s. By the 1610–49 period leases occur in eighteen out of eighty inventories (22·5 per cent) and account for £473 6s. The short lease, however, though encountered, was still unusual, the majority being for ninety-nine years, like the five particularized in the 1632 Solihull survey.

Rents featuring in manorial documents were not always those paid by the actual cultivator of the soil. About 26 per cent of the freehold land at Knowle was sublet in 1605, doubtless at considerably higher charges than those due from the freeholders. In any case, commercial lettings are not impossible to find—even in the mid-sixteenth century. The holdings of Studley priory at Greet, which were acquired by Clement Throckmorton and Sir Alexander Avenon in 1545, had been valued in the *Valor Ecclesiasticus* at £10. A survey of 1562 shows that the 467 acres were then yielding £50 0s. 8d. annually— i.e., a mean of 2·1s. per acre.[3]

Before 1600 the Greswolds of Solihull were in possession of the Greet rental: an acquisition which, together with their existing holdings, enabled the senior branch of the family more or less to withdraw from direct farming and enter

---

[1] Custom of the Manor of Knowle, 1635.—Birmingham Reference Library, 379610. In general customary inheritance was by primogeniture. But at Knowle, Borough English obtained, though "Any Copyholder . . . may intail his land as he or she shall think Proper, by Surrender without the Licence of the Lord."

[2] Presentment made at Manor Court, 11 April, 1609.—Birmingham Reference Library, 392222.

[3] Terrier of the Manor of Greete, 1562.—Warwick Record Office, Greswold of Malvern Deeds (uncatalogued), Box 10.

the ranks of the rentier gentry. The Hugfords of Solihull, who obtained the site and Longdon lands of Henwood priory immediately on its dissolution, did almost as well. But, in the main, this was not a period when the gentry and wealthy yeomen were adding greatly to their estates: certainly not to the extent their predecessors had done in the later middle ages. Too many small and middling farmers were clinging to their land—and enjoying the bonanza. Thus, as far as the landed peasantry is concerned, relatively little change seems to have occurred in social structure and the distribution of wealth between the 1524 subsidy and the hearth taxes of the late seventeenth century. However, there was an ever-increasing number of inhabitants who did not belong to the landed peasantry.

VIII

Arden populations show a persistent upward tendency throughout the period which concerns us. Between 1540 and 1569, at Elmdon, Solihull, and Yardley, there were 403 more baptisms than burials, giving a natural increase rate of 24·6 per cent. In the 1570–1609 period the excess of baptisms, for all parishes, was 891; and in the next forty years 1,030: the rates of natural increase being 29·7 and 28·3 per cent respectively.

Fertility was not particularly high in late Tudor and early Stuart times, but rose during the second quarter of the seventeenth century.[1] At Sheldon, Solihull, and Yardley, the mean birth interval, 1575–1624, was 28·6 months, and the mean closed family size 3·2 children. In the next twenty-five years the birth interval shortened to 27·3 months, while the size of closed families increased to 3·6 children.[2]

Immigration was subject to the usual discouragements. In 1632 an enactment of the Solihull court leet forbade anyone to "receive into his house any person other than a child or children;" and John Miles forfeited 39s. "because he received one William Lea . . . without giving security that the parish would be in no way burdened."[3] Three others were fined 30s. each in 1634 on a similar charge. Nevertheless, families of strangers—along with native ones—were constantly contriving to erect cottages on the Solihull commons. Six erections

[1] Age-specific marital fertility (children born per thousand woman-years lived) at Sheldon, Solihull, and Yardley, 1575–1624, was 405 for women in the 20–4 age-group; 371 for the 25–9 age-group; 328 for the 30–4 age-group; and 214 for the 35–9 age-group. The corresponding figures, 1625–49, were 432, 459, 377, 258. At Colyton, Devon, by contrast, age-specific marital fertility was high between 1560 and 1629 (467, 403, 369, 302), but declined in the period 1630–46 (378, 382, 298, 234).—E. A. Wrigley, 'Family Limitation in Pre-Industrial England', *Econ. Hist. Rev.*, Second Series, XIX, 1966, p. 89.

[2] Mean birth intervals are based on births 1–4. See Wrigley, *op. cit.*, p. 93. Over the 75 years, 1575–1649, age at first marriage stayed fairly static, men marrying at an average of about 29 years, women at 26.

[3] This, and other quotations from the Solihull court rolls in the present paragraph, come from British Museum, Additional Rolls 17771–82.

are noted in the 1632 survey, while Edward Betterton is presented to the court leet in the same year for building "a cottage at Dickens Heath . . . which did not have four acres of land according to the law." In 1647 seven people are charged with erecting cottages "on the lord's waste" in Olton End "without apportioning 4 acres of land apiece to them in accordance with Statute." "They should forfeit £10 each," we are told, "but by grace forfeit 10s." Such cases suggest that manorial authorities may have been less efficient at preventing squatter settlement than in exacting a fine for it.[1] In any event, the parish registers provide ample confirmation of a steady procession of newcomers. Only 257 different surnames are found among Solihull and Yardley baptisms during the 1550's; by the 1600's there are 357 different surnames, and in the 1640's 331.

But people were constantly moving out of these parishes, as well as entering them. A study of the life-histories of 166 individuals born into sixty-six Solihull families between 1601 and 1625 revealed that less than one in three were represented by descendants at Solihull in the next generation. Forty-one (24·6 per cent) died in infancy or childhood;[2] a further seventy-three (44 per cent) left the parish without producing recorded offspring. Indeed, on balance, more individuals seem to have emigrated than immigrated. While natural increase between 1570 and 1649 should have produced a growth of 1,921 for the five parishes, the actual population rise was not much more than half of this: from perhaps 2,150 to 3,200.[3] However, with the estimated population density reaching a record figure of 1 person to 8·5 acres by the time of the hearth tax returns, this was doubtless enough.

A combined analysis of the hearth-tax returns for Sheldon (1674), Bickenhill (1663), and Solihull (1663)[4] shows that twenty-eight out of 439 households (6·3 per cent) had 4 or more hearths. This group, which included a knight and ten of the thirteen named gentlemen, may perhaps be regarded as approximating to the wealthy (i.e., above twice average) group in our earlier inventory analyses. Below these, seventy-six substantial or middling peasants (17·3 per cent) had 2 or 3 hearths. Lesser husbandmen and craftsmen, labourers, etc., paying on 1 hearth, and roughly comparable with the below half and below quarter-average estate values, numbered 156 (35·7 per cent). But beneath these

---

[1] There are three enclosures of about 4 acres in the middle of what was, until the nineteenth-century enclosure, Shirley Heath. Nevertheless, it seems extremely unlikely that there was any long-term intention of encouraging squatters to take in this amount of land. Had anyone done so—at any rate by the seventeenth century—he would almost certainly have been dealt with under the alternative charge of making an encroachment.

[2] The infant mortality rate at Yardley, 1571–1600, was 158 per 1,000; at Solihull and Yardley, 1601–25, 148 per 1,000; and 1626–45, 157 per 1,000.

[3] These figures are based on the Cox estimate, with a 5 per cent allowance for under registration. Family reconstitution suggests that down to the 1640's the parish registers of Sheldon, Solihull, and Yardley (the only parishes reconstituted) provide a reasonably satisfactory record of events.

[4] Warwick Record Office, QS 11/7, QS 11/5.

again was the group whose members were exempt from paying the hearth tax on grounds of poverty, and may be assumed to have left no will. They number 179, accounting for 40·8 per cent of the total households.

As early as 1605, 21 per cent (30 out of 143) of the holdings at Knowle were without land: apart, that is, from a yard, backside, garden, or orchard.[1] Using the hearth tax exemptions as a pointer, it seems safe to assume that by the mid-seventeenth century the proportion of the landless had risen to at least 40 per cent, and probably considerably more. Nor, except at Knowle, where all residents could "put any Beast, Sheep, or any other Cattle"[2] on the common, had the landless any grazing rights.

The increase in arable cultivation may have helped marginally towards providing employment for this growing body of landless cottagers—at least in the harvest months. But the majority must have relied on the pursuit of one of the local crafts.

Woodland by-employments—carpentry, coopery, tanning, weaving, and a certain amount of general smithery—had been present in the area from early medieval times. By the opening years of the fifteenth century tile-making was developing as a major manufacturing activity at Yardley, while a century later specialist metal craftsmen were spreading throughout the Birmingham district. In 1507/8 we come across Nicholas Coterel of Yardley, "Flecher," and Thomas Pratty, "wheeler" (wire-drawer); in the 1530's another wheeler and a scythe-smith are recorded for the same parish.[3] Certain industries, such as tanning and tile-making, tended to be monopolized by farmer-craftsmen, but others—and particularly some of the metal trades—required little in the way of work premises or capital outlay, and were therefore suited to the cottager.

Symon Rotton of Yardley, cutler, who died in 1634, had £2 3s. out of his total estate of £9 7s. 10d. tied up in the equipment of his "shoppe," which included "one paire of bellowes, one handfeld, one glasier, one iron vise, three hammers, fyve paire of tongues, one Cutlers sawe, one iron grate, one fyle and one draweing knyffe." In his hall were a "greate wheele & two little wheeles," which suggest that the regular spinning of wool, hemp, and flax also aided the family budget. Rotton was landless and had no cattle. Yet his house had four rooms, and although he slept on a "chaffebedde," at least there was a "feather boulster" and "feather pyllowe."

Among the smaller craftsmen known to have been operating at Yardley during the first half of the seventeenth century were 6 weavers, a tailor, a capper, a shoemaker; woodworkers included a sawyer, a carpenter, and 2 turners; the metal trades 1 striker, 2 cutlers, 3 nailers, 3 whirlers, and 8 smiths. At Solihull those receiving "Mr Wheatly's dole for decayed tradesmen" (1651–1718) in-

[1] Knowle survey, 1605, *loc. cit.*   [2] The Custom of the Manor of Knowle, 1635, *loc. cit.*
[3] Birmingham Reference Library, 392220, I, fols. 9, 10; II, fol. 83.

cluded 2 cutlers, 2 whirlers, 2 whitesmiths, 4 glovers, 4 masons, 4 sawyers, 7 blacksmiths, 7 tanners, 9 carpenters, 10 turners, 15 shoemakers, 16 tailors, 17 weavers, and 26 nailers.[1]

Without the opportunities provided by these industrial by-employments it is difficult to see how Arden parishes could possibly have supported their seventeenth-century populations. As it was, 179 out of 795 people buried at Solihull between 1597 and 1624—or 22·5 per cent—are described as paupers. The figure for Bickenhill between 1630 and 1649, on the other hand, was as low as 4·2 per cent.

In 1649–50, which was a dearth year when poor law cases were extremely high throughout Warwickshire, £32 16s. 6d. was disbursed by the Yardley overseers. Two-thirds of this sum went on regular pay for 13 persons. Five widows and 2 other females received between 1s. and 4s. 8d. per month; 6 males had between 1s. and 1s. 4d. Twenty-four parishioners had occasional relief, the highest sum of 18s. going to "William Howler and his wyfe in theire necessitie."[2] How far this comparatively modest disbursement represented a genuine lack of distress among the 40 per cent of local populations who—on the hearth tax evidence—were below the poverty line is another matter.

IX

The period 1530–1649 in Arden, then, was one of considerable agrarian advance: bringing, as it did, a change from the traditional pastoral economy to one based on mixed farming and convertible husbandry. For all sections of the landed peasantry, too, it saw an unprecedented—and remarkably homogeneous—rise in the standard of living, with improvements in accommodation, domestic comfort, and—no doubt—diet.

But at the lower end of the social scale, population pressure was creating a large 'landless' class, many of whose members—despite the expansion of industrial activities—may have been prone to greater economic hardships than were their counterparts a few generations before.

Yet craftsmen like Symon Rotton, given good health and reasonable harvests, could manage to make a living. Nor was the lot of the landless labourer necessarily one of unrelieved penury. Among the smallest inventoried estates of the early Stuart period was that of William Bane, labourer, of Yardley, who died in 1614, worth £8 19s. 4d. Bane must have been a bachelor or widower, for he was lodging in somebody else's house, probably his master's. Nevertheless, he had his own "two small coffers," and slept on his own "Course Chaffe bedd," with "the Course furniture to the same belongeinge." "Money found in his coffer" came to 14s. And this was scarcely a tithe of his savings: he

[1] Parish Bailiffs' Accounts, 1525–1813, Solihull Parish Chest.
[2] Birmingham Reference Library, 272091.

also left "money in the keeping of John Marston . . . £6," and "in the keeping of Richard Brown . . . 8s. 2d." Finally, in his room, alongside the tools of his calling—"one hoke," "one old litell Bill," and "other od Implementes"—the appraisers came across "Sertayne small bookes," valued at 10s., and "one penne and inke horne."

The Schooling of the Peasantry in Cambridgeshire, 1575–1700[1]

By MARGARET SPUFFORD

GREAT emphasis has been placed on the increasing prosperity of the farming classes during the sixteenth century, and the expression of this in a higher standard of living. From Harrison's description of the novelty of pewter, feather beds, and chimneys in ordinary houses in the 1580's, to Hoskins's 'Great Rebuilding' and illustrations of the revolution in the size of houses of the yeomanry, it is the material effects of this new prosperity that have called for comment. It is surely worth examining, though, the degree to which these economic changes freed sections of rural society to acquire new aptitudes, to become literate, and so to formulate attitudes and opinions, and participate at the parish level in the reformation of the sixteenth century and the 'further reformation' of the seventeenth century. The growth of a demand for education is in some ways a more significant development than the proliferation of domestic offices in farmhouses, and, like the latter, it demands prosperity, which can enable families to spare children from the labour force.

Any lecturer to adult education classes in rural areas today has probably met the middle-aged members of farming families who were forced to leave school at fourteen after the end of the last war, not for any lack of ability, but because of the desperate shortage of farm labour. In the sixteenth and early seventeenth centuries, on the other hand, farm labourers were desperately seeking employment. Only yeomen farming sixty acres or more were in a position to employ servants or labourers regularly.[2] Since the thickly populated arable counties of eastern England probably still had numerically far more farmers of medium-sized holdings of thirty acres or less than yeomen holding substantial acreages, it seems likely that the children in these rural areas had little chance of much education, even if schools existed for them to go to.

The disadvantages of the ordinary village child, constantly reclaimed by mother or father to help with brewing, bird-scaring, hoeing, haying, and all the crises of the agricultural year, are vividly portrayed in a description of a Suffolk National School between 1860 and 1880. In the village of Blaxhall, the farmers complained before a Royal Commission in 1880 that the loss of the school

[1] I should like to thank very warmly the Trustees of the Eileen Power Fund and the President and Fellows of Lucy Cavendish College, Cambridge, who, by their support, have helped to make this work possible.

[2] *Agrarian History of England and Wales*, IV, *1500–1640*, ed. Joan Thirsk, pp. 652, 661.

children's labour had affected their farming adversely, since they were unable to pay men's wages for the work the children were accustomed to do.[1] One boy, whose father was a miller with a smallholding in the fens near Ramsey, described his schooldays in the mid 1870's: "Attendance at the school warn't compulsory,[2] and all the summer months the older boys . . . had to stop at home and go a-weeding or some such work in the fields. . . I often wished my father were a bit more like other boys' fathers, as a good many o' my associates never looked inside the school. Arter I were about nine year old, I got real ashamed o' going to school when other folks went to work. One morning some men were working in a field as I passed on my way to school, and I 'eard one on 'em say 'Look at that bloody grut ol' bor still a-going to school. Oughta be getting 'is own living'." After this, he hid in the ditches on his way to school to escape being noticed. He left at twelve.[3] It is admittedly dangerous to infer anything about seventeenth-century social conditions from those of the nineteenth century, but it is very difficult to believe that the village child of two centuries earlier can have been a great deal better off than his counterpart after the Education Act of 1870.

Probability suggests, therefore, that the children of labourers and farmers of holdings of only average size would have had little prospect of acquiring even a rudimentary education in the sixteenth and seventeenth centuries, even if provision existed for it. It thus suggests that any improvement in educational standards among classes below the gentry consisted in the emergence of a class of yeomen, who were able to spare their children from the exigencies of the daily grind of keeping alive to acquire the inessential fripperies of education. Latimer's famous observation on the importance of the yeoman class in providing personnel for the church was soundly based on the economic facts of life. In areas of arable farming like southern Cambridgeshire, where the size of farms was increasing during the period and the numbers of the yeomen growing, one would also expect a growing demand for education and an improvement in educational standards, although it might be confined to a small part of the population. Conversely, an area of small farmers like the Fenland is likely to have had fewer literate children. Literacy, or rather illiteracy, rates should, in fact, vary from area to area and follow to some extent differences in types of farming, and therefore in social structure. At the present moment, however, even this simple hypothesis remains unproven.

Much has recently been made of the 'educational revolution' of the late sixteenth and early seventeenth centuries.[4] The evidence for this is based, of

---

[1] George Ewart Evans, *Ask the Fellows who cut the Hay*, 1956, pp. 62, 172–6.

[2] For those children who lived more than two miles from the school.

[3] Sybil Marshall, *Fenland Chronicle*, 1967, pp. 17, 21.

[4] Laurence Stone, 'The Educational Revolution in England, 1560–1640', *Past and Present*, 28, 1964, pp. 41–80.

course, on the intake of the universities and the functions and number of the grammar schools capable of producing such students, not on the extent to which the ordinary villager was taught to read and write, for the simple reason that the grammar schools and their products are easier to trace. There were two great periods of expansion in the universities, when the numbers of students rose steeply, one beginning in 1560 and reaching a peak in the mid 1580's, and the next beginning in 1604, after a lull, and reaching its peak in the mid 1630's.[1] During the latter, it has been very roughly estimated that $2\frac{1}{2}$ per cent of the group of young men aged seventeen were going on to higher education.[2] The social composition of these university students has been exhaustively examined,[3] but more interest has been aroused in measuring the participation of the gentry and the professional middle classes than in measuring the participation of the sons of farmers and their servants, who, as yeomen, husbandmen, and labourers made up the bulk of the population. In a sense, an estimate of the proportion of the peasants' sons who went on to higher education is much less important than the much more difficult question of the extent of basic literacy amongst the mass of villagers. It is relevant, however, for the attainment of a university education can be used as one of the chief yardsticks of educational opportunity amongst the peasantry, and of the possibility of social advancement open to them.

Unfortunately, it is not possible to reach any conclusions about the numbers of university entrants originating from the families of yeomen, husbandmen, village craftsmen, or even smaller fry until the university matriculation registers and the college admission books begin to give the occupation of the entrant's father or, at the very least, to describe him as of an armigerous, gentle, clerical, or 'plebian' family. Forty-seven per cent of matriculands at Oxford between 1575 and 1639 described their parentage as 'plebian'.[4] It is impossible to judge the proportion of these who came from a rural and agricultural background; 'plebian' included sons of merchants, professional men, and artisans, as well as yeomen and labourers, and in fact covered every social group except sons of the new or old gentry, the nobility, or the clergy. In the same way, the admissions registers at Caius College, Cambridge,[5] which are the only printed Cambridge ones which give the parentage of incoming students in the sixteenth century, initially describe the fathers of a large proportion of the entry as "mediocris fortunae." The term apparently covered sons of the clergy and the

[1] Stone, *art. cit.*, pp. 50-1 and graph 1 facing p. 49.   [2] Stone, *art. cit.*, pp. 57 and 68.
[3] By Stone, *art. cit.*, pp. 57-68, and by Joan Simon, 'The Social Origins of Cambridge Students, 1603-1640', *Past and Present*, 26, 1963, pp. 58-67.
[4] Stone, *art. cit.*, pp. 60-1, particularly Table V. Professor Stone suggests that these men may really have represented something like 41 per cent of the intake, when the figures are adjusted to allow for those who misrepresented their parentage and those who did not matriculate.
[5] *Admissions to Gonville and Caius, 1558-1678*, ed. J. Venn.

professional and trading classes, as well as artisans and small farmers. The picture is further obscured by the fact that Caius appeared to cater more exclusively for the sons of the gentry than did other colleges like St John's, whose admissions register begins in 1630.[1] In the peak decade of the 1630's when the Caius register becomes more precise in its terminology, only fourteen entrants, or 5 per cent of the intake, were described as yeomen, farmers, husbandmen, plebians, or "mediocris fortunae." At St John's, in the same decade, 117 men, or 24 per cent, came from the same background. In the 1690's, after the end of the educational boom, the proportion of the intake from these social groups was reduced to 15 per cent at St John's, and 2 per cent at Caius.[2] There is no means of knowing whether the proportion of farmers' sons at St John's or at Caius was more representative of the university as a whole. One can only state that men from rural backgrounds could make up as much as a quarter of the intake in some colleges during the educational boom of the 1630's, although the proportion could also fall much lower.[3] Young men from rural, peasant, backgrounds certainly had the opportunity of a university education in the late sixteenth and early seventeenth centuries. It is fair to assume that the quarter of the entrants at St John's who came from the peasantry represent a maximum, however, and that the overall proportion of peasants among university entrants was much lower than this, while the section of society that they represented was, of course, much greater. Still, the opportunity existed, however rarely it was taken up.

There is a further general argument which suggests that some of the sons of the peasantry were able to benefit from a university education in the sixteenth and seventeenth centuries. It seems to be generally accepted, although exact proof is impossible, that the bulk of the parochial clergy, holding benefices with incomes which in many cases were totally incapable of supporting the incumbent in a way of life in any way superior to that of the bulk of his parishioners,[4] were men of humble origin.[5] At the same time, the evidence shows that the proportion of graduate clergy rose steeply. Only a fifth of the clergy instituted or beneficed in the diocese of Canterbury under Archbishop Bourgchier between

[1] *Admissions to the College of St John* . . . , ed. J. E. B. Mayor.

[2] The whole of the foregoing passage is based on Stone, *art. cit.*, pp. 64–6.

[3] It is impossible to judge whether the farming classes were benefiting to a greater or lesser extent from the earlier educational boom of the 1580's, let alone trace the rise and fall of their prosperity measured in educational terms, for lack of more precise, and earlier, records. Harrison's general remarks on the prosperity of yeomen in the 1580's suggests that they were then sending their sons to university as well as putting glass in their windows and adding brewhouses to their kitchens.

[4] P. Heath, *The English Parish Clergy on the eve of the Reformation*, 1969, p. 173, shows that three-quarters of the parochial livings in England were probably worth less than £15.

[5] Christopher Hill, *Economic Problems of the Church*, 1956, pp. 208–9. Heath, *op. cit.*, p. 137, supports this view, and cites the rare fifteenth-century example of John Pyndere, a bondman of Terrington in Norfolk, who was manumitted to take orders, and was parochial chaplain of Willingham in Cambridgeshire in 1462.

1454 and 1486 were graduates.[1] Sixty-seven per cent of the clergy of the diocese of Ely were graduates at the end of Elizabeth's reign.[2] Between 1660 and 1714, the proportion of non-university men instituted and beneficed in the diocese of Worcester never rose above 16 per cent. The largest group of Worcester clergy were of 'plebian' origin.[3] If we make the moderate assumption that the proportion of men of peasant origin entering the ministry remained the same during the sixteenth and seventeenth centuries (if this is wrong, it is more likely that the proportion rose than fell), then it is clear, since the proportion of the lesser clergy with degrees rose sharply, that a university education must have come more commonly within the reach of the farmer's son. General arguments suggest, then, that just as living standards improved amongst the yeomanry, so also did educational standards.

The hypothesis that different social structures produced different proportions of men free to take up educational advantages[4] can, to some extent, be tested by examining the numbers of college entrants from the county of Cambridge and the Isle of Ely who were admitted to the colleges of Gonville and Caius and of St John's between 1558 and 1700. For if it is valid, the numbers of college entrants ought to be directly related to the number of families in an economic position to dispense with their sons' labour. Therefore, if there were numerically fewer yeomen in this situation in the Isle than in the county, the numbers of college entrants should reflect the situation.

The county and the Isle were strongly differentiated economically. The county was predominantly a barley-growing region. It remained arable, and almost unaffected by enclosure, throughout the period. In 1524–5, 53 per cent of those taxed in the Great Subsidy in southern Cambridgeshire were wage labourers or servants earning 30s. or less a year.[5] This is a much higher proportion than in those other counties, Leicestershire, Lincolnshire, and Devon, studied in detail so far,[6] and is obviously related to the exclusively corn-growing nature of the Cambridgeshire economy, which demanded a very large labour

---

[1] This evidence, drawn from the register printed by the Canterbury and York Society, ed. Du Boulay, 54, 1956, p. xxix, is summarized with other evidence on the literacy of the clergy by Heath, *op. cit.*, pp. 81 *et seq.*

[2] Stone, *art. cit.*, p. 47 (from Usher, *Reconstruction of the English Church*, I, 242). Hill, *op. cit.*, p. 207, gives figures showing a sharp rise in the number of graduate clergy between 1540 and 1640 in the diocese of Oxford.

[3] P. Morgan, 'The Subscription Books of the Diocese of Worcester and Class Structure under the Later Stuarts', unpublished M.A. dissertation, Birmingham, 1952, pp. 90–108, 111–39.

[4] See above, p. 113.

[5] Margaret Spufford, 'Rural Cambridgeshire, 1520–1680', unpublished M.A. dissertation, Leicester, 1962, p. 62.

[6] Averages of 22 per cent in Leicestershire.—W. G. Hoskins, *Essays in Leicestershire History*, 1950, p. 129; 36 per cent in Devon.—H. P. R. Finberg and W. G. Hoskins, *Devonshire Studies*, 1951, p. 419; 28 to 41 per cent in different areas of Lincolnshire.—Joan Thirsk, *English Peasant Farming*, 1957, p. 83.

force. All the available evidence goes to show, moreover, that during the six-teenth and seventeenth centuries a great deal of engrossing took place. Cambridgeshire society was further polarized socially. The number of yeomen increased, and so also did the numbers of the landless, which were already high. Only the villages on the northern edge of the county bounding on the edge of the fen, like Willingham, developed differently. They resembled the villages of the Isle of Ely, which had a totally different economy, based on stock raising. There, there were large numbers of farmers with relatively small holdings, and both fewer labourers and fewer men with larger farms.[1] A man calling himself a yeoman held a far smaller acreage, and left fewer goods at his death in the fen-edge villages of southern Cambridgeshire and the Isle, than he did in the county.[2]

Between 1558 and 1700, a total of 236 men who were born in the Isle of Ely and southern Cambridgeshire came up to Gonville and Caius, and St Johns (TABLE I).[3]

TABLE I

College	Entrants from county				Entrants from Isle					City	Total
	Gent.	Clergy	Others	Total	Gent.	Clergy	Others	Unspec.	Total		
Gonville & Caius	36	10	21	67	10	—	5	3	18	30	156
St John's	11	10	7	28	6	3	8	5	22	71	80
Total	47	20	28	95	16	3	13	8	40	101	236

Forty-three per cent of these were from the city of Cambridge alone, and can be discounted for these purposes. Seventy per cent of the remainder were from the county of Cambridge, and only 30 per cent from the Isle of Ely.[4] Allowing for the very different populations of the county and the Isle,[5] it seems that there were seven men coming up from the county to every four from the Isle.

[1] Joan Thirsk, *Fenland Farming*, Leicester University Occasional Papers, 3, 1953, pp. 39–41. Dr Thirsk's work is based on the Lincolnshire fenland, but the farms in the Isle of Ely seem to have been very similar.

[2] Margaret Spufford, dissertation *cit.*, p. 76. The median yeoman farm in the 1660's was 92 acres, and the median wealth of yeomen dying in southern Cambridgeshire in that decade was £180. There were very few examples of yeomen from the edge of the fens coming into this category. My evidence suggests that a fenland yeoman with between 29 and 40 acres of arable and his fen common was, very roughly, in the same situation as his upland counterpart.

[3] Excluding the considerable numbers of boys from outside, who came to finish their grammar school education at Ely or one of the schools in Cambridge itself. The registers of Christ's College and Peterhouse, which also provide information on schools, do not usually give information on parentage. See below, p. 123, note 1.

[4] Including the City of Ely.

[5] 5,091 occupied households in the Isle in 1674.—*V.C.H. Cambridgeshire and the Isle of Ely*, IV, 1953, p. 273. 6,952 occupied households in the county in 1664.—My figures, dissertation *cit.*, p. 47, amended to include the hundreds of Stapleho and Cheveley.

The chances of a man from the county coming up were nearly twice as great. Dividing the entrants up socially is a risky business; those whose father's status was described as 'gentleman' include men whose fathers are known to have been yeoman farmers, and the clergy included sons of people like the Master of Peterhouse at one end of the spectrum and those from the humblest livings at the other. However, if the pitifully small numbers of entrants of rural parentage who did not claim to be of gentle or clerical background are considered alone, it still seems that the chances of a county man from the peasantry coming up to college were nearly half as great again as those of his counterpart from the Isle. Such minute figures must of course, be treated with great caution. Twenty-eight men of peasant stock from the county, and thirteen from the Isle, acquiring an education up to university level over a period of 140 years, can hardly be claimed as a great educational boom.[1] Furthermore, conclusions based on two registers could be totally misleading. If the Isle schools had special connections with a college, or colleges, whose registers are unprinted or do not give parentage, and if they in fact sent up far more entrants, this picture could be totally reversed. In so far as it goes, however, the evidence suggests that the different social structures of the Isle and southern Cambridgeshire did have a considerable effect, and that the areas with an enlarging class of substantial yeomen were more able to benefit educationally. But the evidence also suggests that few Cambridgeshire yeomen were able to take the final step in social aggrandisement of sending their sons to college, even though the numbers might be greatly expanded if more registers were printed.[2] There are odd

[1] Half of these (15) came up to Gonville and Caius before 1590, and all but one, who was specifically said to be the son of a husbandman, were described as sons of men 'mediocris fortunae'. The term covers many different types of parentage (see above, pp. 114–15, and Joan Simon, 'Social Origins of Cambridge Students, 1603–40', *Past and Present*, 26, 1963, p. 60). I have assumed that these men were of peasant stock, because they originated in villages where there was no cottage industry, apart from the normal number of craftsmen supplying the community with essentials. The major flaw in my argument is that they could have been the sons of clerics. However, I think this figure of twenty-eight is a minimum rather than a maximum one for the peasantry, despite the difficulty over the Gonville and Caius terminology, because I suspect that gentle status was claimed whenever this was possible. Henry Crisp, son of a yeoman of Willingham (see below, p. 120), who came up to Caius in 1627, is a case in point. I have not tried to draw any deductions on the period when farmers found it most possible to educate their sons to university level, because of these difficulties in terminology. On the face of it, it seems significant that half the men I have assumed to be sons of peasants came up before 1590, when the economic difficulties at the turn of the century began to loom, especially since only one of the registers supplies information for this earlier period, and that is one from a college which later appeared to have a bias towards the gentry. I think it likely, however, that there were a good many Henry Crisps amongst those described as gentlemen's sons in the seventeenth century, and that therefore no conclusions can be drawn.

[2] Again, this judgement could be totally reversed, if many of the county schools happened to have affiliations with other colleges rather than with Caius and St John's. Examination of entrants from other counties needs to be made, but can only be made by people aware of the social and economic structures concerned, to account for the high proportion of students of peasant origin at St John's in the 1630's (see above, p. 115).

examples of men of peasant stock whose careers were so notable that they can be picked out without the aid of printed registers. John Richardson was born in Linton in about 1564, and went up to Clare. He became Regius Professor of Divinity in 1607, and was one of the translators of the Authorized Version.[1] His father died in 1616, and "John Richardson, Dr. of Divinity," was duly admitted to his lands as his son and heir. When his successor inherited in turn in 1626, the copyhold amounted to only about fifteen acres, so John Richardson seems to have been born of relatively very humble stock.[2] The type of family which could normally afford to spare a son for college is exemplified by the histories of the Butler family of Orwell, in the uplands, and the Crisp family of Willingham, in the fens. Both stood out as exceptional in their own villages.

Nicholas Johnson alias Butler of Orwell, who died in 1601, and who was described by his neighbours as a yeoman, was able to send his eldest son, Thomas, who was born in 1570, up to Gray's Inn. The Inns of Court are usually regarded as the most socially exclusive of the establishments for higher education. One of Thomas's younger brothers was literate and able to write a letter and address it to "his loveing Brother Thomas Butler att his Chambers in Gray's Inn." A second brother was able to write his name when he witnessed Thomas's will.[3]

Thomas put his legal education to good use. He acquired a lease of a large part of the Orwell demesne, and then brought a suit against some of his fellow tenants, when his actions eventually brought him into dislike.[4] He sent his eldest son, Neville, first to school at the Perse in Cambridge, and then to Christ's College in 1623, when he was fourteen. By the time Thomas died, in 1622, he was known as a "gentleman." He left his son all his books. His widow held ninety acres of copyhold arable in 1628 during the minority of her son, over and above an unknown amount of freehold and demesne leasehold.[5] Neville Butler sent his eldest son away to grammar school in Hertford, before he went up to Christ's in his turn in 1649. By the time his fourth son John was educable, there was a "schola publica" in Orwell which prepared him for Christ's in 1661. John eventually became rector of Wallington. When Neville Butler died, after marrying an heiress, and buying the lands of the priory of Barnwell, one of the clauses in his will left £2 to his "good friend" Mr John Noon of Clare Hall to preach at his funeral.[6] The Butlers had made the

---

[1] Venn, *Alumni Cantabrigienses*, III, 452.

[2] Cambridgeshire Record Office (henceforth C.R.O.), Linton Court Minutes, R.59.5.1, entries for 1616, 1625, and 1626.

[3] P.C.C. wills, 18 Savile.

[4] All details of the Butler family, except those on the size of their holdings, are taken from the depositions in this suit.—P.R.O., E 134, 3 Jas. I, East. 18; and a reconstruction of the family from the parish registers.—*The Register of the Parish of Orwell, 1560–1653*, ed. R. W. Whiston, 1912.

[5] C.R.O., L 1/130, pp. 73 *et seq.*   [6] P.C.C. wills, 1675, fol. 42.

transition, both economically and in taste, from the yeomanry to the gentry.

George Crisp was the only man in Willingham, which lay on the edge of the fens, whose farm was comparable in size with those of yeomen in the upland part of southern Cambridgeshire. He held seventy-five acres of arable, both freehold and copyhold, in 1575, and stood head and shoulders above the other tenants. The most prosperous of them held under forty acres. George split his holding between his two sons, leaving the fifty-six acres of freehold to his son Henry, and a full yardland of thirty-six acres of copyhold to William. Even so, Henry Crisp still held the most considerable farm in Willingham in 1603. It was his son, another Henry Crisp, who went up to Gonville and Caius in 1627, described in the College register as the son of a "gentleman." For all that, when either his brother or his cousin, both of whom were unfortunately christened William, got into an altercation with a youth from a gentle family in the Isle of Ely in 1639, and told him that he was "a better gentleman," the gentle family was so piqued by this language from what they described as "an ordinary country fellowe" that they took the case to the Court of Chivalry.[1] The Crisps had obviously not made the grade to gentility, in local eyes.

During the rest of the seventeenth century, the whole of the tenurial history of Willingham is one of the breakdown of holdings into smaller and smaller units. It is no wonder that after 1627, despite the well-established school in Willingham,[2] no other Willingham boys, so far as is known, went up to college.

Illustrations of individual families who were able to afford university education do nothing, however, to illuminate the related, and in many ways much more important, question of the degree of literacy amongst the mass of villagers who could not hope to free their sons from farm labour for schooling which would lead to a university course. At the moment, the main statistical evidence bearing on literacy in the countryside is that a proportion ranging from 17 to 38 per cent of the signatories to the Protestation Oath of 1642 in each parish were able to sign their names.[3]

This whole question of literacy is at present being examined by the Cambridge Group for the History of Population and Social Structure. When the work of the Group is completed, those interested in the quality of life lived in local communities will have as accurate a picture as it is possible to obtain of the extent of literacy at this level, measured solely in terms of the ability to sign

---

[1] Case referred to by George Squibb, *The High Court of Chivalry*, 1959, pp. 175 and 209. I am indebted to my husband for this reference. I am also deeply obliged to Mr Francis Steer, Archivist to His Grace the Duke of Norfolk, who made a special journey to Arundel and sent me a transcript of William Crisp's submission to the Court (Arundel Castle MS., E.M.134), and notes on two other newly discovered documents in the suit (Arundel Castle MSS., E.M.3154 and 3155). It is most unfortunate that the documents cited by Mr Squibb, including the plaintiff's petition, cannot at present be found at the College of Arms.

[2] See below, pp. 131 *et. seq.*

[3] Stone, 'Literacy and Education in England, 1640–1900', *Past and Present*, 42, 1969, pp. 100–1.

one's name. The limitations of such a criterion are self-evident. It is impossible
to gauge exactly the relationship between the ability to write one's own name,
and the ability to read, which is the real subject of inquiry for those who want
to know how far the ordinary villager was open to external influences and
pressures.[1] Furthermore, the two main classes of documents surviving from
before 1700 which bear enough signatures to be analysed in this way are the
depositions in ecclesiastical cases, and the original wills. The former were
signed by witnesses, who were necessarily completely arbitrarily chosen and
came from every social group. The latter, which are more likely to be available
for any particular community, have the considerable disadvantage that they
were signed or marked by a man who was, more often than not, on his death-
bed, judging by the rapidity with which the date of probate followed that of
the will. He was probably therefore much less able to make the effort to sign
his name than usual,[2] and statistics drawn from the wills are suspect because
of this. However, there is no better material available for the historian to
work on.

Some insight both into the relationship between the abilities to write and to
read and into the failing powers of testators is given in a dispute in 1578 concerning the will of Leonard Woolward of Balsham. He was a retired man who
asked the young chirurgeon, who was trying to give him some relief from pain
in his last illness, to write his will for him.[3] He did this because he was living
with his son and daughter-in-law in his old age, and wanted his will made
"as pryvelye as mighte be," for he feared that if it were known to his son and
his wife that he was going to leave some of his free land to someone other than
them "he shoulde not be well tended & have that he woulde have, and yf enye
of his frends or acquaintances . . . should write his sayd will, his sayd sonne
yonge Lennard . . . woulde knowe of yt, and soe laye on him yt he shoulde not
or coulde not make his wyll accordinge to his owne mynde." The old man held
about twenty-four acres of free land, and so is likely to have been a fairly humble
yeoman. The will was actually written on the day Leonard Woolward died,
although he could still sit up in bed. It was disputed by the family in the consistory court. In response to questioning, the young barber-surgeon replied:
"Yt whether oulde Lenard Woolward in his lyef time coulde wrighte or noe

---

[1] There seems to be a general impression that, although the relationship between the ability to
sign and the ability to read is unknown, the two were related, and that reading ability very probably
exceeded writing capacity. Discussed by Laurence Stone, *art. cit.*, pp. 89, 98. V. E. Neuberg,
'Literacy in Eighteenth Century England: a Caveat', *Local Population Studies Magazine and News-
letter*, 2, 1969, p. 44, points out that eighteenth-century educationalists stressed that the teaching of
reading was much more important than that of writing, which did not necessarily follow it. At
Orwell school, boys were taught to read and write, girls 'only' to read. See below, p. 140, n. 1.

[2] See below, pp. 134 *et seq.*

[3] Cambridge University Library, Ely Diocesan Records, D2/11, fols. 259–61. I am deeply
indebted to Mrs Dorothy Owen for drawing this particular case to my attention.

this deponent knoweth not, for he saythe he never sawe him wryte, yet saythe yt he hathe hard the sayd oulde Leonard saye yt he cowlde wrighte, And further saythe yt yf he the sayd oulde Leonard cowlde wrighte in his lyef tyme, yet that at the tyme of his will makeing, this deponent verelye belevethe that he cowlde not well write wth ease or to his contentation, for yt he was then verye oulde, & for yt his sighte then fayled him muche, for this deponent saythe yt ymediatelye after the wyll was wrytten he the sayd oulde Leonard toke the sayd will in his hand & woulde have red yt him selfe but sayd yt his sighte was soe evell (excepte he had spectacles) yt he coulde not reade yt, & deliveringe yt to this deponent desyred him to reade yt, wch he this deponent did accordinglye." It is therefore perfectly evident that this old man was known to be able to read, and that the chirurgeon attending him was in no way surprised by this, although he was not entirely sure that he could write. Elsewhere in the chirurgeon's testimony it appears that Leonard Woolward had an "oulde parchment booke" in his house. On the very day of his death Leonard Woolward made an attempt to read the will written according to his directions, although he made no attempt to write it. Reading was an easier skill.

In many ways it is premature to attempt to produce anything on literacy until the work of the Group is complete. However, there are two ways in which it seems that this work can be supplemented. In the first place, bare statistics on literacy are in some ways uninformative unless they can be combined with information on the schools existing in the area from which they are taken. There is still a dearth of regional studies of schools,[1] particularly those which include full studies of elementary schools, since the latter involve working through all licences, visitations, and subscriptions of schoolmasters in episcopal records.

In the second place, although the work of the Cambridge Group in examining literacy rates is irreplaceable, and cannot be done effectively on any small scale, there is still some advantage to be gained from examining literacy in a few communities which a local historian has already portrayed. There are obvious benefits in knowing something of the social structure of a community as well as the number of its inhabitants able to sign their names at a given date. I have therefore added an examination of literacy, based mainly on the testators' ability to sign their names to their wills, of three villages in Cambridgeshire between 1600 and 1700 to a survey of schools in the county.

[1] Like, for instance, Brian Simon's 'Leicestershire Schools, 1625–40', *British Jnl of Educational Studies*, III, 1954, pp. 42–58; the survey of education in the Diocese of Norwich in E. H. Carter, *The Norwich Subscription Books*, 1937, pp. 81 *et seq.*; P. J. Wallace and W. E. Tate, 'A Register of Old Yorkshire Grammar Schools', *Leeds University Researches and Studies*, XIII, 1956, pp. 64–104, which confines itself to schools sending pupils to the universities.

Cambridgeshire Schools and Schoolmasters

The Ely diocesan records, for the period when references to schoolmasters abound, from 1574 to about 1628,[1] give a startlingly strong impression that education was readily available in southern Cambridgeshire (see MAP I). There were twenty-three places where a school seems to have been kept more or less continuously during the sixty years.[2] Most of these were in the larger villages. The settlements on the fen edge, which had had over a hundred households in 1563 (see MAP II) like Cottenham, Waterbeach, Bottisham, and Fulbourn, had them. The larger villages in or near the Cam valley, like Great Shelford, Barrington, Sawston, and Linton, which had accommodated over fifty households, had them, and so also did the larger villages of over fifty households in the Upper Rhee valley, like Melbourn and Bassingbourn. There is a remarkable degree of coincidence between the sites of these well-established schools and the sites of the present Cambridgeshire village colleges. At least eight of the present ten village colleges[3] lie where a school was well-established in the late sixteenth and early seventeenth centuries. The explanation lies either in the continued size of the village, which makes, and made, it a suitable settlement to provide enough work for a school, or in a combination of size and status. Market towns, like Linton, were obvious foci for schools, and were both easily accessible and much visited, so that they had a large catchment area. It is noticeable that the ancient market town of Bourn was the only settlement to

---

[1] I have taken all my information on schools and schoolmasters in the diocese of Ely from the register compiled by Mrs Elizabeth Key, which I hope will shortly appear in print in the *Cambridge Antiquarian Society Proceedings*. I should like to thank Mrs Key very warmly for giving me unstinted access to this material, and information on it. Her register is based on an examination of the Ely Registers of Licences (Cambridge University Library, E.D.R. G/2/18–21), which mention schoolmasters from 1574–1618; the Libri Cleri (E.D.R. B/2/various) which include the names of schoolmasters at visitations from 1601 to *c.* 1628 and after 1665 to 1692, and the Ely Subscription Books (E.D.R. A/5/1–8 and Bodleian Rawl. D340) which only cover the period after 1662. The careers of the schoolmasters named in the diocesan records were traced in Venn, *Alumni Cantabrigienses*. She has also searched the printed registers of *Admissions to Gonville and Caius, 1558–1678*, ed. J. Venn (in which schools are noticed throughout), *Biographical Register of Christ's College, 1505–1905*, I, ed. J. Peile (schools noticed from 1622 but no indication of parentage given), *Admissions to the College of St John . . .*, ed. J. E. B. Mayor (opens in 1630 and mentions schools throughout). *The Admissions to Peterhouse*, ed. T. A. Walker, give the names of schools after 1637. Mr David Cressy, of Clare College, who has worked through all the visitation and licensing material of the diocese of Norwich, has very generously given me all the references he has found to teaching in the Deanery of Fordham, which lies in the diocese of Norwich and the county of Cambridge. MAP I is therefore based entirely on the work of Mrs Key and Mr Cressey.

[2] I have assumed continuity where there was a gap in the records for ten years or less. Records exist for the same man teaching for twelve years, like Mr John Jackson, vicar of Gamlingay, who was licensed from 1607–19.

[3] Excluding Soham and Burwell village colleges, which lie in the Deanery of Fordham in Norwich, for which there is little information. References to teaching were made for only four villages in the deanery in the entire seventeenth century. It may be significant that two of these were Soham and Burwell. Soham was endowed in the mid-seventeenth century.—*V.C.H. Cambs.*, II, 1948, pp. 331–2.

have a well-established school on the western clay plateau of Cambridgeshire.

Apart from these twenty-three well established schools, masters were continuously referred to in another nine villages either up to 1600 or after 1600.

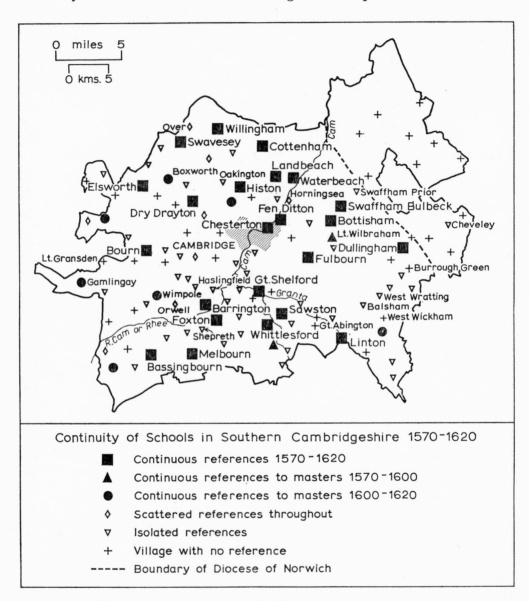

Map I

They also had scattered references in the later, or earlier, period. These villages may well have had schools consistently for a much longer period. The records do not give the appearance of scrupulosity in licensing. A college entrant in

1589, who had been at school in Hauxton, is a salutary reminder of the unreliability of the records. There is not a single mention of a master at Hauxton in either the sixteenth- or seventeenth-century documentary records.

Yet a third group of eight villages appeared in the records as having a schoolmaster both before and after 1600, and was referred to between four and six times altogether. In these villages, and those with even fewer references, it seems probable that individual masters, rather than established schools, were

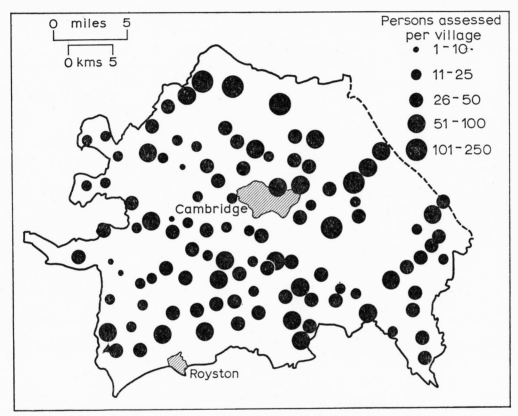

MAP II. DISTRIBUTION OF POPULATION IN CAMBRIDGESHIRE, 1563

concerned. The high academic quality of many of these men[1] makes it seem very likely that they were the products of the bulge in university entrants in the 1560's to 80's, and were reduced to searching for jobs wherever they could find them. The number of college entrants taught by men in villages which have no other record of a school gives the same impression that isolated individuals were often teachers in villages with no established school.[2] Detailed work on

[1] See below, p. 129.

[2] This confirms Professor Stone's impressions in 'The Educational Revolution in England, 1560–1640', *Past and Present*, 28, 1964, p. 46, that college entrants were often privately prepared in small

the careers of schoolmasters show that many of them were very young men doing a short spell of teaching between graduation and getting a benefice elsewhere.[1] The spells for which they taught were therefore brief and there was little or no permanence. It is no wonder that endowment, even of a very humble kind, had the immediate effect of establishing a school, when there were so many graduates obviously seeking work which offered a steady income, however small.

Over is an example of one of these villages with a record of occasional teaching throughout the period 1574 to 1628. A master was licensed to teach young children there in 1583; in 1604 and 1607 Ezra Parkes was teaching there when the place was visited. The clerk who drew up the visitation book expected to find him there in 1610, but his name was crossed out, presumably because he had gone. By 1616, though, the vicar was schoolmaster there. These scattered references may well have indicated some continuity in teaching over a short period, and certainly did mean that the children in villages of this type had periods of several years when they could go to school at home, instead of walking to the nearest established school.

Finally, another forty-seven villages had up to three references to masters teaching in them between 1574 and 1628. Sometimes there was certainly a master in one of these villages for five or ten years; sometimes there was only a single reference. But in all, only twenty-two villages in the county had no schoolmaster licensed at any time between 1574 and 1628.[2] Most of them were very small.

The overall distribution of schools in the county shows that north of Cambridge the villages on the fen edge both to the west and to the east were well provided with established schools, or schools where there was a fair degree of continuity. A child born here would rarely have to walk further than to the next village to acquire an education, if he could be spared from more pressing work. The river valleys and whole area south of Cambridge were also well provided for; again, a child would rarely have to walk further than the next village. The two exceptions to this abundant provision were the line of villages from Balsham out to Borough Green, and the villages west of Cambridge on the clay plateau out to Bourn. Most of these villages had schoolmasters licensed, or noted in visitations occasionally, but there was much less continuous schooling available here, and very often a child would be out of walking distance of a school.

This pattern of distribution fits very well with the economic differences

hamlets. It is quite wrong to assume, as W. A. L. Vincent did in *The State and School Education, 1640–60*, 1950, that any village in which a college entrant was prepared automatically had a grammar school. His county lists are suspect for this reason.

[1] Forthcoming article by Mrs Elizabeth Key, to whom I am indebted for this information.

[2] One of them was Little Gransden. See below, pp. 128–9.

between these areas of Cambridgeshire in the sixteenth and seventeenth centuries. The settlements on the fen edge and in the valley area were expanding during the period, whereas those on the boulder clay to the west were shrinking. The villages on the chalk ridge were noticeably poorer than those in the rest of the county, judging from the much higher proportion of houses with only one hearth taxed there in the 1660's.[1]

It is important to know what type of education was available in these schools for the village child, but it is also difficult to establish this. The licences issued for schoolmasters between 1574 and 1604 sometimes simply gave permission to teach and instruct; but frequently the licence was issued for a specific function. These varied from "to teach grammar," "to teach the rudiments of grammar," "to teach boys and adolescents to write, read and caste an accompte," "to write and read the vulgar tongue," and "to teach young children." It looks, on the face of it, as though they were grammar and English schools, and as if the latter were divided into the two types described by Professor Stone, petty schools teaching children to write and read, and those teaching English grammar, writing, and arithmetic up to the age of sixteen.[2] Unfortunately, there is a great deal of inconsistency in the type of licence issued for the same village within relatively short spaces of time. Licences not uncommonly specified the teaching of the "vulgar tongue" or "young children" at one visitation, and grammar at the next, or vice versa. Moreover, the college admissions registers gave evidence that boys were prepared in some villages in which, according to the episcopal records, there had never been a schoolmaster, or there was not a schoolmaster at the right time, or there was only a schoolmaster who taught the "vulgar tongue."[3] These suspicious contradictions make any attempt

[1] Margaret Spufford, dissertation *cit.*, pp. 55–7; *idem*, 'The Significance of the Cambridgeshire Hearth Tax', *Cambs. Antiq. Soc. Proc.*, LV, 1962, p. 59, and Fig. 2, p. 61.

[2] Stone, *art. cit.*, pp. 42–4.

[3] Grammar was certainly taught up to university entrance level in half a dozen Cambridgeshire villages in the period up to 1628, but village grammar schools were of very little importance compared with the schools in Cambridge and Ely. The latter, for instance, prepared nine boys from the county for the three colleges with printed registers before 1622, while no village school sent up more than three entrants. The only cast-iron evidence that a village had a grammar school was provided by the combination of a continuous succession of masters recorded for the place, preferably licensed to teach grammar, together with evidence that a boy who went up to college was taught grammar there. The schools which sent entrants directly up to college in this period were Cheveley 1593, 1603, 1629 (*V.C.H. Cambs.*, II, 1948, p. 331); Elsworth 1581; Fulbourn 1573, 1592; Hauxton 1589; Oakington, 1583; and Willingham 1627. Of these 'grammar schools', Cheveley lay in the diocese of Norwich. Elsworth, although it prepared a boy for Caius in 1581, had a master licensed to teach reading and writing of English only at the end of the decade. Fulbourn had a continuous record. There is no mention of a schoolmaster at Hauxton in the Ely records at any time. Oakington had had a pupil taught by Mr Longworth for seven years before 1583, but Mr Longworth managed to escape episcopal attention entirely. The first master who appeared in the diocesan records, in 1596, was licensed to teach, not grammar, but the "vulgar tongue." Willingham had a continuous record. In addition, Bassingbourn prepared two pupils for other schools, who went up in 1574 and 1634, and Dullingham, Fen Ditton, and Little Wilbraham also acted as preparatory schools for boys who went up in 1580,

to establish a typology of local schools futile. For one thing, the definitions given in the episcopal records may not be reliable, for another, these small village schools probably changed in character remarkably fast. Many existed over a brief period only, or for the working life of an individual teacher. Others, which apparently had no continuous history, may well have done so, and escaped episcopal notice. It is obvious that the records are only impressionistic, and the impression that they give is of flexibility and change. The school held in Little Gransden should serve as a salutary reminder against too rigid definition. It escaped episcopal notice altogether, and Little Gransden was one of the few villages with no record of any teaching there. The existence of the school is known only because the tenants of Little Gransden fell out with the new lords of the manor in the early seventeenth century over the whereabouts of the demesne which they themselves had leased since the late fourteenth century. One of the witnesses in the consequent series of suits was an old gentleman settled in Lincolnshire, who deposed that he had known Little Gransden for sixty years "for he was born in Great Gransden nearby and went to School in his youth in the chancel of Little Gransden."[1] Another was Christopher Meade, gentleman, steward of the manor court, who likewise went to school in Little Gransden, and therefore knew all the local gossip of the place.[2] He was responsible, in 1607, for searching the thirteenth-century episcopal surveys of Gransden, and the medieval reeves' accounts, and tying these descriptions together with surviving earthworks to reconstruct the layout of the medieval demesne. Such was his expertise as an antiquarian that the judge ruled testily that "no more such old books should be brought in unless they were . . . not above forty or fifty years continuance." This school at which Meade was trained, which did not even exist according to the diocesan records, evidently flourished in the 1570's and 80's, and served as a preparatory school, at least, for the local gentry. It is impossible to believe either in the reliability of the records, or in any interpretation of sixteenth-century local schooling which rests on a rigid typology of schools according to class. It is perfectly

1587, and 1599, as did Fulbourn. Of the preparatory schools, Bassingbourn and Fen Ditton had impeccable records of schoolmasters licensed to teach grammar, or simply to teach. Both had a continuous life and were well-established schools. Dullingham had a continuous life and had a master licensed only to teach reading and writing in 1579. (*V.C.H. Cambs.*, II, 1948, pp. 332–3, for its later endowment.) Edward Barton, son of a gentleman of Dullingham, who went up to Caius after going first to Dullingham, then Ely, and then to Hitchin grammar school for four years, must have learned to read and write in his own village. Little Wilbraham, which prepared its rector's son to go to grammar school in Cambridge, had a continuous record of masters licensed in the 1580's but even so, Mr Cockman who was master there at some point in the 1590's, according to the register of Caius College, escaped episcopal notice. The records for the schools acting as preparatory schools therefore showed just as much variety and lack of consistency as those of the 'grammar' schools.

[1] P.R.O., E 134, 1649, East. I. He must have been to school in the late 1580's, according to his deposition.

[2] P.R.O., E 134, 5 Jas I, Hil. 26.

obvious that the children of Little Gransden who could be spared to go to school, including the children of the gentry, went along to the church chancel. How much they learnt there cannot be known. However, those who were later to go to university acquired an adequate foundation. And they all strengthened the common bonds of community which bound them, for, amongst other things, they talked about the rumour that houses had once stood in the Bury Close, and about the size of the yardland.

Although the schools may have changed rapidly in character between 1574 and 1604, the general quality of the masters teaching in them was extraordinarily high. Nearly two-thirds of the men licensed specifically to teach grammar are certainly known to have been graduates.[1] A number of the remainder may, of course, have graduated as well. Much more surprisingly, a third of the masters licensed merely "to teach younge children to read write and caste accompte" were also graduates.[2] After 1604, when the licences stopped specifying the kind of teaching to be done, no generalizations can be made on the qualifications of teachers in different schools.

After 1628, until the Ely subscription books start in 1662, the only evidence available on schools is that provided by the college entrance books. Whereas a few villages had provided entrants in the earlier period (although nothing like as many as the grammar schools of Cambridge and Ely), no local school sent up an entrant in the boom years of the 1630's at all, while the schools of Cambridge and Bury became much more predominant. Local schools only really started sending up entrants again in any numbers in the 1660's. The period when college registers are helpful coincides with the period when the diocesan registers reopen.[3] Even after 1662, the references in the records to schools are too scanty to give any real knowledge of the villages in the county which had schools functioning permanently. There is usually only one reference to a schoolmaster subscribing between 1662 and 1700; and the gap from the late 1620's is far too long to postulate continuity, although where there is a later reference to a school which had had a continuous record up to 1628, it is tempting to suspect it.

At least half the schools with continuous records between 1574 and 1628 reappeared at the end of the century. There was very little overlap between them and the places which sent up entrants to college. Again, it looks as if many of the latter were privately tutored by individual masters. However, Bottisham, which had had an early continuous record, and had been left a little bequest producing an income of a pound a year for teaching three poor children in

---

[1] Fifty-one out of eighty-one.   [2] Ten out of twenty-nine.

[3] Nine villages produced entrants for the colleges which had printed admissions books between 1660 and 1700. They were Orwell 1661; West Wratting 1666; Oakington (2 entrants) 1666; Bottisham 1668; private school Bourn 1671; Shepreth 1671; private school Swaffham Prior 1678; Willingham, preparatory to Eton, 1685; Fordham 1690.

1639, managed to send a boy from the village up to college in 1668. Willingham, which was early endowed by public subscription, had masters who subscribed in 1666 and 1675, and an attorney from Cambridge sent his son there in the 1680's to be prepared for Eton. Endowments had an immediate effect. Dullingham had had a continuous record in the earlier period, but did not appear in the episcopal records of the 1660's. In 1678 Barradill Millicent left rents worth five pounds a year for teaching poor children in "grammar and learning," and in 1679 a master subscribed, if only to teach writing and arithmetic. The most considerable endowment noted in the inquiry into charitable donations of the eighteenth century was at Haslingfield, where Simon Ertman left an income of twenty pounds a year in 1658. There had been scattered references to a master teaching there in the earlier part of the period, before 1628, but as a result of the Ertman endowment, masters from Haslingfield appeared five times in the episcopal records after 1662, more than from any other school.

The references in the subscription books are so thin that they can be used only as positive evidence. It is not safe to suggest that no school existed where no schoolmaster subscribed. Therefore, although masters appeared in far fewer villages between 1662 and 1700 than between 1574 and 1628, it is impossible to say whether the ordinary village child had more or less chance of an education at the beginning or end of the seventeenth century. The only conclusion that can be drawn is that at the end of the century, as at the beginning, the areas best served by schoolmasters were the thickly settled edges of the fen north of Cambridge, and the valleys of the Cam south of Cambridge. The western clay plateau and the poverty-stricken chalk uplands were still relatively unprovided for.

Even though schools seem so often to have been taught by young men before they obtained benefices elsewhere, it still seems true to say that, in the late sixteenth and early seventeenth centuries at least, the combination of the number of village schools in southern Cambridgeshire and the quality of the masters teaching in them should have given the Cambridgeshire peasantry ample, if erratic, opportunities for education. If their economic situation allowed them to benefit from their opportunities, then the literacy rates should have been fairly high.

Elementary Ability to Write

The communities chosen for special study were strongly contrasted socially. Willingham was a fen village, in which the economy was based largely on stock raising, rather than on the arable holdings. This economy produced a very different social structure from that of the uplands. In 1575, only one man held an arable acreage appropriate to a yeoman in the south of the county; the backbone of the community was formed by the holders of the twenty-eight half yardlands. These men were only copyhold tenants of between thirteen and twenty-three acres of arable, but here, on the edge of the fen, they were men of substance, and they, in their wills, described themselves as yeomen. These wills give the impression of prosperity in the last quarter of the sixteenth century, at a time when the upland counterparts of such men were losing their holdings because they were unable to withstand the combined economic pressures of the price rise and frequent bad harvests. During the seventeenth century there was an influx of people into Willingham, and probably a rise in the resident population also, because the opportunities provided by the fen meant that it was possible to exist on a relatively small holding. The old half yardland units, which had remained intact since the thirteenth century, broke down, and there was actually a diminution in the number of the landless, and an increase in the number of tenants holding between two and fourteen acres, at a time when, in the uplands, the most noticeable movement was towards the polarization of the size of holdings and an increase in the number of landless labourers.

Lawrence Milford was the first schoolmaster known to have taught in Willingham. He was licensed to teach "young children" in 1580.[1] He had obviously been living in Willingham before he was licensed there, for he acted as the regular scribe for the villagers' wills for the last thirty years of the century. He had no cottage there when the place was surveyed in 1575, but must surely have been resident. In March 1578, John Loder of Willingham made a will which was written and witnessed by Lawrence Milford, in which John left him the crops of one "land" of meslin, one acre of wheat, and "my best hat." In 1579, before he was officially licensed, Lawrence Milford held a lease in Willingham.[2] When John Loder's brother, Robert, died in 1583, he left a pregnant wife, and specifically provided in his will "that if it be a man child that she go with all I will that she bring it up in learning til it comes to the age of sixteen years,"[3] He must have been thinking of Lawrence Milford's school.

There was obviously some interest in education at Willingham, and in 1593 this bore remarkable fruit, for in that year, the inhabitants endowed a school by public subscription.[4] The rector, Dr William Smyth, may well have been the initiator and driving force behind the foundation, for he seems to have been

[1] Cambridge University Library, E.D.R. G/2/18.

[2] P.R.O., E 310/9/13. This reference is given in *Charity School to Village College*, produced by the Cottenham Village College Local History Group, 1968, pp. 5–7, which discusses the early history of the Willingham school. The school has also been discussed by E. H. Hampson.—*V.C.H. Cambs.*, II, 1948, p. 339.

[3] Robert Loder appears from his will to have held only a copyhold house and close, and one rood of free land. This is not the kind of holding one would suppose would keep a child at school until he reached the age of sixteen.

[4] C.R.O., P 177/25/1, pp. 1–2. I am informed by Dr Roger Schofield that this subscription list is, so far as he knows, unique.

resident in Willingham for a considerable part of his incumbency from 1586 to 1601.[1] He had been a Fellow of Kings before his appointment in 1586, and went on to be Master of Clare in 1601. His name came high on the subscription list with a donation of one pound a year during his incumbency. Whether or not he was the initiator of the scheme, the really striking thing about it was the degree of support given by the villagers.[2] The 102 people who subscribed raised £102 7s. 8d. between them, and only five donations were of more than £2.[3] The core of the list was made up by the sixteen men who gave sums ranging from £1 up to and including £2, and the fourteen who gave £1 apiece. All the rest gave less than £1. Thirteen of the sixteen men who gave the largest sums were, or had been,[4] half yardlanders. Another six of those who gave £1 were also half yardlanders. Almost all the tenants of half yardlands were represented somewhere on the list, and almost all the larger sums given by villagers were given by them. This is the most concrete proof it is possible to have that the half yardlanders of Willingham were indeed relatively prosperous. They could afford to give sums which amounted to more than two years' rent in most cases.[5] It was also proof they were sufficiently interested in education actually to dig into their pockets to give their children some chance of it. The half yardlanders, although they were the most substantial villagers contributing, were not the only ones. Involvement in the plans for the school to the point of making a financial sacrifice on its behalf spread right down through Willingham society. There were examples of the younger sons of half yardlanders, like Henry Bedall, who contributed 10s. 2d., and held three and a half acres. There were also plenty of examples of cottagers like Matthew Ewsden, who had a lease to help provide a living for his five children,[6] and subscribed 4s., and of less fortunate landless cottagers like William Ridley, Simon Bissell, and William Haynes who all contributed 8s. or 10s.

It is impossible to gauge the motives of these men, but concern to provide some kind of education for their children was evidently uppermost. The school articles agreed by the inhabitants[7] laid down that only the children of men resident in Willingham should be taught in the school, and only if their families had made a contribution, with the notable exception that the children of the

[1] Canon F. J. Bywaters, 'Historical Notes' in the *Willingham Parish Magazine*, January 1949.

[2] It is possible to identify a large number of the subscribers on the list of 1593 by using a combination of the surveys of 1575 and 1603, and abstracts of the court roll entries which give the descent of each holding between these two dates. Many of the tenants of 1593 can be identified with certainty by these means, and their wills give additional personal information.

[3] These were all made by people described as "gentlemen" except for Anne Pearson, widow. I have been unable to identify any of them, except the lord of the Manor of Burne. I have excluded his contribution, and the £1 a year given during the term of his incumbency by the rector.

[4] Two of them had, according to the rolls, surrendered their holdings in favour of their sons.

[5] C.R.O., R 59.14.8(b). The rents of half yardlands varied between 14s. 4d. and 17s. 10d., and were usually nearer the former.

[6] Will proved 1595.   [7] C.R.O., P 177/25/1, pp. 2–5.

poor should be taught free. If a man either bought or rented a house or land in Willingham, his children were not to be eligible for instruction unless he made a contribution, if he was able to do so. Subscribers presumably made their gifts, therefore, specifically so that their children could go to school.

There is a certain amount of information which gives an indication of the number of these parents, who desired education for their children, who were able to write their own names. Eighteen of the subscribers acted as witnesses to wills in the next decade or so.[1] Of these eighteen, only five, or just over a quarter, could sign their names. Naturally, however, the more prosperous men in Willingham acted as witnesses more often than their poorer neighbours. They are also easier to identify. Eight of the eighteen witnesses held a half yardland, and they accounted for four of the five signatures.[2] One of them, William Ashman, may have even written a few wills on his own account. Half the half yardlanders who witnessed wills, therefore, could sign their names. Not all the prosperous could sign their names, but on the other hand, all those who could do so were relatively prosperous. It is startlingly obvious that if only just over a quarter of the identifiable subscribers could sign, a very much lower proportion of the whole group of men who subscribed must have been able to do so, considering that the group contained a large number of unidentifiable, less substantial men. This lack of the elementary ability to sign amongst at least three-quarters, and probably more, of the subscribers to the school makes their desire that their children should acquire some elementary schooling even more poignant, considering the financial sacrifices that they were prepared to make to provide the opportunity.

Willingham school was upgraded in status when William Norton was licensed to teach grammar in 1596.[3] He remained there until 1607, and the seventeenth-century history of the school is as continuous as the records permit thereafter. It survived various vicissitudes in the eighteenth century, and functioned until its eventual closure by the Charity Commission in 1876.[4]

The vital question is how much difference the continuous existence of this subscription school, which had been set up by costly communal effort, made to the inhabitants. Unfortunately, this very question is almost impossible to answer. The education provided in the school was obviously an adequate one, or it could not have prepared Henry Crisp, son of a 'gentleman' of Willingham,

---

[1] A mark or signature as a witness is a more reliable guide to the ability to sign than the mark or signature of a testator, which might so evidently be influenced by his illness or his physical weakness. See below, pp. 134–6.

[2] The fifth was a signature of a tenant of the sub-manor of Burne, who in fact held an acreage appropriate to a half yardlander.

[3] Lawrence Milford remained in the village and continued to act as principal scribe for the villagers' wills until his death in 1604.—Willingham Parish Register.

[4] *Charity School to Village College*, pp. 8–10, 50–1.

for entry to Caius in 1627.[1] It is true that Richard Pearson, another son of a 'gentleman' of Willingham[2] went to school in Huntingdon, rather than Willingham, for four years before going up to John's in 1658. Despite this, the place must have had some continuing merit at least as a preparatory school, or James Drake, attorney of Cambridge, would hardly have sent his son out from Cambridge itself to Willingham school before transferring him to Eton for the two years before his entry to Caius in 1685. The real interest does not lie, however, in whether the school was fitted to prepare college entrants, but in how much it did to raise the standard of literacy of the more ordinary village families, who were not able to consider a university education for their sons.

The only material which bears on this is the ability of men, who were usually dying, to sign their wills, and this, as evidence, is fundamentally unsatisfactory. There are specific examples, apart from the detailed history of old Leonard Woolward, which show the obvious fact that a man's ability to sign his name deteriorated when he was on his death-bed.[3] Robert Caldecot, or Cawcot, of Willingham itself, was one such man.[4] He held between thirteen and fifteen acres of copyhold between 1575 and 1603, and subscribed 13s. 4d. to the school fund in 1593. In 1588, he witnessed a will, and was able to sign his name on it. In 1607, when he died, described as a 'yeoman', his staggering attempt at his initials was set down as a mark by Francis Chapman, who wrote the will (FIG. I).

Orwell yields an even more striking example. Thomas Butler of Orwell had a first cousin, Nicholas Johnson.[5] Nicholas never left Orwell to acquire an education, as far as is known, but he was literate. He acted as rent collector for his cousin, and was able, in an Exchequer deposition, to identify the handwriting of Thomas Butler's brother, George. He was a churchwarden, and he acted as the scribe of some of the villagers' wills between 1614 and 1626. It was probably his nephew, another Nicholas Johnson, who frequently acted as a witness to wills with his second cousin, Neville Butler, Thomas's son. The

---

[1] See above, p. 120.

[2] I have been unable to find much material on the Pearson family. They were not considerable freeholders or copyholders in the 1575 or 1603 surveys; yet Anne Pearson, widow, gave £3 towards the school.

[3] A further disadvantage is that very few people in any of the village communities discussed here made wills. In five villages, under two people per household assessed in the Hearth Tax made wills during the entire seventeenth century, including those proved in the Prerogative Court at Canterbury. If only the most prosperous, who were therefore more literate, tended to leave wills, the proportion of those unable to sign must in reality have been much higher.

[4] I am indebted to Miss Marie Rowlands for giving me a similar example which she found amongst the wills and inventories in the Lichfield Record Office. Samuel Freeman, an apothecary of Uttoxeter in Staffordshire, who must surely have been a fully literate man to practise his profession, marked his will, rather than signed it, in June 1696. On 5 July, a codicil was added, and whereas his mark on his main will approximated to rough letters, his mark on the codicil was a mere cross. On 15 July he was dead, and his inventory, as one would expect of a professional man, set a value on his books.

[5] See above, pp. 119–20.

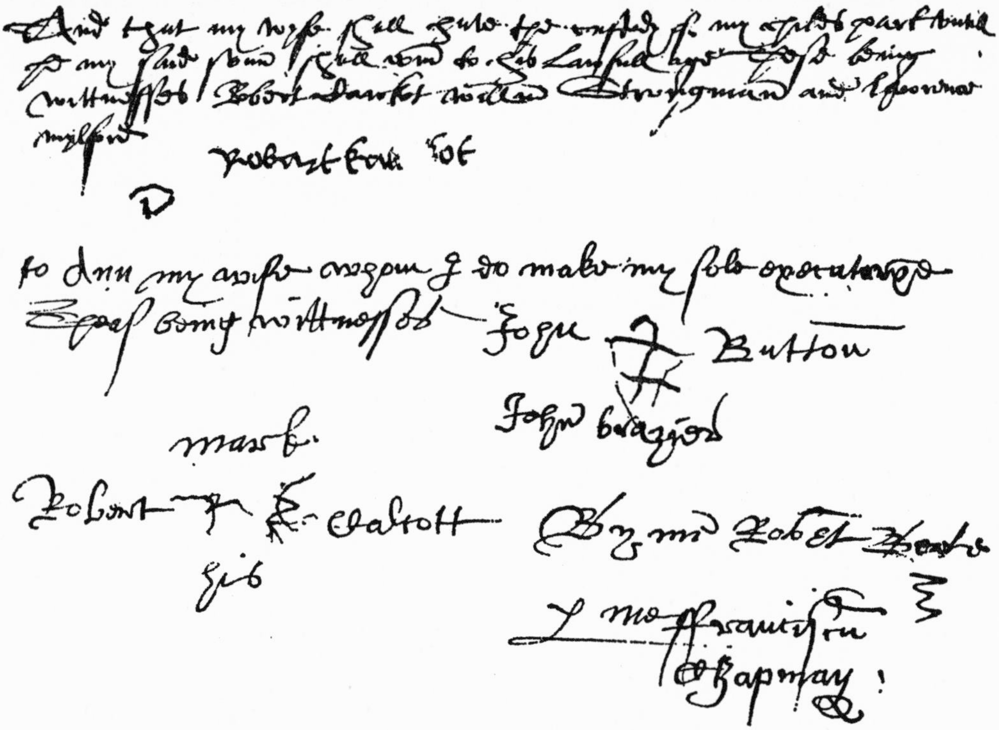

FIG. I. Top: Robert Caldecot witnesses Anthony Haidon's will, 1588; bottom: Robert Caldecot marks his own will, 1607.

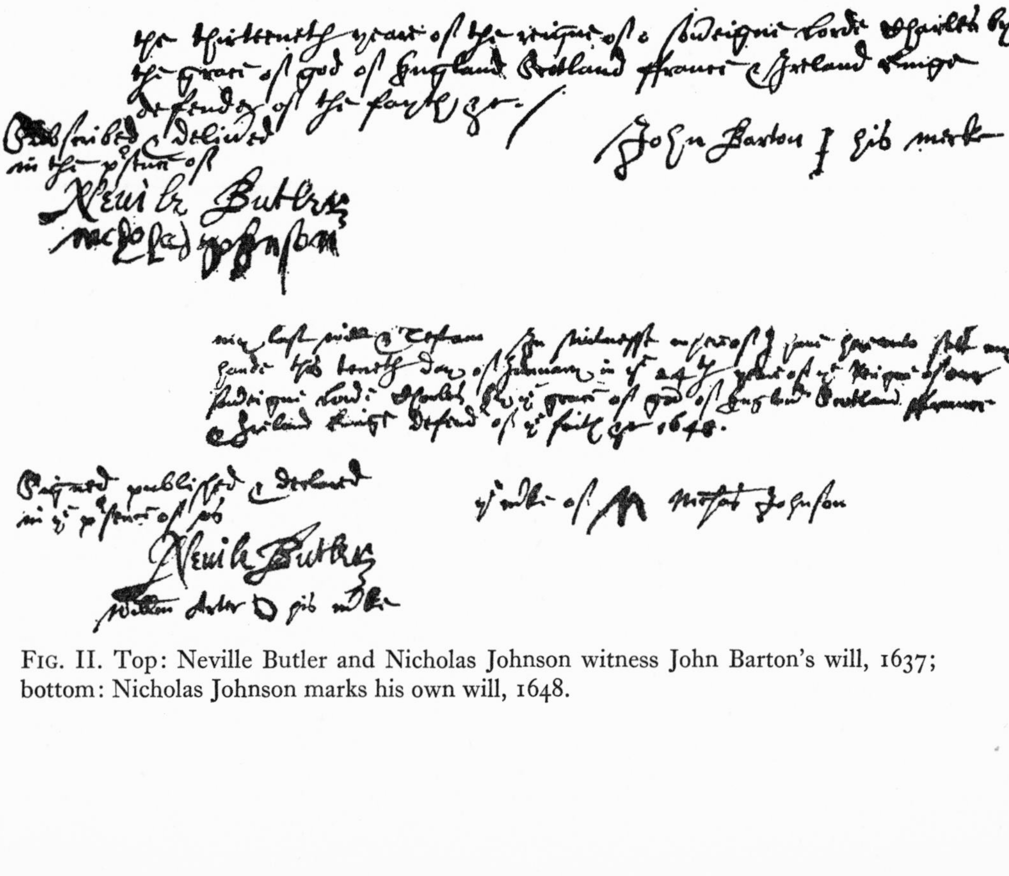

FIG. II. Top: Neville Butler and Nicholas Johnson witness John Barton's will, 1637; bottom: Nicholas Johnson marks his own will, 1648.

contrast between the polished hand of one cousin, educated at the Perse and Christ's, and the rough village hand of the other, is a very illuminating one. Nevertheless, the younger Nicholas Johnson could write. When he died in 1648 he marked his will with an almost unrecognizable attempt at an N, though his cousin Neville witnessed it in his usual style (FIG. II).

Any estimate of ability to sign based on wills, therefore, presents absolute minimum figures of the proportion of the will-making population able to write their names; and it reflects the toughness of their constitutions, as well as their literary prowess. An analysis of signatures on the Willingham wills for the period 1600 to 1690 shows that 15 per cent of the wills were signed. (TABLE II).

TABLE II

TESTATORS SIGNING AND MARKING WILLS AT WILLINGHAM

	Yeomen & above		Husband-men		Labourers		Craftsmen		Women		No occupation given		Total	
	Sign	Mark	Sign	Mark	Sign	Mark	Sign	Mark	Sign	Mark	Sign	Mark	Sign	Mark
−1600	0	1	0	0	0	0	0	0	0	0	0	1	0	2
1601–1625	2	10	1	4	0	6	2	11	0	8	0	5	5	44
1626–1650	4	4	2	19	0	10	2	9	0	7	0	4	8	53
1651–1675	9	8	0	5	0	6	0	5	1	7	0	2	10	33
1676–1700	6	16	0	5	0	3	2	5	0	7	0	3	8	39
Total to 1700	21	39	3	33	0	25	6	30	1	29	0	15	31	171

It is a very great pity that hardly any wills bear marks or signatures before 1600. As a result it is impossible to make any comparison of ability to sign before the endowment of the school and after it. However, one might expect some slight increase in the ability to sign amongst testators beginning in the 1620's and 1630's, if they had attended school in the 1590's. It does not seem to be there. The figures give a slight impression of improvement in the second half of the seventeenth century, but this is too small to be statistically significant, and might be a mere chance.[1]

However disappointing the wills prove generally as a source of information on ability to sign, one inescapable conclusion emerges. At Willingham, yeomen were both better represented and far more able to sign their names than any other group. Over a third of the yeomen who made wills could do so. A sixth of the smaller group of will-making craftsmen could sign their names. A few husbandmen and one woman signed; no labourer could do so. Yeomen there-

[1] I should like to thank Dr R. S. Schofield for much general help and encouragement, as well as for detailed comment on these and similar figures.

fore stood out as a class persistently more able to afford an interest in education than any other, as common sense suggests.[1]

It seems, therefore, that the school, even though it began with whole-hearted support and encouragement from the relatively rich and the relatively poor alike, and even though its rules laid down that the children of the genuine-ly poor should be taught free, really benefited the sons of yeomen far more than any other class. It is necessary to add that, considering the way holdings broke down in Willingham in the seventeenth century, and that the acreage farmed by a 'yeoman' became smaller and smaller, the school may have been responsible for keeping up basic standards of educational techniques that would otherwise have fallen far lower.

The community at Orwell was strongly contrasted with that of Willingham in many ways. A dependence on barley production and lack of common led it near to famine in 1612 and 1617, and the first thirty years of the seventeenth century saw the disappearance of many of the half yardlands and yardlands, apparently under the same economic pressures as those at Chippenham,[2] although the evidence is not nearly so conclusive. The same years saw four or five prosperous yeomen families increasing their acreages, and the numbers of cottagers rising. Later in the century, the demesne farms were expanded, again at the expense of the farmers of traditionally sized holdings.

Orwell was, of course, much smaller than Willingham. In 1563 it was less than half the size, and in the 1660's it had fallen even further behind the ex-panding settlement in the fens, as its own surplus population emigrated. The difference in the size of the two villages meant that Orwell had fewer yeomen families than Willingham, although they made up a slightly larger proportion of the village population.[3] Only the outstanding yeoman family in each village took what was perhaps the decisive step into the ranks of the gentry by sending a son up to university. The Butlers of Orwell seem to have started with more pretensions, and taken them further, than the Crisps of Willingham.[4] It is not surprising that no more than one family in each village considered university education as a possibility; the number of university entrants from rural back-

---

[1] See above, p. 113. Professor Stone shows that there was a very marked difference between the ability to sign of yeomen and husbandmen marrying by licence in the Archdeaconry of Oxford and Diocese of Gloucester in the seventeenth century. Between 71 and 72 per cent of yeomen, as against 43 to 52 per cent of husbandmen could sign.—'Literacy and Education in England 1640–1900', *Past and Present*, 42, 1969, p. 110.

[2] Margaret Spufford, *A Cambridgeshire Community: Chippenham from Settlement to Enclosure*, Leicester, 1965, pp. 44–9.

[3] Orwell had four or five families with over 40 acres, in so far as one can judge on the basis of the copyholds alone. These accounted for 9 per cent to 12 per cent of tenants in 1602 and 1603, and the 1670's. Willingham had between five and eight families with over 25 acres, which I have suggested is roughly equivalent (see above, p. 117, n. 2). These accounted for 5 per cent or 6 per cent of the tenants in 1603 and in the 1720's.

[4] See above, pp. 119–20.

grounds must have been directly related to the number of yeomen families in a position to make this sort of economic sacrifice. But if it is not too facile to suppose that the proportion of families who could free their sons to attend school should bear some relationship to the proportion of the people in the community who were later able to sign their wills at death, then the differing proportions of yeomen families in Willingham and Orwell should have made some difference to the basic literacy rates there. An examination of the Orwell wills, however, shows that the true position was not so simple. (TABLES III and IV).

TABLE III

TESTATORS SIGNING AND MARKING WILLS BEFORE 1700

	Yeomen & above		Husband-men		Labourers		Craftsmen		Women		No occu-pation given		Total	
	Sign	Mark	Sign	Mark	Sign	Mark	Sign	Mark	Sign	Mark	Sign	Mark	Sign	Mark
Willing-ham	21	39	3	33	0	25	6	30	1	29	0	15	31	171
Orwell	3	13	3	15	0	5	2	6	2	10	1	6	11	55
Milton	6	9	1	9	0	6	0	4	1	4	2	6	10	38

TABLE IV

TESTATORS SIGNING WILLS BEFORE 1700

	Yeomen Total		Non-Yeomen Total		All Testators Total	
	No. of Wills	% Signed	No. of Wills	% Signed	No. of Wills	% Signed
Willingham	60	35	142	7	202	15
Orwell	16	19	50	16	66	17
Milton	15	40	33	12	48	21
Total	91	33	225	10	316	16

The information given by the wills was frankly disappointing. It did nothing to prove this suggestion, and something to refute it. The number of wills surviving was really too small to show any changes over a period of time. The yeomen of Orwell shared the general inability to write the letters of the alphabet on their death-beds, and they did nothing to leaven the illiterate lump of their fellow villagers. Seventeen per cent of those who made wills at Orwell could sign, as against 15 per cent at Willingham, but a much lower proportion of yeomen, and a correspondingly higher proportion of husbandmen, signed at

Orwell. Prosperity and elementary ability to write were therefore less clearly related at Orwell, where there was more economic polarization of the community than at Willingham.[1]

If the proportion of those able to sign their names at death was approximately the same in Willingham and Orwell, it seems that the basic tenet that the number of smaller farmers in the fens should have led to a higher illiteracy rate is wrong, unless the wills which survive from Orwell are too small a selection to be representative.

Apart from the small numbers, part of the solution appears to lie in yet another major difference between the two villages: Willingham had a permanent school; Orwell did not. There were scattered references to a master teaching at Orwell from 1575 onwards, but they never amounted, in the episcopal records, to anything like Willingham's consistent record. Robert Clark was licensed to teach grammar there in 1587 after graduating from Queens' in 1583. There was a master there in 1590, and again in 1596. In 1609, William Barnard, the vicar, was teaching in Orwell. He may have done some sporadic teaching for some time, for he held the living until his death in 1644. He seems also to have acted as scribe for a number of the villagers' wills from 1615 to 1642.[2] However, no later visitation took notice of him as a teacher and, if he taught, it is obvious that his standard never came anywhere near that of the Willingham school. If it had done so, Thomas Butler would not have found it necessary to send his son Neville to the Perse in Cambridge before he went up to Christ's in 1623.[3] Nor would Neville Butler, in his turn, have sent his son away to school in Hertford before he went to college in 1649. Things must have changed considerably before 1661, for in that year Neville Butler's fourth son, John, went up to Christ's, after being prepared by "Mr. Griffen" at the 'schola publica' at

[1] These figures are to some extent falsified by the fact that the most prosperous in the community tended to assume the aura of gentility, and get their wills proved in the Prerogative Court of Canterbury. The Butlers of Orwell did this, and so also did one or two Fairchilds, Godfreys, and other yeomen. It is fair to assume that a higher proportion of these men could sign their names than of those men whose wills were proved in the Consistory Court. The number of Orwell wills proved in the Consistory Court was so low that these Prerogative Court of Canterbury wills could make a considerable difference to the pattern. On the other hand the wills of prosperous Willingham men, like Henry Crisp, also went to the Prerogative Court of Canterbury. The proportion of wills in relation to the size of each community going to the Prerogative Court of Canterbury was approximately the same over the seventeenth century, so it is unlikely that an analysis including all these Prerogative Court wills for both communities would be fundamentally different from one based on the Consistory Court wills alone. This conclusion is based on the *Prerogative Court of Canterbury Wills*, Index Library, IV–XII, covering wills proved in the Prerogative Court, 1584–1629, 1653–60, 1671–1700; J. & G. F. Matthews, *Year Books of Probates*, 1–8, 1903–27, covering the years 1630–55; J. H. Morrison *Wills, Sentences, and Probate Acts, 1661–1670*, 1935. I have excluded the years 1653–60, when all wills were proved in the Prerogative Court in any case.

[2] Nicholas Johnson appears to have written a parallel series of wills at approximately the same time.

[3] See above, p. 119.

Orwell. The school was still not permanently established,[1] but a Mr Wright was there in 1665 and John Lowe, "schoolmaster," was buried in Orwell in 1689. It looks as if more schooling may have been available at Orwell in the second half of the seventeenth century.

There is another complicating factor in Orwell. The wills which survived are probably too small a group for statistical analysis and this may account for the disappointing results. These results are in any case in many ways at logger-heads with the general impression given by the wills that witnesses were highly literate. Such impressions, of course, are not capable of this type of analysis. There seem also to have been more scribes at work in Orwell. Many of the hands at work are unidentifiable, but many of those which are identifiable belong to the Johnson and Butler family. This leads to the suspicion that there may have been a tradition of literacy in some families, which was not neces-sarily based on economic factors at all. On the Butler side of the family, of course, education was based on prosperity, from Thomas who went up to Gray's Inn in 1589 onwards.[2] On the Johnson side of the family, however, it was not. Nicholas Johnson, the churchwarden who wrote a series of villagers' wills, had inherited about thirty-four acres in all. His brother Richard, who could sign his name on his death-bed, seems to have had a conventional four-teen-acre holding. The tradition continued, for Lawrence Johnson wrote a couple of wills at the end of the 1640's, and one of these was witnessed by Elizabeth Johnson, who was one of the rare women who could write her name clearly and well.

Family tradition, cutting across economic divisions, may therefore be an-other reason for the apparently low numbers of yeomen, and the comparatively high proportion of husbandmen, who could sign their names at Orwell.[3]

The generally unsatisfactory and contradictory nature of the evidence at Orwell suggested the desirability of adding a third village study. Milton, immediately north of Cambridge, had about 400 acres of fen common, which was obviously important in the economy, but it must have relied more heavily on its thousand acres of arable in the open fields than Willingham. The

[1] Until the incumbency of Dr Cobbatch, rector of Orwell, who died in 1748/9. The parish register records, "Dr Cobbatch gave the school for ever." His foundation appears to have spread literacy down the social scale. In 1775, the death of John Lawrence, "labourer and Church Clerk," is like-wise recorded in the register. Boys were taught to read and write and cast accounts; girls to read, as well as to sew, knit, and spin.—C. E. Parsons 'Notes on Horseheath Schools and other Village Schools in Cambridgeshire', *Cambs. Antiq. Soc. Proc.*, n.s., 16, 1920, p. 117.

[2] Joseph Foster, *Gray's Inn Admission Register, 1521–1889*, 1889, p. 75. He had previously been at Staple Inn. The Butler wills themselves were proved in the Prerogative Court at Canterbury, and are therefore excluded from the Orwell analysis, which is based on the wills proved in the Consistory Court.

[3] Family literacy deserves separate study; the same thing was true of the Crisps at Willingham who likewise sprawled across class divisions.

village was very small. It had only thirty-six households in 1563, and thirty-eight houses in 1664. The community based in this environment was a remarkably placid one, able to agree peaceably on the enclosure of its commons with its lord, and remarkably free from change. If the evidence of the surveys made of the place in 1599 and 1707 is to be trusted, the distribution of land changed very little during the seventeenth century. There were only four tenants with over fifty acres at both dates.[1]

There was even less evidence for the existence of a school at Milton than at Orwell; only two references were found to a master teaching there in the entire seventeenth century. Even fewer usable wills survive for Milton than for Orwell but, such as they are, they confirm the impression suggested by the Willingham evidence. Six of the fifteen yeomen who made wills at Milton signed their names; only four of the remaining thirty-three will makers did so. Again, literacy and prosperity were related, despite the absence of a school. At Milton, as at Willingham, the yeomen stood out as a group, which even at death, retained the acquired skill of scrawling out letters far more markedly than any other section of the community.

The Importance of Reading in the Village Community

However helpful information on the proportion of villagers actually able to sign their names may be, statistics of this sort remain bleak and arid unless some idea can be gained of the extent to which writing, and more particularly reading, entered into the ordinary life of the village community. Information of this kind can never be complete, and will never be capable of expression in statistical terms. It must necessarily be fragmentary and impressionistic. J. W. Adamson collected such information for the fifteenth and early sixteenth centuries, and showed, for instance, that "Englische billes" were placed on the Norwich city gates in 1424. They were presumably intended to be read not only by the urban inhabitants but also by country folk coming in to market. By 1534, girls in Langham village on the borders of Essex and Suffolk could read Matins in English.[2] The number of devotional works, from Richard Whitford's *A Werke for Householders* printed in 1530 to Josias Nicholas's *Order of Household Instruction* which appeared in 1596, argues a market for such works.[3] It is highly unlikely that these books were all aimed at the urban market. Herbert Palmer the minister, of Ashwell on the Cambridgeshire and Hertfordshire border, who set up a model Puritan household in the 1630's

[1] Margaret Spufford, dissertation *cit.*, pp. 85, 108–14.

[2] J. W. Adamson, 'Extent of Literacy in England in the Fifteenth and Sixteenth Centuries', *Library*, 4th series, X, 1930, pp. 169–70.

[3] I am indebted to Professor Kenneth Charlton for these references and his opinion on this point. Professor Stone uses a similar argument.—'Literacy and Education in England', *Past and Present*, 42, 1969, p. 99.

and provided a schoolmaster to teach those who repaired to him, also regularly presented a bible or 5s. to any new communicant who could read.[1] In 1578, a man was "sellinge of lytle bookes in Balsham churcheyard." A young barber-surgeon, who does not appear to have been very prosperous, since he was also a patcher of old clothes, and swore on oath that he would be "worthe nothinge" if his debts were paid off, bought one.[2] There were, then, itinerant booksellers about, who appear to have caused no special remark. It is an interesting co-incidence, if no more, that Balsham had a few members of the Family of Love. The way dissenting opinions could be spread about, if such book pedlars were at work, is obvious.

Unfortunately, the probate inventories for Cambridgeshire survive only from the early 1660's, and they give hardly any information on the books to be found in the ordinary household. The bible is occasionally mentioned, in the houses of people who were not outstandingly prosperous. Richard Broomhead of Fenditton had a bible, and his goods were worth £54 19s. 10d. when they were valued in 1669.[3] Robert Reynolds of Hauxton was worth only £18 7s. 8d., or little more than the norm for a labourer. He had a bible, but he may of course have been a retired yeoman. It is impossible to get an accurate impression of the number of households with bibles from the inventories, however. The usual form of the inventories was to give a small notional value at the end for "a bible and other lumber" or "a bible and other trashe," in the same way that small furniture in a room was often not described but simply valued as "other lumber." It is quite evident that books were not worth listing, even if they were there, and that bibles would not necessarily be entered separately. The only book apart from the bible mentioned by name in these probate inventories of the 1660's is a copy of Gray's *Complete Horseman*, which was listed, along with a pair of pearl-coloured silk stockings, amongst the few possessions of a gentle-man who apparently died while on a visit to the county. Reading obviously did not assume sufficient importance in the lives of most villagers for the books to be allocated special house room. Of nearly 350 inventories which survive from between 1660 and 1670, only one single house apart from those of the clergy and gentry had a study in it. Thomas Laurence, a yeoman of Trumping-ton, whose goods were worth £138 when he died in 1669, had at least ten books in his study. The only other example was that of Richard Wootton,

---

[1] Samuel Clarke, *A Generall Martyrologie... The Lives of Sundry Modern Divines*, London, 1651, pp. 423–4.

[2] E.D.R., D2/11 fol. 261. See above, p. 121.

[3] The median wealth of the 18 labourers whose inventories occur amongst those presented in the Consistory Court of Ely for the 1660's was £15. That of the 24 husbandmen was £30. That of the 55 craftsmen was £40, and that of the 58 yeomen was £180. Analysis of all the inventories surviving for the decade gave a median of £40 for the area of southern Cambridgeshire. See my 'Significance of the Cambridgeshire Hearth Tax', *Cambs. Antiq. Soc. Proc.*, LV, 1962, pp. 53–64.

a yeoman of Ickleton, who had "his books" and money, with a desk in his chamber.

The inventories also give some indication of the importance of money-lending, and the way that even the humbler members of the community were owed cash, and held bonds for this. William Bourne of Cherryhinton, who died in 1666, was a fell-monger. It was not surprising that he held £154 in bonds, since he must have travelled around the county collecting skins, and was an obvious person to give credit. But it seems that when men retired from active farming and took up residence with their sons or daughters, they often put their savings into bills and bonds. George Morling of Langstanton was described as a yeoman when he died in 1669, but he had no household goods apart from a few pairs of sheets. He had kept eleven hives of bees to care for in his retirement, but apart from these and his little flock of sheep, his property was in bills and bonds. Richard Caldecot was a husbandman, and was worth only £21 6s. 8d. All this was in bills and bonds, except his own personal clothes, and a chest to put them in. Robert Cole of Duxford had a "sole and only dwelling and lodging room" in 1662 and the furnishings were of the most meagre. "One Hutch, one shouell and one Iron Rake, and an old bedsted" were priced at 3s. 6d. and his clothes and money in his purse at 5s. His whole estate was worth less, at £12 18s. 6d., than that of the typical labourer. But in spite of his poverty, he held bonds worth 12s. 10d. Thomas Doggett of Over, who was described as "labourer" by the appraisers who made up his inventory in 1666, held bonds worth over £77, although his personal goods were again of the poorest. He must have been putting his saved earnings out at interest for years. Most striking of all in some ways was Alice Scott, a spinster of Bottisham, who left only clothes, and bonds worth £40, in 1669. These examples seem to represent standard practice. A series of thirty-one inventories which survive for Chippenham from 1576 to 1700 show that a third of the people who were well enough off to be appraised at death were involved in money-lending.[1] The three groups of people concerned were retired yeomen and husbandmen, prosperous craftsmen, and widows and spinsters. Although no inventories exist for the diocese of Ely before 1660, the wills which survive give ample confirmatory evidence of the widespread use of credit, since they sometimes contain lists of debts both owing to, and owed by, the testator. In 1566, a yeoman of Orwell, Richard Kettle, drew up his will. He was owed £4 by a neighbour, over £6 by someone from the next village of Barrington, sums of between £1 and £8 by three men in Little Gransden, six miles away, and another £1 by a man in Royston, where Orwell people frequently marketed. John Hart, a husbandman of Milton, who died in 1588, was an extreme ex-

[1] Amongst the records of the Episcopal Commissary Court for Bury St Edmunds at Bury St Edmunds and West Suffolk Record Office.

ample of indebtedness. He owed money to fourteen men from seven villages including his own. All these villages lay within five or six miles, except Bourn, over ten miles away, where he owed the very large sum of £11.

It can be argued that people who entered into bonds were not necessarily able to read them,[1] providing they understood what they had signed or marked their names to. On the other hand, those who were owed sums on bond, who were most frequently yeomen, had a very powerful practical incentive to be able to read them. There must, indeed, have been a more powerful incentive for lenders of money to be able to cope with written figures than with letters. The written word cannot have been so inherently useful. If it was indeed normal for retired farmers and even widows and spinsters to hold their money in bonds, written notes of hand must have been extremely commonly exchanged amongst ordinary villagers, and it is no wonder that the ability to "caste an accompte" was included as a basic skill with reading and writing in the curricula of many schools which set out to teach the humblest village child.[2] Simple accounting must have been a very necessary skill in the farming community if credit was so generously used.[3]

Even if the inventories give little direct information on the importance of reading in the community, a study of the growth of dissenting opinion in Cambridgeshire under the Commonwealth gives a very strong impression of the vitality and fervour with which religious topics were canvassed in the villages in the 1650's and 60's, and the extent to which the humblest, and even the women, joined in the debate. Many communities seem to have been hotbeds of religious dispute and conviction. When the Baptist evangelist, John Denne, went on a preaching tour in the early 1650's, he was engaged in constant dispute with Ranters, and proto-Quakers like the 'maid' Isobel in the village of Kingston, who was convinced of the need to "judge the Scriptures by the Spirit, not the Spirit by the Scriptures."[4] She could presumably read them. The records of all the dissenting churches of Cambridgeshire give some intimations of the importance of the ability to read, and an impression that this was widespread. They are sprinkled with references which give at least indirect information on literacy. John Aynslo, "farmer," who lived in Over and

---

[1] For instance, John Aves of Chippenham, who may have been a scribe, died owning goods worth only £9 6s. 2d. in 1676. A baker of Fordham, George Durrant, held a bond of his for £4 10s. George Durrant had been unable to sign his name when he appraised the goods of another Chippenham man in 1669. It is, of course, always possible that he was able to read, even if he could not write.

[2] See above, p. 127, and the curriculum of Orwell School, p. 140, n. 1.

[3] Miss Marie Rowlands, who has been working on tradesmen's probate inventories of Staffordshire in the late seventeenth century has found the same or even greater use of credit amongst mercantile members of the community. It seems that credit extended throughout local society by this period and probably did so much earlier.

[4] *Records of the Churches of Christians gathered at Fenstanton, Warboys and Hexham, 1644–1720*, ed. E. B. Underhill for the Hanserd Knollys Society, 1854, p. 74. (Henceforth, *Fenstanton Records*.)

was recognized as the teacher of the Quakers of Over, and indeed of Cambridge-shire, which sect was described in such a derogatory way by the bishop in 1669 as "all of very poor condition, scarce a yeoman amongst them," could write a vivid letter. His accounts of the prosecution of the Quakers in 1660 and the conditions in Cambridge Castle at that time are horrifying documents.[1] It is perhaps not surprising that a recognized Quaker teacher, even if he was a local farmer, could write so fluently, and indeed there is some doubt about whether he did not originally come from a gentle family in Northumberland.[2] He was writing tracts for publication by 1664. It is perhaps more surprising that the otherwise unknown Baptist John Blowes of Bourne could in 1657 be disciplined into writing a letter of sorrow, apparently in his own hand, to the brethren he had duped on a visit to London by sneaking away leaving his bill unpaid.[3] Much more general evidence is provided by the standard disciplinary practice amongst both Baptists and Quakers of writing letters of admonition to erring members who for some reason could not be visited. These were addressed to both men and women. The General Baptists of Fenstanton wrote a stinging letter to Jasper Dockwra of Bassingbourn in 1657,[4] after he had given persis-tent offence by going frequently to hear the minister of the Church of England. It is quite evident that this letter was intended to be read by Jasper Dockwra himself. The Baptists can scarcely have written it under the assumption that he would be obliged to take it to be read by the minister in question, or even by the parish clerk in Bassingbourn. The same argument applies even more strikingly to the letter of reproof addressed to Thomas Sterne of Haddenham in the Isle of Ely, after he had "dishonoured" the name of God by giving consent to the "sprinkling" of his child. Thomas was invited to come to a general meeting at Fenstanton in 1658 to account for himself.[5] John Bunyan's Open Baptists also communicated with their congregations in the same way. In 1669 they addressed letters of encouragement to two men and to two women who were suffering in the persecution.[6] There seems to have been a general assumption that members of the meetings could read, and could therefore commonly be addressed by letter. Indeed, much business between the elders of different congregations was conducted by correspondence as the appeal addressed by the Baptists of Caxton to the various Baptist congregations in Cambridgeshire on behalf of John Wilson in 1654 bears witness.[7] John Wait, a yeoman of Toft, who was a local preacher affiliated to the Open Baptists of Bedford, sent them information by letter on the misdeeds of one of

[1] Printed in J. Besse, *A Collection of the Sufferings of the People Called Quakers*, 1753, I, 89–91.
[2] Margaret Spufford: 'The Dissenting Churches in Cambridgeshire from 1660 to 1700', *Cambs. Antiq. Soc. Proc.*, LXI, 1968, p. 92, n. 1.
[3] *Fenstanton Records*, pp. 224–37.   [4] *Ibid.*, pp. 212–13.   [5] *Ibid.*, pp. 247–9.
[6] *The Church Book of Bunyan Meeting, 1650–1821*, ed. G. B. Harrison, pp. 39 *et seq.*
[7] *Fenstanton Records*, pp. 104–5.

their members, who was begging from the brethren in St Neots in 1669[1] without the permission of his church.[2]

One direct and striking piece of evidence shows the way in which the written, as apart from the spoken, word could be responsible for the spread of dissident religious opinion, and could bring about conversion at the lowest social level. The General Baptist, Sister Sneesby of Over, was in 1654 in a state of great spiritual distress. She was tormented by the new Quaker teachings, and by the necessity to choose between them and her Baptist principles. In the end, she became a Quaker, and therefore formed one of that group which Bishop Laney had found of such humble origin. During her conversion to Quakerism, she was visited by Baptist messengers, who "found [her] in a very sad and deplorable condition. . . We told her, that we heard that one of those commonly called Quakers was at her house and preached there; and we were afraid his preaching had brought her into that condition. She answered, that she could hear very little that he said [perhaps she was deaf]; but she said that she had read many of his books. Then we asked her whether the reading of them were not the cause of her trouble." When she confessed that this might indeed be the root of her distress, she was advised "to continue reading" the Scriptures.[3] In 1660, Widow Sneesby was amongst the Quakers imprisoned for not swearing the Oath of Allegiance. John Aynslo sent a list of the prisoners to Quaker headquarters in London and annotated this with notes on their status.[4] He wrote of the small group of women of which she was one, "they were most of them poor women and had nothing to live on but what they did labour for." In his letter to London describing the prisoners he expanded this to explain that the women "had little but as they did erne it by day labor." This woman from Over, then, was in all probability either of a labouring family or reduced to day labour in her widowhood. Despite the poverty of her social background she had enough education to read the Bible and Quaker literature, and the printed word conveyed a sufficiently powerful impression to bring about her conversion.[5] No

---

[1] *The Church Book of Bunyan Meeting*, p. 44.

[2] A certain amount of caution is necessary in interpreting this evidence, particularly in view of the statement of a miller's son from the fens in the nineteenth century that of the local preachers who served the local Wesleyan chapel, "Some on 'em couldn't read at all, and had to learn by heart everything they were likely to want for the service, hymns and psalms and readings from the Bible and all the lot. . . Some on 'em could only put two or three words together at one time."—Sybil Marshall, *Fenland Chronicle*, 1967, p. 97. Still there is no doubt that the elders of the Baptist congregations in the seventeenth century wrote both the church books and letters of admonition, just as a yeoman of Croyden-cum-Clopton wrote, about 1690, the evilly spelt account of the life of the Congregationalist Francis Holcroft which opens the Great Gransden Church Book.—Unprinted typescript in the possession of H. G. Tibbutt, Esq., of Bedford, partly quoted Margaret Spufford, *art. cit.*, p. 71.

[3] *Fenstanton Records*, p. 120.

[4] *Volumes of Sufferings*, 1, Friends' Meeting House, London, pp. 110–12.

[5] It is very difficult, unfortunately, to discover exactly what the Widow Sneesby was reading, apart from the Scriptures. John Aynslo later lived in Over, of course, but there is no record of any

more positive proof could exist of the importance of literacy in bringing about the spread of new religious opinion in the seventeenth century amongst people who were of far too humble status to be touched by any growth or decline of grammar school or university education. It will always be impossible to know, for lack of documentation, whether the ordinary villager was better educated in the sixteenth and seventeenth centuries than before the Reformation. We can only state that the written word was a powerful and influential weapon at the parochial level in seventeenth-century Cambridgeshire, not whether it was more, or less, powerful than in the preceding period.

We can also show that yeomen, as a class, were more literate, and, indeed, the only class generally able to afford the luxury of developing skills which were not strictly necessary to the upkeep of their farms. The detailed village studies carried out in Cambridgeshire, however, do not offer any proof of the thesis that the uplands, with their more diversified social structure, produced communities of more literate people. The proportion of substantial yeomen in a community did not appear to bear any strong relationship to the basic literacy of that community, gauged by the ability to sign wills alone. If anything the reverse was true. The small number of college entrants from the Isle of Ely, compared with those from the southern Cambridgeshire uplands, did suggest, on the other hand, that yeomen from the uplands could afford to send their sons to university more often than could those from the fens.[1] The more numerous, less prosperous yeomen in the Isle may have been less able to afford university education than their more substantial brethren in the uplands, but larger numbers in communities in the Isle could perhaps afford elementary education. The history of the Willingham school shows that at the end of the sixteenth century there was in some places an interest in education which permeated whole villages, even though it did not enable the villagers to give their children any protracted schooling.

---

work of his being printed until 1664. James Parnell was the Quaker apostle of Cambridgeshire.— Margaret Spufford, *art. cit.*, p. 74. He was active from the autumn of 1654 to the spring of 1655, and Sister Sneesby developed qualms of conscience in November 1654, at just the right date to be the result of his ministry. However, only one of James Parnell's tracts seems to have been printed before 1655, so unless he circulated broadsheets before they were formally printed, these cannot have been responsible. If broadsheets of his were responsible for Sister Sneesby's distress, she was able to follow a highly intricate argument. Despite James Parnell's extreme youth, he was responsible for such indigestible matter as *The Watcher: or, the Stone cut out of the mountains without hands, striking at the feet of the Image, whose head is gold, and brest of silver, and thighs of brass and legs of iron and feet part iron and part clay, or, A Discovery of the ground and end of all Forms, Professions, Sects and opinions. . .* , London, 1655.

[1] See above, pp. 117–18.

Seventeenth-Century Agriculture
and Social Change

By JOAN THIRSK

THIS essay is an attempt to analyse in more detail than hitherto agricultural developments in the seventeenth century, and to present them within a more clearly defined social and geographical framework. The whole century is recognized as a period of economic and political crisis. Agriculturally, this crisis is most readily attributable to the relentlessly falling prices of grain, which posed long-term problems of readjustment to specialized grain growers. But these were only one group among many engaged in agriculture. How did the thousands of farmers who were engaged in other branches of the farming business fare during the seventeenth century? The answer is that some of them met the new circumstances with solutions which were economically successful and far less destructive of the small farmer than those adopted in the specialized corn-growing areas. Thus the farming systems of England became more sharply differentiated economically and socially; and the stage was prepared for changes in the eighteenth century which wrought an agricultural revolution in arable regions and an industrial revolution in pastoral ones.

During the first half of the seventeenth century, fears at the overproduction of grain and its low price commanded the forefront of the stage in all government discussions on agriculture, and particularly during the troubled depression years of 1620–4.[1] In fact, these fears were exaggerated and premature, and they turned to alarms at grain shortage between 1630 and 1632 and in the late 1640's. But the idea of giving some financial encouragement to corn growers was being canvassed by the middle of the century—by Henry Robinson[2] in a pamphlet written in 1652 if not earlier—and after the Restoration farmers were constantly urged to export grain overseas so that corn production could be maintained and its price improved. After 1673 farmers received bounties for so doing.[3] This effort to maintain grain prices proved vain, however, and they fell steadily between 1660 and 1750.[4]

[1] W. Notestein, F. H. Relf, and H. Simpson, *Commons Debates, 1621*, 1935, IV, p. 105.

[2] Henry Robinson, *Certain Proposals in Order to the People's Freedom and Accommodation*, 1652.

[3] *Statutes of the Realm*, v, p. 781.

[4] A. H. John, 'The Course of Agricultural Change, 1660–1760', in *Studies in the Industrial Revolution*, ed. L. S. Pressnell, 1960, p. 134 *et seq.*; W. G. Hoskins, 'Harvest Fluctuations and English Economic History, 1620–1759', A.H.R., XVI, i, 1968, graph facing p. 15. But see also M. Flinn, 'Agricultural Productivity and Economic Growth in England, 1700–60: a Comment', *Jnl Econ. Hist.*, XXVI, i, 1966, p. 97, who argues for only a slight secular downward trend in grain prices, 1660–1720.

But many corn growers were also wool producers, and in this role they also had cause to complain for low wool prices persisted for most of the century. Rising wool prices which had characterized the sixteenth century were at an end by 1603 and a debate on falling prices had begun by 1610. A sharp crisis accompanied the outbreak of the Thirty Years' War, for it abruptly reduced the demand for cloth in Europe, spreading unemployment among the cloth-workers, and quickly reacting upon the wool growers. Thus the shrillest and most alarmist complaints from the countryside in the years 1618–24 came, not surprisingly, from a sheep–corn area, the Lincolnshire wolds, where Sir William Pelham of Brocklesby described small tenants giving up their farms and selling their bed straw for food, eating raw dog flesh and horse flesh for very hunger.[1] It was one of many episodes in the corn-sheep areas which gradually drove the small farmer out of existence.

Grass sheep farmers, however, were almost equally distressed by the cloth crisis, and the complaints of both groups were represented in the report of the Northamptonshire justices of the peace in 1620. Wool, they told the Privy Council, was the chief commodity of the county, yet it would not sell at the lowest price. Compared with this misfortune, the low price of barley was a minor matter; indeed, the latter was rather welcomed since it allayed the discontent of the poor, the "tumultuacious levelling" of 1607 being still green in the memory.[2]

Low wool prices remained a source of anxiety for the rest of the century. Spanish wool was a strong competitor with English wool both at home and overseas. Yet the government persisted in curtailing the market for English wool by prohibiting exports. After the passing of the Irish Cattle Act in 1666, Ireland was forced to turn from cattle to sheep production and her wool also competed successfully against English wool. English wool prices followed a long downward trend after the Restoration, interrupted only during periods of temporary shortage.[3]

Stock farmers and dairymen benefited from a sustained demand for meat and other livestock products which caused prices to maintain a steadier level over the century as a whole.[4] The interests of rearers and graziers were not equally served, however. Already in 1621 the scale of imports of Irish cattle was being criticized as a drain on the bullion reserves of the nation. With butter, they were said to cost £10,000 a year.[5] In the course of the next generation, Irish cattle were increasingly blamed for the stationary or falling level of rents for

[1] P. J. Bowden, *The Wool Trade in Tudor and Stuart England*, 1962, p. 186; Joan Thirsk, *English Peasant Farming*, 1957, p. 193.

[2] P.R.O., SP 14/113, no. 21.

[3] Bowden, *op. cit.*, pp. 46–8, 213–17, 230; P.R.O., SP 29/176, no. 130; CSPD 1673–5, pp. 169–70; Bodleian MS. Top. Kent, A 1, fol. 26; John, *op. cit.*, p. 142.

[4] *Ibid.*   [5] Notestein, Relf, and Simpson, *op. cit.*, IV, p. 105.

good grazing land, which seriously hit the incomes of the gentry. Graziers, it was argued, were failing to take up pastures because they were unable to compete with the Irish producers. The remedy adopted at the Restoration was an act in 1663 imposing a duty on imported fat cattle and sheep, followed by the Irish Cattle Act of 1666 which prohibited all livestock imports, both lean and fat, from Ireland. This greatly diminished the supplies of lean stock in England and had the effect of driving up the prices of store animals, greatly to the profit of the rearers of cattle in highland England, Wales, and Scotland. Counties like Devon, Lancashire, and Northumberland benefited at the expense of the graziers of the Midlands and the south who had to pay higher prices for lean stock than ever before.[1] Thus for a time the profits of meat production were redistributed in favour of the highland rearers at the expense of the lowland graziers. The vociferous complaints against the Irish Cattle Act did not die away until the early 1680's, when in fresh discussions on the merits of the act none could be found to support its repeal.[2] Yet there is no evidence that Midland graziers found the going easier.[3] Around London, however, specialized fattening procedures were evidently producing substantial profits: for example, bullocks which were bought up, stall fed for a year in the Home Counties, and sold fat were yielding high returns while calf fattening was a remunerative speciality in Suffolk and Essex.[4]

Prices of dairy produce, like those of meat, also held up better than grain. In the middle of the century, Sir Richard Weston confidently maintained that the produce of meadows, namely, butter, cheese, tallow, hides, beef, and wool, were all of greater value than corn.[5] But the dairymen were not unaffected by short-term difficulties. From East Anglia they were unable to get their produce away to London by coastal vessels in 1630 because of the Dunkirk privateers preying on the east coast.[6] The Irish Cattle Act in 1666 caused Irish farmers to turn from cattle production for the English market to dairying whereby they captured English markets for dairy produce in Flanders, France, Portugal, and Spain.[7] This development injured the dairy producers of the south and east and, according to J. H. Clapham, killed England's export trade in butter.[8] Nevertheless, butter and cheese were easily transported inland, the home

---

[1] P.R.O., SP 29/176, no. 130; Bodleian MS. Top. Kent, A 1, fol. 26; Roger Coke, *A Discourse of Trade*, 1670, p. 33; 'The Grand Concern of England Explained. . .', 1673, *Harl. Misc.*, 1746, VIII, p. 534.

[2] John Houghton, *A Collection for the Improvement of Husbandry and Trade*, ed. R. Bradley, 1727, II, p. 3.

[3] Tenants were extremely reluctant to take up land at Ashby de la Zouch, Leics., a grazing parish on the Hastings family estates, in the years 1685–9. I owe this information to the kindness of Mr Christopher Moxon.

[4] Houghton, *op. cit.*, I, pp. 285, 297, 300.   [5] Samuel Hartlib, *His Legacie*, 1651, p. 49.

[6] P.R.O., SP 16/162, no. 41.   [7] Coke, *op. cit.*, p. 34.

[8] J. H. Clapham, *A Concise Economic History of Britain*, 1957, p. 285.

demand was insistent, and prices remained stable after 1665.[1] Moreover, in the neighbourhood of towns, and particularly in London, milk sales rose markedly as increasing numbers of pedlars hawked it through the streets. A London milkwoman in the 1690's sold on average sixteen pints of milk a week to each of her customers.[2]

These brief remarks do no more than draw attention to some facets of agricultural development which come to light in contemporary pamphlets, newspapers, and Parliamentary debates. But they are valuable in directing attention at branches of the farming business other than corn growing: each farming type had its own chronology of crises; each crisis threw up different problems for different specialists. Thus, legislation on Irish cattle imports exerted different effects on the rearers of stock (primarily a business of the highland zone of England) and on the graziers (mostly based on the Midlands and south); the evident difficulties of corn producers in selling grain in a saturated market implies differences between the fortunes of farmers cultivating high-grade crops on the most fertile soils and of those producing inferior qualities of grain on the less fertile ones; the hazards of war and changes of policy towards Irish food imports damaged the dairymen of East Anglia and the south at one moment and the West Midlands dairymen at another.[3] And throughout the century it is evident that farmers near towns had a more buoyant market than those at a distance. In short, we can discern differences in the nature and gravity of the seventeenth-century crisis based on geography and farming types.

These, however, are not the only means to a more refined analysis of seventeenth-century agricultural trends. Given the predominance of large farmers in the specialized corn-growing areas and the numerical preponderance of small farmers in the pastoral districts, the geographical differences clearly carry social implications as well. And wider perspectives open up when we consider the contemporary literature on agriculture, offering advice to farmers facing the economic problems of their time. Some suggestions, like the growing of vegetables, were immediately within the grasp of the small farmers with little or no capital; others, like the watering of meadows, lay only within the grasp of the rich gentleman or yeoman who could afford to wait years for the full return on his investment. To separate the factors which facilitated agricultural improvements in some places and obstructed them in others, and to

---

[1] John, *op. cit.*, p. 144.   [2] Houghton, *op. cit.*, I, p. 410.

[3] One of the arguments against the Irish Cattle Act was that much pasture had been turned from breeding to dairying purposes before the Irish Cattle Act and such land was now being hit by the competition of Irish butter. I assume that this is a reference to lands in the West Midlands, where there is positive evidence of this change of farming system (see *supra*, pp. 91–2). That Irish butter and cheese were the cause of the low prices of the English product was, however, contested by Houghton. —John Houghton, *A Collection of Letters for the Improvement of Husbandry and Trade*, 1681, I, no. 9, 19 Oct. 1682, p. 87.

measure the ramified consequences of this uneven development, is a complex and ambitious undertaking, especially since farming systems were so numerous and varied. Yet we know that in the end the choices made by different types of farmers shaped conditions in the eighteenth century for an industrial revolution in pastoral areas and an agricultural revolution in arable ones. Thus, as a first step, it should not be impossible to separate, if only in a generalized way, the social and technical factors which changed the structure of English farming regions between 1600 and 1700 and set certain rural communities on paths which diverged ever more sharply after 1750. This should clear the way for local studies which can probe the problem more deeply, and in due course make possible a more far-reaching comparative analysis.

*   *   *

Specialist corn growers have received most attention from historians because their history is among the best documented and lends itself most readily to generalization. Moreover, bread was a staple food and so bread producers have always been regarded as the central pillar of the farming structure. The growers of high-quality grains for food and drink were found on the wolds and downlands, on the loams and brecks of East Anglia, and in the vales and lowland plains. The life of such communities was centred upon villages which are also deemed typical of the English rural scene. Presided over by the squire, all classes—yeomen, husbandmen, cottagers, labourers, and paupers—were represented in the one community. By the sixteenth or seventeenth centuries, such villages usually lacked any considerable reserves of waste land waiting to be brought into cultivation and so increased production was possible only by intensifying cultivation on the existing land.[1] Much ingenuity was shown in achieving this. A steady increase took place in the proportion of land given to fodder crops, which fed more stock which manured the land more effectively, and so produced more corn. The Lincolnshire hills and vales yield plentiful evidence of this development.[2] In the common fields of Oxfordshire the self-sown leys which were used to feed more stock in the 1630's gave way in the second half of the century to deliberately sown grasses such as rye grass, trefoil, lucerne, clover, and particularly sainfoin.[3] Somewhere between 1650, when Sir Richard Weston wrote his propaganda in favour of clover, and 1662 the

---

[1] A more detailed analysis is contained in Joan Thirsk, ed., *The Agrarian History of England and Wales, IV, 1500–1640*, (henceforth A.H.E.W. IV), 1967, pp. 1–112. Cf. also E. L. Jones, *Agriculture and Economic Growth in England, 1650–1815*, 1967, pp. 154 *et seq.*

[2] Thirsk, *English Peasant Farming*, p. 192.

[3] Michael Havinden, 'Agricultural Progress in Open-Field Oxfordshire', A.H.R., IX, ii, 1961, pp. 74–7.

price of seed fell from 2s. a pound to 7d. Men had learned to thresh the seed for themselves and no longer relied entirely on Dutch imports. Thus clover became a practical proposition, which Andrew Yarranton could with some assurance recommend to West Midlands farmers below the rank of rich gentleman and yeoman. For this reason, clover spread more widely after the 1660's.[1] At the same time, turnips, which were first popularized as a field crop in Norfolk and Suffolk by the Flemish aliens in the early seventeenth century, were grown more freely on the lighter loams by the middle decades, and, like clover, they improved the performance of the livestock side of arable farming and so indirectly the corn yield.[2]

Meanwhile a search was under way for better varieties of seed that would yield heavier crops of corn. We probably do not know one-tenth of the experiments that were going on. Robert Plot wrote of more productive strains of wheat and barley which were cultivated in Oxfordshire and slowly, too slowly for his taste, spread to other counties in the course of the seventeenth century.[3] It is pure luck that Plot happened to record these facts; they must represent a minute proportion of new strains of traditional crops being exploited at this time in the arable centres of England.

The main improvements listed in reply to the questionnaire put out by the Royal Society in 1664 described better rotations in the arable fields, more generous use of fertilizers on the arable, more use of the sheepfold as a fertilizer, and the careful choice of seed. Questions were put about meadows and pastures but the answers that have survived were brief, and only enumerated the traditional remedies for poor quality grass.[4] Nevertheless, it was in these corn-growing areas that the watering of meadows took hold in the 1630's, spreading through Wiltshire, Berkshire, Dorset, Hampshire, and later into the Midlands.[5] Like so many of the innovations in corn-growing regions, it is associated with substantial farmers and the owners of great estates. The first watering of meadows by artificial dykes had been devised by Rowland Vaughan,

[1] Andrew Yarranton, *The Improvement Improved. A Second Edition of the Great Improvement of Lands by Clover*, 1663, pp. 4, 44, 31; P. E. Dove, *Account of Andrew Yarranton. The Founder of English Political Economy*, 1854, p. 8; Bodleian MS. Aubrey 2, fol. 152; G. E. Fussell, 'Adventures with Clover', *Agriculture*, LXII, no. 7, 1955, p. 343. The quality of the imported seed in the 1650's was very variable and Walter Blith urged growers to send a reliable man to the Low Countries to buy it, another impracticable suggestion to the small farmer.—W. Blith, *The English Improver Improved*, 1652 edn, p. 179.

[2] E. Kerridge, *The Agricultural Revolution*, 1967, pp. 270–6.

[3] Thirsk, A.H.E.W. IV, p. 168. It is perhaps significant that the early ripening variety of barley used in Oxfordshire which could be sown and returned to the barn in nine or ten weeks—ideal in wet and backward springs—had been introduced to Oxfordshire from Patney in Wiltshire, which was an estate belonging to the Earl of Craven.—R. Plot, *The Natural History of Oxfordshire*, 1676, pp. 152–3; Bodleian MS. Aubrey 2, fol. 84.

[4] Royal Society, Georgical Enquiries, Classified Papers, x(3).

[5] E. Kerridge, 'The Sheepfold in Wiltshire and the Floating of the Water Meadows', *Econ. Hist. Rev.*, 2nd ser., VI, 1954, pp. 286–9; idem, *Agricultural Revolution*, pp. 266–7.

a substantial gentleman farmer living in the Golden Valley of Herefordshire. The digging of the trenches for watering cost him many hundred pounds and it is not surprising that he could not persuade others in the valley to follow his example. His description of his neighbours makes it clear that he lived among small dairymen who were busy with their cheese and butter making from May to July and wove hemp and flax in winter. They could not have afforded such expensive innovations.[1] Hence the idea was taken up among wealthier farmers in the corn-growing regions, on the chalk downlands of Salisbury plain where the Earl of Pembroke owned estates, and subsequently in other counties further east. Sir Richard Weston adopted the idea on his lands in Surrey and spent £1,500 on it, not to mention the costs of litigation with his neighbours who claimed damage to their lands by flooding.[2] In Wiltshire Dr Kerridge has found manor courts agreeing upon co-operative schemes for watering their meadows. But since it remains doubtful how many small husbandmen could have afforded to be involved in such a costly enterprise, it may be that by this time such Wiltshire villages had already succeeded in driving out the small occupier. This would be consonant with Dr Kerridge's general observation that by 1657 the watering of meadows "was normal amongst gentlemen farmers and cultivating land owners."[3]

Zeal for experiments together with the capital to back them were conspicuous among substantial yeomen and gentry on the most fertile cornlands of the kingdom, and it is no accident that the two outstanding farm account books that have survived from the seventeenth century were written by men farming lands in these districts: Robert Loder at Harwell on the Berkshire downs, and Henry Best at Elmswell on the Yorkshire wolds.[4] The agricultural revolution of the eighteenth century was likewise publicized by the same class of men farming similar soils. Jethro Tull's *Horse-Hoeing Husbandry* emerged from experience of farming in Berkshire at Crowmarsh Gifford (on the Thames near Wallingford)—superb corn-growing country, producing grain for the London market. After his book was published, Tull moved to a hill farm on the chalk downlands between Berkshire and Wiltshire—an arable, sheep-corn area. Turnip Townshend was similarly concerned with the improvement of potential arable land at Rainham, near Fakenham, on the brecklands of Norfolk, which when consolidated by sheep and improved by their manure became fertile granaries of corn. Considerably later in the eighteenth century Thomas Coke worked on the same principles in the same countryside.[5]

The logic in this enthusiasm for more intensive arable farming in a period of

[1] E. B. Wood, ed., *Rowland Vaughan, His Booke*, 1897, pp. 30–1.   [2] P.R.O., E 178/5669.
[3] Kerridge, *Agricultural Revolution*, pp. 254, 262 *et seq.*
[4] G. E. Fussell, ed., *Robert Loder's Farm Accounts, 1610–20*, Camden Soc., 3rd ser., LIII, 1936; C. B. Robinson, ed., *Rural Economy in Yorkshire in 1641*, Surtees Soc., XXXIII, 1857.
[5] Lord Ernle, *English Farming Past and Present*, 1936 edn, pp. 170, 173–4, 218.

stagnating prices lay—for farmers on the light lands of the downs and wolds and brecklands, at least—in technical necessity. The sheep-corn system was ideal on these soils and no other commended itself as a substitute. The readiest solution to falling profits, namely, more intensive and more efficient production of the same commodities, was well within the capacity of the large farmer. The consolidation and enclosure of land and the engrossing of farms were all means to this end. Moreover, by growing more fodder crops, more sheep could be kept on the hills and more cattle in the vales, and thus the sources of income were diversified. In certain geographical situations, other solutions, involving the use of more distant grazing lands as a supplement to the resources of the hill farms, were favoured. Gentlemen farmers on the Lincolnshire wolds and the Kesteven heath rented marshland and fenland to fatten cattle which they could not finish on their home pastures. This practice continued throughout the seventeenth century and only slackened off in the eighteenth when hill farmers recognized the value of growing turnips at home for stock feeding. The renting of these distant pastures was not within the means of the small husbandman.[1]

In the clay vales farmers had more alternative choices in the changing economic circumstances of the seventeenth century. They were not inescapably tied to corn growing, but could enclose their land and turn it to grass. On heavy soils this was an attractive solution, particularly as it solved the problem posed by high wages, of which lowland farmers generally complained in the second half of the seventeenth century.[2] "Pasturage is more profitable than tillage," wrote one pamphleteer in 1654, "why should they [i.e. the enclosing farmers] not have liberty to lay down their arable land for grass."[3] In fact, they continued to do just this in many parts of the East Midlands—in Leicestershire, Northamptonshire, and north Buckinghamshire. It is roughly estimated that nearly a quarter of Leicestershire was enclosed in the seventeenth century.[4] The pamphlet controversy for and against enclosure between two Leicestershire parsons, John Moore and Joseph Lee, in 1653–4 seems something of an anachronism in seventeenth-century England—for public opinion was generally moving in favour of enclosure so long as it safeguarded the interests of the poor commoners—yet it did not appear so in the East Midlands; here enclosure was still a lively present issue.[5]

[1] Thirsk, *English Peasant Farming*, pp. 176–7.

[2] Coke, *op. cit.*, p. 15; Bodleian MS. Top. Kent, A1, fol. 26; *Plain English in a Familiar Conference betwixt three Friends, Rusticus, Civis, and Veridicus, concerning the Deadness of our Markets*, 1673, p. 6.

[3] *Considerations concerning Common Fields*, 1654, p. 21.   [4] *Leics. V.C.H.*, II, pp. 204, 223.

[5] John Moore, *The Crying Sin of England of not caring for the Poor*, 1653; idem, *A Scripture Word against Inclosure...*, 1656; idem, *A Reply to a Pamphlet entitled Considerations...*, 1656; *Considerations concerning Common Fields*, 1654; J. Lee, *Vindication of a Regulated Inclosure*, 1656; *A Vindication of the Considerations concerning Common Fields and Inclosures...*, 1656. See also W. E. Tate, *The English Village Community...*, 1967, p. 77.

There is general agreement among those who have worked on particular parishes and estates in the arable districts of England that these economic changes caused land to become more and more concentrated in the hands of the larger farmers. A. H. Johnson who many years ago sought to explain the decline of the small landowners found evidence for it between the sixteenth and the mid-eighteenth centuries, and more particularly between 1688 and 1750, in Oxfordshire parishes generally, and on various estates in Norfolk, Sussex, Kent, Wiltshire, the Isle of Wight, and Leicestershire.[1] It is noticeable that his evidence was drawn from the best corn-growing regions. His comparisons were of a rough and ready kind, but the difficulties in estimating changes in the number of owner-occupiers during the seventeenth century have discouraged others from attempting other large comparisons. Most modest examples from single parishes, however, have shown the same trends.

At Sherington in Buckinghamshire, for example, modest freeholders who had been gaining ground in the late sixteenth century when manorial lords sold out their interests, and who continued to flourish until the 1660's, were driven out by indebtedness between 1660 and 1710. The engrossing of holdings proceeded apace and many merchants and town dwellers became owners.[2] At Chippenham in Cambridgeshire, where the common fields were not enclosed until 1791, large farms nevertheless grew at the expense of the rest during the seventeenth century. Circumstances in this case suggest that it was not always debt that drove men to sell. Rents were falling, and the weight of taxation borne by owners of land was rising. Since there were sound arguments for becoming a tenant rather than an owner in the second half of the seventeenth century, the three Chippenham farmers who sold out farms of between 120 and 155 acres apiece in 1696 to enable the lord to create a park may have made their choice deliberately and willingly.[3]

Some gentle propaganda in favour of small farms began to flow in the late 60's and early 70's from people familiar with conditions in the lowland zone, who viewed with increasing anxiety the fall of rents. Sir Thomas Culpeper, junior, in the preface which he wrote in 1668 to his father's *Tract against the High Rate of Usury* described the increase of large farms as more appropriate

---

[1] A. H. Johnson, *The Disappearance of the Small Landowner*, 1963 edn, pp. 132–8

[2] A. C. Chibnall, *Sherington. Fiefs and Fields of a Buckinghamshire Village*, 1965; Margaret Spufford, reviewing the above in A.H.R., 16, i, 1968, p. 72.

[3] Margaret Spufford, *A Cambridgeshire Community, Chippenham from Settlement to Enclosure*, Leics. University, Dept. of English Local History, Occasional Paper, no. 20, 1965, pp. 45–6, 48–9. For evidence of the continued decline of the small farmer in the first half of the eighteenth century, see G. E. Mingay 'The Size of Farms in the Eighteenth Century', *Econ. Hist. Rev.*, 2nd ser., XIV, 1962, pp. 481–4. *Cf.* also the statement of William Ellis that it is doubtful "whether since the early part of the eighteenth century it has profited the man of middle acres to own the land he farms." Cited in Charles Wilson, *England's Apprenticeship*, 1965, p. 252. See also H. J. Habakkuk, 'La Disparition du paysan anglais', *Annales E.S.C.*, 20e année, 1965, no. 4, pp. 649–63.

to New England than Old England, and mourned the diminution of small ones. Carew Reynel believed that "the smaller estates the land is divided into the better for the nation, the more are maintained, and the land better husbanded."[1]

The decline of the small landowner in the seventeenth century, then, was a feature of specialized arable regions, and also of vale lands newly enclosed for pasture, not, as we shall see presently, of traditional pasture-farming districts. The smaller farmer was being driven out by a combination of factors, notably the technical economies possible in large-scale cereal production, or in conversions to pasture, sluggish grain prices, and the high cost and quantity of labour in corn growing. Capital was essential both to the farmers who chose to intensify grain production and to those who chose to turn over entirely to grazing. Not surprisingly, it was from among these farmers, and not from the ancient pasture-farming communities, that the livestock improvers like Robert Bakewell and the Culley brothers emerged in the eighteenth century.[2] They had been nurtured in communities so structured as to promote the interests of the thrusting and ambitious improver.

This generalized conspectus of arable-farming regions in the seventeenth century takes its guide lines from the examples of the best corn-growing lands and the most ordered village communities. It omits certain variants: these were the villages with less fertile soils which continued under arable cultivation without yielding great rewards to their cultivators; crops other than corn could quickly win general favour if they prospered in the environment. The variant villages, socially speaking, were those which lacked the controlling influence of a squire, either because the ownership of land was divided among several lords of almost equal status, or because the village entirely lacked a lord (this could occur if the manorial rights were sold up and the manorial courts ceased to be held), or because the manorial lord allowed things to slide through sheer negligence. Many such communities maintained a strong freeholder class, which ruled the village when necessary, but which failed, often from self interest, to check the influx of immigrant cottagers and squatters. These became the 'open' villages of the eighteenth century, providing much-needed casual labour for the farmers in the 'closed' villages roundabout. Wigston Magna, Leicestershire, is one such example: it solved the problem of employment for its inhabitants by turning to framework knitting, which was already entrenched in forest areas nearby, and which spread in the second half of the seventeenth century into the almost equally congenial environment afforded by such 'open' villages.[3] Industries, however, were not the only solution to the problem of

[1] Culpeper, Preface to the 1st edn, 1668; Carew Reynel, *The True English Interest*, 1674, p. 20.
[2] H. C. Pawson, *Robert Bakewell*, 1957, pp. 18 *et seq.*; D. J. Rowe, 'The Culleys—Northumberland Farmers, 1767–1813', forthcoming article in the A.H.R.
[3] W. G. Hoskins, *The Midland Peasant*, 1957, pp. 97–110, 228.

employment in such communities. Another solution lay in the cultivation of special, labour-intensive crops.

Pamphlet literature during the seventeenth century recommended with growing conviction and growing precision the cultivation of specialized cash crops, commanding a high and profitable price at the markets. These were fruit and vegetables; herbs and spices for cooking and medicinal purposes, such as saffron, caraway, mustard, and liquorice; industrial dyes such as woad, weld, madder, and safflower; flax and hemp for cloth weaving; mulberries for feeding silkworms; and teasels which were used for brushing up the nap of cloth and were considerably cheaper than wire cards. The first exhortations to grow these crops were made by men who had travelled in European countries, particularly Flanders and France, and drew object lessons from their observations. Some were cloth merchants who readily saw the commercial advantages of producing flax, hemp, and dyes at home instead of importing them; others were gentlemen who collected unusual plants and foods for their gardens and dining tables and either bought them from special importers in London or sent their gardeners abroad to collect them.[1]

The lessons were only slowly driven home. When the example of the Dutch was preached to Englishmen in the early 1620's as a model to be copied for alleviating the economic crisis, the cultivation of flax, hemp, and tobacco at home were principally commended as a means of saving on foreign imports. The obvious remedies for the sick economy at that time seemed to lie in increasing the volume of trade and improving the money supply.[2] By the middle of the century, however, proposals for overcoming a new and even deeper depression were far more broadly conceived, and gave a prominent place to schemes for the diversification of agriculture. The need to provide more employment for the poor loomed large, and, with this objective in mind, political writers set great store by labour-demanding crops which would increase work on the land and indirectly in industry. Thus Henry Robinson's pamphlet in 1652 entitled *Certain Proposals in order to the People's Freedom and Accommodation* wished to foster weaving industries of silk, cotton, hemp, and flax as well as wool, and to grow most of these fibres at home. To provide additional land for them he urged the more productive use of wastes, which meant, of course, enclosure as a first step. But so long as the commoners' interests were protected, Robinson believed this to be a desirable improvement.[3] These two arguments

---

[1] Mea Allan, *The Tradescants, their Plants, Gardens, and Museum, 1570–1663*, 1964, *passim*. See also *infra*, p. 160.

[2] Thomas Mun, *England's Treasure by Foreign Trade* in J. R. McCulloch, *Early English Tracts on Commerce*, 1952, pp. 115 *et seq*. It was published in 1664 but was written in 1623.—B. Supple, 'Thomas Mun and the Commercial Crisis, 1623', B.I.H.R., XXVII, 1954, pp. 91–4.

[3] Some of the same ideas occur in the earlier pamphlets by Henry Robinson, namely, *England's Safety in Trade's Increase*, 1641, and *Brief Considerations concerning the Advancement of Trade and*

in combination became standard among writers on the economy during the Interregnum and for the rest of the century. Flax and hemp would increase the variety and quantity of domestic handicrafts; dye crops required much hand labour and would also save the cost of imported dyes; vegetables and fruit used land and labour intensively, were in great demand, and extremely profitable. Changes in dietary habits had occurred during the civil wars and people now ate only one main meal a day, consuming less meat and eating more fruit and vegetables.[1] Sales in towns were brisk: Londoners of all classes bought fruit from pedlars and munched it in the streets—like goats, the Venetian Busoni remarked unkindly.[2]

The literature advocating these crops was voluminous after 1650 and cannot be recited in detail. But two editions of Walter Blith's textbook on husbandry serve as signposts to the success of the propaganda. In 1649 Blith published *The English Improver or a New Survey of Husbandry*, and enumerated "six pieces of improvement." These were (i) the floating and watering of land, (ii) the draining of fens, bogs, and marshland, (iii) the ploughing of old pasture, and enclosure without depopulation, (iv) the careful use of manures appropriate to different soils, (v) the planting of woods, and (vi) the more modest improvement of lands presenting special problems. In 1652 the new edition of this work, entitled *The English Improver Improved*, contained the same recommendations but added "six newer pieces of improvement." These were (i) the growing of clover, sainfoin, and lucerne, (ii) the correct use of ploughs appropriate to different soils, (iii) the planting of weld, woad, and madder, (iv) the planting of hops, saffron, and liquorice, (v) the cultivation of rape, coleseed, hemp, and flax, and (vi) the planting of orchard and garden fruits. In the revised text Blith implied that some at least of these new crops had only just been brought to his notice, perhaps, we may guess, as a result of comments by readers of the first edition. Of weld, he wrote with a trace of pique, "it is my desire to make public whatever comes under my experience, yet this hath been used this many years by many private gentlemen in divers parts but not discovered for public practice. . . I fear men's spirits are strangely private that have made excellent experiments and yet will not communicate."[3]

Where and by whom were these crops adopted and how did they relieve the problems of corn-growing communities in the seventeenth century? The dye

---

Navigation, 1649. See also William Goffe, 'How to Advance the Trade of the Nation and Employ the Poor', *Harl. Misc.*, IV, pp. 385–9.

[1] Sir William Coventry, 'Essay concerning the Decay of Rents and their Remedies', 1670, Brit. Mus., Sloane MS. 3828, fols. 205–10. See also 'The Grand Concern of England explained', 1673, *Harl. Misc.*, VIII, 1746, p. 544, referring to the "leaving off eating of suppers."

[2] Ronald Webber, *The Early Horticulturists*, 1968, p. 41.

[3] Walter Blith, *The English Improver, or a New Survey of Husbandry*, 1649, title page; *idem, The English Improver Improved*, 1652, pp. 224–5.

crops, vegetables, fruits, herbs, and spices were all taken up with alacrity in arable areas. For technical reasons, the dye crops did not generally commend themselves to small growers, and, except in market gardens, were cultivated by more substantial farmers with capital, and even by adventurers who moved around the country renting land for short periods at high prices.[1] Madder, for example, took three years to mature and yield its first crop. Moreover, the best plants had to be brought from Zealand or at least bought in London from an importer. After three years of waiting, the grower preferably needed access to a madder mill for drying and pounding, although as an alternative he could employ women and children to do the job by hand during the winter. At all events, he faced strong competition from the Dutch product, for Zealand madder was noted for its high quality and was imported in quantity. Nevertheless, if successful, madder could yield a profit of £300 an acre after three years, and £160 for an indifferent crop.[2]

The early attempts at madder growing in England are associated with a London dyer, Mr Minne, who evidently had the capital to invest in a long-term project. Around 1620 he sent George Bedford to study its secrets in the Netherlands and spent £1,000 in nine years keeping him there. When Bedford returned with some plants, he tried to grow them in Romney Marsh, a significant choice of district, for it was a happy hunting ground for outsiders who leased land in the seventeenth century and did not reside there.[3] Another adventurer with madder was Sir Nicholas Crisp who set up a madder plantation at Deptford. Later in the century it was grown for a short while near Wisbech, but since Wisbech lies on the edge of the Bedford Level, we may fairly suspect that this was an enterprise promoted not by traditional fen peasants but by some of the big farmers who came into the Level after drainage and took up large tracts of land as a speculative venture.[4] The only madder growing which was carried on on a small scale occurred in market gardens around towns and mainly around cloth-working centres. Growers cultivated vegetables such as cabbage, kidney beans, radishes, onions, and herbs between the madder plants to yield a harvest in the years before the madder was ready, and since both kinds of plants needed continuous weeding, this system worked well.[5]

Woad was another dye which required capital and had to be grown on a large scale if it was to yield the best profit. "Experiments of a little parcel,"

[1] Kerridge, *Agricultural Revolution*, 1967, pp. 194, 210–11.

[2] Philip Miller, *The Method of Cultivating Madder*, 1758, *passim*; J. Mortimer, *The Whole Art of Husbandry*, 1707, pp. 123 *et seq.*; Blith, 1653 edn, *op. cit.*, p. 235.

[3] P.R.O., SP 16/164, nos. 53 & 53, I–III; L. B. Larking, *Proceedings principally in the County of Kent...*, Camden Soc., 1862, pp. 54–5.

[4] Blith, 1652, *op. cit.* p. 235; Houghton, ed. Bradley, *op. cit.*, II, p. 372.

[5] W. Coles, *Adam in Eden*, 1657, pp. 584–5; Blith, 1652, *op. cit.*, p. 233.

wrote Walter Blith, were useless; one must grow enough to keep at least one mill at work. It also made heavy demands on labour during the summer for two weedings and at least two cuttings in mid-June and mid-July. Thus clothiers disliked it because it made labour short for spinning in summer. It was therefore not well suited to pastoral areas where the cloth industry was entrenched, and much better suited to arable-farming systems where a summer supply of casual labour was already at hand. In these conditions it was one of the most rewarding crops of any. "The best estates that hath been got in all our rich upland countries," maintained Walter Blith, "have been got by it [i.e. woad]." By this he meant estates in the Midland counties of Northamptonshire, Leicestershire, Rutland, Felden Warwickshire, Oxfordshire, parts of Worcestershire, and Gloucestershire, and in Bedfordshire and Buckinghamshire where woad was incorporated in a system of alternate husbandry, being a good first crop when pasture was being broken up for corn. Its other home was in gardens particularly around cloth towns such as Godalming, Farnham, and Winchester.[1]

A dye crop which found a congenial home on upland arable farms was weld, producing a bright yellow dye. It prospered on chalky barren hillsides wherever the soil was warm and dry. Thus it was widely grown on the downlands around Canterbury and Wye where it was inserted into the arable rotation, being sown in with barley or oats one year for a harvest the following year. It did not call for much cultivation while growing, though it was a "ticklish vegetable" prone to blasting and to other accidents if bad weather damaged it in spring. When harvested the stalks simply had to be dried and some of the seed shaken out for the next year's crop. It was a plant which diversified the interests of sheep-corn farmers without posing any special problems of cultivation and harvesting.[2]

A new dye crop which gained ground notably in the 1660's and 1670's was safflower or bastard saffron. It yielded a reddish pink dye and was much in demand from the silk dyers, who had hitherto obtained the bulk of their supplies from around Strasbourg in Germany. It was an indigenous English plant but it began to be grown more deliberately around London, in Gloucestershire, and in Oxfordshire in an effort to undercut the price of the imported article. Successful growers found it extremely profitable, yielding clear gains of £20–£30 per acre in a year; its only disadvantage was that it was harvested at the same time as wheat. Thus it is not clear whether it was adopted by pasture

[1] P.R.O., SP 14/113, no. 21; Blith, 1652, *op. cit.*, pp. 226–7, 230; L. Meager, *The Mystery of Husbandry. . .*, 1697, p. 106; Guildford Muniment Room, Loseley MS., 1965; 1966, 1–4; Hants. County Record Office, 1583, B. I owe this reference to Miss Adrienne Batchelor.

[2] John Banister, *Synopsis of Husbandry*, 1799, pp. 197–202. This is the most circumstantial account of weld growing known to me. I wish to thank Mr Dennis Baker for the reference. See also Blith, 1652, *op. cit.*, pp. 222–5; Houghton, ed. Bradley, *op. cit.*, II, p. 459; Mortimer, *op. cit.*, p. 127.

farmers or was taken up by arable farmers with unusually ample supplies of casual labour during the summer.[1]

Saffron was a traditional English crop which feared no competitors. It was deemed far superior in quality to any of foreign origin. Its chief use was medicinal, demand was high, and it commanded good prices. It was grown in arable fields, even in common fields, in Suffolk, Essex, and Cambridgeshire, and also in Herefordshire. It called for much hand labour, first in setting the roots in trenches, and then in gathering the saffron every morning for about a month in summer. Clear profit ranged from £3 10s. to over £30 an acre.[2]

Another special crop was liquorice which was grown around towns where plenty of dung was available. Since it stayed in the ground for three summers before the roots grew to any size, vegetables such as onions, leeks, and lettuces were cultivated in between. It was grown in quantity around London, at Godalming in Surrey, at Pontefract in Yorkshire, and around Worksop in Nottinghamshire. In the words of John Parkinson, the herbalist, writing in 1640 it "is much used nowadays to be planted in great quantity even to fill many acres of ground, whereof riseth a great deal of profit to those that know how to order it and have fit grounds for it to thrive in." At the end of the century profits of £50–£100 an acre were quoted in exceptional cases.[3]

Market gardeners have already appeared in this account as growers of dyes and medicinal crops. But vegetables and fruit were their main livelihood and contemporary descriptions leave no doubt of the remarkable success of this specialized branch of farming. Vegetable seeds were cheaply and easily bought from seedsmen in London and other towns and from country innkeepers.[4] The land required was small, and every foot was profitably used; fruit trees separated the beds of vegetables. The towns which devoured the produce readily supplied dung for the next season's crops. In short, horticulture was ideally suited to small peasants with little land, no capital, but plenty of family labour, and with easy access to a town. Good market-garden land fetched high rents, but vegetables could be grown on poorer land, richly dunged, and were sown on many strips in common fields. While good-quality produce fetched handsome prices, better returns still came from the cultivation of vegetables

---

[1] Houghton, ed. Bradley, *op. cit.*, III, pp. 354–5; IV, p. 361; Hist. MSS. Comm., IX, *House of Lords MSS.*, p. 28; Carew Reynel, *op. cit.*, p. 87. A petition against a duty on safflower *c.* 1670 says that not more than 2,000 lb. were then grown in England compared with 600 cwt which was imported from Germany. This was in the early days of its commercial cultivation in England.—*CSPD 1660–85, Addenda*, p. 505.

[2] W. Coles, *The Art of Simpling*, 1656, p. 51; *idem, Adam in Eden*, p. 172; Houghton, ed. Bradley, *op. cit.*, II, pp. 331–2; IV, pp. 283–7; Blith, 1652, *op. cit.*, p. 244; Mortimer, *op. cit.*, pp. 129–30.

[3] Blith, 1652, *op. cit.*, pp. 246–8; Houghton, ed. Bradley, *op. cit.*, IV, pp. 41–3; Mortimer, *op. cit.*, pp. 127–9; John Parkinson, *Paradisi in Sole*, 1656, p. 472.

[4] P.R.O., SP 46/100, fol. 242, lists an order for vegetable seeds, 1656(?); 1½ lb. of best onion seed cost 5s., ½ lb. lettuce seed 2s., and ¼ peck of radish seed 2s.

for seed.[1] Four or five acres of land used in this way, declared John Houghton, would sometimes maintain a family better and employ more labourers than fifty acres of other land. £100 from an acre was thought a not impossible return.[2]

The prosperity of the market gardeners along Thames-side is well known but they also throve in many other districts of the Home Counties and, indeed, all over southern England in the neighbourhood of busy towns. Tewkesbury, for example, produced excellent carrots which were distributed to markets via the Avon and the Severn. In Surrey the gardeners were clustered on the Lower Greensand, on the Bagshot Beds, and on alluvial soils in the valleys of the rivers Mole and Wey. In consequence, the whole county was especially re-nowned for its "gardening for profit," a reputation which is reflected in numer-ous tithe disputes relating to vegetables and also to hops, the latter being ex-tensively grown around Godalming and Farnham. A dispute in 1687 at Farn-ham listed twenty-two people in the parish growing hops and this did not claim to be a complete list. Witnesses alleged that there were forty owners or occu-piers of land planted with hops and that they covered between 250 and 300 acres of land. The tithe owners evidently shared handsomely in the benefits for the tithe of 6½ acres of hops was said to be valued at £15.[3]

Books on horticulture found a ready sale in the second half of the seventeenth century. French works were translated into English and Englishmen wrote their own handbooks, "wrung out of the earth" as one reviewer put it. The work to which this description was particularly applied was *The Garden of England* by Sir Hugh Platt, which incorporated much that he had learned by diligent correspondence and assiduous visits to gardeners around London. Clubs of experts were formed in London, where men received the latest information from other parts of the country and from Europe, and being "apt to essay novelties and rarities" they turned this knowledge to good account.[4]

The intensity of cultivation in the best organized market gardens is illus-trated in the probate inventory of Robert Gascoine, a gardener of St Martin in the Fields, who died in February 1718. He had row upon row of cauliflower and cabbage plants—1,000 plants were set in two banks three rows wide—radishes, carrots, colewort, young lettuce, asparagus, onions, spinach, and

---

[1] The Venetian Busoni said that gravelly land around London was dug out to about 6–7 feet and filled up with the filth of the city, so making it very fertile for garden crops.—Webber, *op. cit.*, p. 51; Mortimer, *op. cit.*, p. 146.

[2] John Houghton, *England's Great Happiness or a Dialogue between Content and Complaint*, 1677, p. 12; Blith, 1652, *op. cit.*, p. 261; *Philos. Trans.*, x–xii, no. 116, p. 363.

[3] *Philos. Trans.*, x–xii, no. 131, p. 796; no. 136, p. 922; Hist. MSS. Comm., *Portland II*, p. 30; P.R.O., E 134, 33 & 34 Chas. II, Hil. 26; 13 & 14 Chas. II, Hil. 7; 21 Chas. II, Trin. 7; 3 Jas. II, Easter 2.

[4] See bibliography in Webber, *op. cit.*; *Philos. Trans.*, x–xii, pp. 303, 373–4, 922.

artichokes, while fruit trees lined the palings between the beds. Forty rods of asparagus were of the first year's planting, 124 rods were one year old, and 32 rods were ready for cutting, with colewort in the alleys between. In addition other beds of asparagus and lettuce were being forced under glass. The surname of this gardener strongly suggests a French immigrant, but if his expertise and the scale of his enterprise placed him in the first rank of market gardeners, he was not alone. Other gardeners' inventories show the same system in operation, their crops being sometimes more specialized and sometimes less. John Lee of St Martin in the Fields, dying in July 1684, had specialized in asparagus and cucumber as well as growing cherry and other fruit trees between the beds. Curtis Akers of Chelsea in April 1686 was growing herbs, asparagus, carrots, parsnips, and beans. Another gardener in St Martin in the Fields in February 1682 grew only asparagus.[1]

This evidence does not give any clue to the total volume of production, nor can we compare the value of vegetables, fruit, and other special crops with the grain, meat, and dairy produce sent to the market by other farmers.[2] But the weight of contemporary comment leaves no doubt that specialists in these branches of farming weathered the crisis of the seventeenth century with ease. By 1670 Sir William Coventry put the argument in their favour in the simplest cash terms: corn and cattle were being produced to excess and the population was not increasing rapidly enough to consume it all. The solutions to this dilemma were to sell the surplus abroad (corn bounties, in fact, followed soon afterwards), or to increase the population consuming it at home, or to divert land from corn and meat to the growing of other crops, the ones which he most favoured being wood, flax, and hemp.[3] Farming textbooks in the second half of the seventeenth century consistently gave specialized cash crops their full share of space and added circumstantial details on yields, labour costs, and the net profit. The correspondence columns of John Houghton's weekly journal, *A Collection for the Improvement of Husbandry and Trade*, contained frequent homilies on their advantages; and the current market prices of saffron, caraway seed, linseed, and mustard were quoted regularly between 1694 and 1697.[4]

Except for hemp and flax, which are dealt with below in the account of pasture-farming regions, all these specialized crops were the produce of arable-

[1] Middlesex County Record Office, M1, 1718/10; 1684/93; 1686/36; 1682/18.

[2] Gregory King's estimates do not help us to make any very accurate guesses. He estimated the value of hemp, flax, woad, saffron, and dyes at £1,000,000, and the produce of arable land (grains and legumes) at £10,000,000. But hemp and flax are treated in my analysis as the products of pastoral regions, and King omitted vegetables entirely.—George E. Barnett, ed., *Two Tracts by Gregory King*, 1936, p. 36.

[3] Brit. Mus., Sloane MS. 3828, fols. 205–10.

[4] The value of these crops in relieving poverty among the increasing population of the Netherlands is discussed in B. H. Slicher van Bath, 'Historical Demography and the Social and Economic Development of the Netherlands', *Daedalus*, Spring 1968, pp. 612, 614.

farming regions. As we have seen, some were taken up by the market gardeners and other small growers, others were adopted by wealthier and bolder spirits who were prepared to invest capital and take risks, and were assured of adequate casual labour in busy seasons. Such pools of labour were most readily at hand in 'open' villages and it was doubtless in the neighbourhood of such communities that the most successful enterprises were established and maintained.

Further work will undoubtedly yield instructive illustrations of the association between labour-intensive crops and over-populous villages in arable regions. An example from a town in Gloucestershire, however, gives a vivid example of this association, arising through unusual circumstances in a pastoral area. 'Open' communities were not, of course, confined to arable districts; but their labour problems stood out most conspicuously in the latter case because they contrasted strongly with the 'closed' villages round about and because the two types complemented each other economically. There were 'open' villages in pastoral regions, but, as we shall see below, they did not present employment problems that were any different in kind from those of all other pastoral communities. Underemployment was common to them all.

Winchcombe was a market town in the pastoral vale of Gloucester. Its markets had fallen into decay, and it may thus be presumed to have had an economy that was hardly different from that of a village, though its population was larger. Tobacco growing took firm hold, as it did in many other villages in Worcestershire and Gloucestershire. Moreover, the lord of the manor failed to hold any courts or to enforce the bylaws, and uncontrolled immigration into Winchcombe followed. Single family houses were divided into tenements to accommodate two, three, and four families. The houses fell into disrepair and were in danger of falling into the street. Lodgers and beggars thronged the place: according to the poor law overseers there were twenty households of paupers begging for alms for every household able to bestow them. The lord of the manor attempted to remedy this state of affairs in 1662 by imposing entry fines for the first time in many years, and met with indignant resistance from his tenants. The dispute of 1662 was thus concerned with an inquiry into the customs of Winchcombe. "Hath not the neglect of executing the orders and bylaws upon offenders much encouraged the people there to become careless of offending in taking in of inmates and undertenants?" asked the Exchequer commissioners. This was clearly one of the causes of the trouble. But it is impossible for us not to see some association between tobacco growing and the inordinate growth of Winchcombe's population. The lord of the manor had neglected to control movement into the town. The trade of the market was declining. Tobacco was a labour-intensive crop which offered work and cash to all comers. People had crowded into Winchcombe for cheap accommodation and jobs, and the prohibition on the growing of tobacco after 1619 had not noticeably detracted from its popularity. The planters paid fines and later excise and continued to grow it. In 1652 an Act prohibited tobacco growing afresh, but it was followed by yet another in 1653 allowing offenders to pay excise and quietly harvest their crops. Not so in 1654. The Council of State took the legislation more seriously this time and sent soldiers to destroy the crop. Winchcombe people raised three hundred armed horse and foot to resist the attack, declaring that they were bred to the trade, and "if they lose it they will lose their lives." Signatories to a petition to Cromwell from Winchcombe tobacco growers numbered 110 persons.[1]

Tobacco growing was not stamped out until the late 1670's. Winchcombe was left in a pitiful plight, overpopulated and without adequate work. Its inhabitants subsequently resorted to stocking knitting. A visitor passing through the town in 1678 remarked upon the sight of the women folk carrying their puddings and bread to the common bakehouse, smoking and knitting as they went.[2]

In this account of arable-farming systems in the seventeenth century, three main streams of development may be discerned. On the best corn-growing lands, the large farmers prospered, offsetting the fall of grain prices by growing more grain with greater efficiency and driving out the small growers. In the vales, events followed the same course, except that in some places arable farms were converted to pasture for feeding cattle and keeping sheep. The work that was provided for the agricultural labourer was little enough on pasture farms[3] and liable to sudden interruption on arable ones. On suitable land less fertile for corn, special cash crops were grown by men with capital who could rely on the plentiful supply of casual labour from 'open' villages. However, the Diggers in Surrey, Kent, Northamptonshire, and Buckinghamshire who dug up the commons in 1649 during deep economic depression expressed the resentment of many poor labourers in arable areas when misfortune hit their employers and left them both landless and workless.[4] As for the small farmer in arable areas, he had little hope of survival, except in those districts which were suited to market gardening. Here, indeed, he had positive advantages over his richer and larger competitor.

* * *

[1] P.R.O., E 134, 14 Chas. I, Mich. 31; SP 25, 1, 75, pp. 374–5, 409; SP 18, 72, no. 65; R. Steele, *A Bibliography of Royal Proclamations of the Tudor and Stuart Sovereigns*, p. 150, 30 Dec. 1619, gives the first proclamation banning tobacco growing throughout England and Wales.

[2] Hist. MSS. Comm., *Portland II*, p. 303.

[3] A good example of a corn-growing village which was converted to pasture is the Verney family's home at Claydon, Bucks. It was a 'closed' village in which the rich farmers were graziers and the poor were dairymen. The surplus population which could not find work in the parish or in neighbouring ones drifted to London. I wish to thank Mr John Broad for this information.

[4] Brit. Mus., Thomason Tracts, E 669 f 15 (21) and (23); Keith Thomas, 'Another Digger Broadside', *Past and Present*, 42, 1969, pp. 57–68.

It remains for us to consider how the peasantry fared in pastoral regions. The pasture-farming regions present a different set of social and geographical circumstances. Grass growing was the primary objective of all farmers but their ultimate goals were varied, and may be broadly grouped under four headings: in the mountains and moorlands of northern England and on the moorlands of the south-west, cattle and sheep were reared; in the vales of the West Midlands and in other areas where the heavy soils lay under permanent grass, dairying was one speciality, rearing and fattening, sometimes in combination, were the others. In forest areas horse breeding and pig fattening played an important role alongside stock keeping; in the fenlands of eastern England and the Somerset Level stock enterprises were mixed.[1]

Pasture farmers lived in isolated farms and hamlets as well as in villages, and the population was thus more widely scattered than in the arable lowlands. Manorial courts could not exercise close surveillance over their tenants, and tenants generally held their land by freer tenures. In many of these dispersed centres of settlement, moreover, it is noticeable that the population consisted of one class only; the poor and the rich did not always live cheek by jowl, as in the nucleated villages. In Staffordshire, for example, it is remarkable how many hamlets recorded in the Hearth Tax Return of 1666 consisted either of the rich or of the poor but not of both. In fact in many parishes, some of which had ten or fourteen separate settlements, it was usual to find that half the townships mixed the classes, while in the other half they lived firmly segregated. All in all, the inhabitants enjoyed much greater freedom and this bred in them a fiery spirit of independence, which armed them for struggle. As one nineteenth-century writer expressed it, when comparing this life favourably with that of the inhabitants of the squire's village, "a dominant and resident landowner was the centre of intelligence, of charity, and of social life," but for these advantages there was a social price to pay. "It is as true in the parish as in the nation that a paternal government makes a childish people. A man whose brothers and neighbours are dependent upon him is prone to become overbearing whilst the neighbours and even the brothers are apt to become obsequious." There was little danger of this in the pastoral districts of the kingdom.[2]

The seventeenth century was a testing time for pasture farmers living in fens and forests. Strife and controversy had surrounded enclosure and engrossing in the arable regions for more than a hundred years. Now the pastoral areas came under attack from the agricultural improvers. "Improvement of the wastes and forests" became the slogan of the age. The Crown led the way in the early decades of the century with its schemes for the drainage of the fens

---

[1] These farming types are mapped in Thirsk, A.H.E.W. IV, p. 4.

[2] Joan Thirsk, 'Horn and Thorn in Staffordshire. The Economy of a Pastoral County', *North Staffs. Jnl of Field Studies*, 9, 1969, pp. 3–4.

and disafforestation of the forests, in both of which countrysides it had considerable landed interests. The principal investors in, and beneficiaries from, its schemes were members of the court circle, nobility and gentry, as well as the drainers and their friends. The native peasantry had nothing to gain and much to lose by their designs, for in both forests and fens they were intended to turn pastoral economies into arable ones, and would inevitably have altered the structure of the local communities. The agricultural system in pastoral areas prospered on the basis of certain well-defined conditions. Society was dominated by family farmers; the economy depended on imports of corn from other districts, the use of spacious commons for feeding stock, and the availability of supplementary work in industries of many kinds. The drainers in the fens and the improvers disafforesting the forests did not fully appreciate that the destruction of the old economies meant the destruction of their societies as well; the inhabitants, on the other hand, perceived this instinctively. Most of the riots in the years before the civil war (though not the Midland Revolt of 1607) broke out in pastoral and forest areas, threatened by changes which undermined their whole way of life. The worst outbreaks occurred in the years 1629–32, when the three pillars of the economy—imported corn, spacious commons, and domestic industries—threatened to crumble simultaneously. First bad weather hit the pasture farmers, creating a shortage of hay and cattle feed, and spreading cattle murrain among their herds. Then it spoiled the corn harvests in 1630 and 1632 and made it impossible for some pastoral communities to buy corn at any price. Plague took hold in 1631. And acute unemployment hit the domestic, and particularly the cloth, industries. "Want of work," bad weather, and the intrusions of drainers and improvers hit the pastoral areas with unprecedented harshness. Hence the many riots in the pastoral and forest districts of Wiltshire, Dorset, Hampshire, Gloucestershire, Worcestershire, and Rutland.[1]

The conviction that improvement of the wastes and forests was the first priority in agriculture persisted if anything more strongly during the Interregnum than under the early Stuarts.[2] The only difference was that writers hedged their recommendations about with safeguards for the commoners. 'Improvement' had become a dirty word. "Scarce anyone," wrote John Houghton later on recalling these years, "durst offer for improvements lest he should be called a Projector as if he came from the fens to borrow 5s. to purchase

[1] H. C. Darby, *The Draining of the Fens*, 2nd edn, 1968, pp. 49–58; P.R.O., SP 16, 185, no. 2; Acts of the Privy Council, 1630–31, nos. 329, 330, 536, 646, 816, 818, 835, 855, 1041, 1057, 1129, 1130, 1156, 1158, 1165. See also E. Kerridge, 'The Revolts in Wiltshire against Charles I', *Wilts. Arch. and Nat. Hist. Mag.*, LVII, 1958–9, pp. 64–75.

[2] For three examples of reports and tracts on this subject, see SP 18/69, no. 6 ('Proposals by Dr John Parker and Edward Cressett for best Improvement of the Forests', 1654); Silvanus Taylor, *Common Good or the Improvement of Commons, Forests, and Chases . . .*, 1652; Appendix to Blith, 1652, *op. cit.*, pp. 263 *et seq.*, entitled 'A Remonstrance . . . for regulating forests, Wastes, or Commons. . .'

£5,000 yearly, so averse were our English then from all care of improvements."[1]
The angry commoners instilled a fear which lingered well beyond Houghton's
time. It still permeated the atmosphere of debates in the House of Lords on the
draining of the fens in 1701 and 1711. The plan to enclose and drain was called
"the most arbitrary proceeding in the world. It invades the properties of
thousands of people."[2]

The vision which inspired would-be improvers of forests, fens, and chases
during the Interregnum was the prospect of increasing employment. One-fifth
more people, argued Silvanus Taylor, might be fed if waste lands were enclosed. But he did not plan or predict the class structure of such communities.
The experiments which were brought to conclusion in the fens created large
farms running into hundreds of acres, occupied by strangers rather than local
inhabitants, including many Dutchmen.[3] Thus the crisis of the seventeenth
century in these regions was created by short-sighted planners with an obses-
sive predilection for corn-growing economies, blind to the looming economic
difficulties of corn growers elsewhere, and wilfully ignoring the fact that corn-
growing systems fostered large farms far more successfully than they sustained
small peasants. Their schemes were designed to create class-divided communities of the lowland kind with their due proportion of yeomen, husbandmen,
labourers, and paupers, presided over by an affluent gentleman. Fortunately,
they did not succeed in moulding much of pastoral England in the image of the
arable lowlands.

Outside these disturbed areas, agricultural improvements by pasture farmers
were necessarily made at modest cost, did not generally disturb neighbours,
and thus leave less trace in our records. The social obstacles to expensive
capital improvements have already been illustrated in the experiences of
Rowland Vaughan who devised the scheme for watering meadows in the
Golden Valley of Herefordshire. He cheerfully spent large sums in order to get
his young lambs ready for the butcher a month before his competitors. His
neighbours, on the other hand, who were family farmers, dairying in the
summer and weaving hemp and flax in the winter, pursued another course of
life altogether.[4]

Despite the difficulties, described by Andrew Yarranton, in spreading innovations among farmers without much spare cash for experiments that could

[1] J. Houghton, *A Collection for Improvement of Husbandry and Trade*, 1692, p. 76.

[2] Thirsk, *English Peasant Farming*, pp. 126–7.

[3] P.R.O., SP 46/88, fols. 173 *et seq.*, illustrate the experiences of Rumbold Jacobson, merchant of
London and lessee of 428 acres of Hatfield Chase, *c.* 1640–1. The report in 1654 by Parker and
Cressett (see above, p. 168, n. 2), discussing the possibility of improving the forests by leasing out
large portions, assumed that the commoners would not take up such leases out of hostility to the
whole project, while "others will be very tender of disgusting their neighbours the commoners in
hiring it from them."—P.R.O., SP 18, 69, no. 6.

[4] See *supra*, pp. 153-4.

easily fail, stock in pasture-farming areas benefited from the ley grasses that were improving the feed of animals in arable areas. In general, however, they continued to be fed mainly on grass and hay, though care was devoted to the improvement of the herbage by careful grazing, frequent cutting down of thistles, rushes, etc., and by the application of dung, lime, potash, and ashes, and by drainage with open or covered drains. These measures, which feature prominently in the replies to the Georgical inquiries in 1664, were all traditional, but they nevertheless produced substantial improvements in the feeding capacity of pastures. Walter Blith in 1652 particularly extolled the efforts of farmers in the woodland parts, "as in Worcestershire, Warwickshire, Staffordshire, Shropshire, and Wales-ward and northward," in improving their coarse lands by these traditional methods. He judged the land to be as highly improved as many parts of the fielden country *"and fuller of wealthier inhabitants."*[1]

Little evidence survives concerning the selection and care of stock; but the social structure of pastoral communities affords part of the explanation. They did not produce men who kept accounts or had the flair for publicly advertising their achievements. Samuel Hartlib complained in 1651 that "we advance not the best species," but it is not clear which farmers he had in mind; and he did single out for measured praise the pasture farmers of Lancashire and some other northern countries, who "are a little careful in these particulars."[2] What is clear is that the pastoral regions, as the main breeding centres for stock, had been responsible for developing a remarkable number of different breeds of cattle, sheep, and horses, which were adapted to suit different environments. If a man changed the environment by improving his land, then he could change the breed of his animals, as farmers of enclosed pastures in the sixteenth century evidently changed the breeds of sheep which they kept.

If we look in vain for spectacular innovations and the willingness to invest capital such as that which possessed corn growers like Henry Best, Jethro Tull, and others, this does not mean that the populations of pastoral areas were living in a derelict and miserable backwater, outside the main stream of enterprise. Traditionally, pastoral areas were the abode of small family farmers and their way of life suited their environment. The common pastures were a community asset available to all, and many farming systems, like dairying and pig keeping, required small capital. But another key to the success of this way of life, which enabled men to weather successfully the seventeenth-century crisis, was the many additional opportunities for earning a living. Some simply involved ex-

---

[1] Royal Society, Georgical Enquiries, Classified Papers, x (3), *passim*. These reports are summarized in R. V. Lennard, 'English Agriculture under Charles II . . .', *Econ. Hist. Rev.*, IV, 1932–4, pp. 23–45; Blith, 1652, *op. cit.*, p. 38, my italics.

[2] Samuel Hartlib, *His Legacie*, 1651, p. 96. These remarks were made with particular reference to dairy cattle.

ploiting the diversity of natural resources: fishing, fowling, cutting reeds for thatching and for fuel in the fens; timber felling and the manufacture of wood-ware in the forests. Mining offered work in some areas; in others there were domestic industries such as potting, nail making, metal working, lace making, stocking knitting, and the weaving of woollen, linen, and hempen cloth. In some districts the growth of flax and hemp weaving was facilitated by larger imports of the raw material from the Baltic which was more widely distributed inland as rivers were improved. Nidderdale in West Yorkshire and parts of Derbyshire, for example, enjoyed an easy link with the port of Hull.[1] In other counties the domestic weaving of hemp and flax went hand in hand with an increase in the cultivation of these crops. Some of the propaganda in favour of growing them was directed at counties lacking adequate domestic industries, such as Leicestershire, Northamptonshire, and Oxfordshire.[2] In fact, however, it was in pastoral areas where handicraft industries were already well established that it spread most successfully, particularly in the West Midlands, in parts of Herefordshire, Worcestershire, Warwickshire, Nottinghamshire, Derbyshire, and Staffordshire.[3] Staffordshire, indeed, was described by Robert Sharrock as exemplary in its system of growing these two crops; and it seems legitimate to argue from the increasing references in this county to tithes of hemp and flax in the later seventeenth and early eighteenth centuries that production was expanding.[4] Other pastoral areas which grew flax and hemp were the marsh-lands of Thames-side in Essex and Kent, the fens of eastern England and the Somerset Level, parts of Dorset, the Weald of Kent around Maidstone, which was the renowned thread-making centre of the kingdom, and the forests of Northamptonshire. When Sir Richard Weston came back from the Nether-lands urging flax growing, he recommended experiments in St Leonards Forest in Sussex.[5] Like the industrial crops which flourished in arable regions, hemp and flax were universally regarded as profitable ventures: some hemp and flax ground was rented for £3 an acre, labour costs added another £2 or £3, but the crop was worth £10–12. Thus profits were in the region of £5–6 an acre.[6]

In pastoral regions farming combined with industrial employment was almost common form. The combination was well integrated into a life focused on the

[1] Bernard Jennings, ed., *A History of Nidderdale*, 1967, pp. 171–2, 176.

[2] P. E. Dove, *Account of Andrew Yarranton, the Founder of English Political Economy*, 1854, p. 44.

[3] Blith, 1652, *op. cit.*, p. 254.

[4] Robert Sharrock, *An Improvement to the Art of Gardening*, 1694, pp. 43–4. The evidence for larger crops of hemp and flax comes from the glebe terriers of Staffordshire which refer with in-creasing frequency, 1698–1735, to tithes of hemp and flax in the parishes of the county. I wish to thank Mr B. B. Evans for assembling this evidence for me and allowing me to use it here.

[5] Blith, 1652, *op. cit.*, pp. 251, 254; Michael Williams, 'The Draining and Reclamation of Meare Pool, Somerset', Thirteenth Annual Report, Somerset River Board, 1962–3, Bridgwater, 1963, p. 1; Thirsk, A.H.E.W. IV, p. 13; Richard Weston, *Discourse of Husbandry used in Brabant and Flanders*, 2nd edn, ed. Samuel Hartlib, 1652, p. 18.

[6] Hartlib, *His Legacie*, pp. 40–1; Houghton, ed. Bradley, *op. cit.*, II, p. 389.

family as the wage-earning group. The nailer's forge and the pottery were sheds next door to the farmhouse, while the weaving loom might be in the parlour or chamber or in a separate weaving shed.[1] A rare glimpse of the detailed pro-gramme of daily life is offered in the diary of a farmer-weaver in 1782–3 who worked out of doors one day till three o'clock and then wove two yards of cloth before sunset. On wet days he might weave eight and a half to nine yards. One Christmas eve he wove two yards before 11 a.m. and spent the rest of the day doing winter jobs around the house and midden. In addition, he had occasional work on other people's farms, hauling timber, preparing a calf stall, fetching and carrying with his own horse and cart, and picking cherries.[2] The variety of work compensated for the absence of some material comforts. Indeed, the use of the term 'by-employments' for the industrial occupations of pasture farmers may convey a false impression. They were not accidental or subsidiary, secon-dary, or a miserable makeshift. They were an integral part of the pastoral way of life. They remain so in many pastoral regions of England, though the num-bers of people so occupied form such a small proportion of the total population that they are not seriously considered.[3] But in countries where peasant-workers still represent a much larger slice of the population, this way of life is recognized and studied as a permanent social and economic phenomenon with merits of its own. In Poland, for example, it is agreed that the family budget of the peasant-worker at the present time is decidedly larger than that of the farmer of a medium-sized holding with only his land to support him.[4] In England today it is reasonable to regard the peasant-worker as a negligible element in rural society, but not so in the seventeenth century. Indeed, we may guess that such farmers must have comprised somewhere near half the farming population of the kingdom. The economy and fortunes of this group deserve more attention than has yet been given to them for theirs is a different story with a different chronology from that of the small owner-occupier and small tenant in arable regions.

It is too early to make dogmatic generalized statements about the economic fortunes of traditional pasture-farming areas in the seventeenth century or about the size of their populations. But there are suggestive clues to some economic trends. Multiple sources of income attracted immigrants to the pastoral areas. Numerous contemporaries remarked (usually with disapproval)

[1] Cf. Marie B. Rowlands, 'Industry and Social Change in Staffordshire, 1660–1760', *Trans. Lichfield & S. Staffs. Arch. & Hist. Soc.*, IX, 1967–8, p. 39.

[2] Quoted by Edward Thompson in 'Time, Work-Discipline, and Industrial Capitalism', *Past and Present*, 38, pp. 71–2.

[3] They represented 11·2 per cent of the total number of occupiers of land in England and Wales in the National Farm Survey of 1941–3.

[4] Władisław Adamski, 'Investigations on Off-Farm Income in Poland', summary of a paper read to a seminar at Birmingham University on Peasant Farming in Europe, March 1968.

on this migration, particularly into the forests and fens of the Midland, south-ern, and eastern counties. Against this background the Act of Settlement in 1662 takes on a special significance. Its preamble refers to the movement of people from parish to parish "to settle themselves where there is the best stock, the largest commons or wastes to build cottages, and the most woods for them to burn and destroy." Roger Coke, writing eight years after the passing of this Act, believed it to be without effect: squatters on the waste were increasing daily.[1]

In some places we can measure a substantial growth of population at least until the Act of Settlement. In others it continued into the early eighteenth century. In part of the Lincolnshire fenland, for example, numbers almost doubled between 1563 and 1723, whereas in arable parts of the same county the population at these two dates was more or less the same. Warwickshire figures of average populations in arable and forest areas do not illustrate growth rates but they do demonstrate the larger populations living in the forests: the average size of communities in old enclosed arable parishes in 1663 was 46 households, in unenclosed arable parishes 54 households, and in pastoral (Arden) parishes 120 households.[2]

Professor Everitt's comparison of labourers with less than an acre of land in the period 1500–1640 shows a considerably higher proportion in fielden parishes (72 per cent) than in fell parishes (65 per cent) or forest parishes (44 per cent), and of course, in fell and forest regions the common rights that went with land were much more valuable.[3] Among the more substantial pea-sants an increase, rather than a decrease, took place in the number of land-holders in the course of the seventeenth century. In the forest of Pendle, Lancashire, for example, the number of medium and small copyholders in-creased markedly. In four stock-rearing communities in Pendle the 55 copy-holders in 1608 more than doubled to 129 in 1662.[4] In Nidderdale, Yorkshire, a noticeable decline in the average size of farms had taken place by the late seventeenth century.[5] In Rossendale, Lancashire, 72 copyholders in 1507 had increased to 200 by 1608 and to 314 by 1662. The increase was partly brought about by the enclosure of waste land, partly by the subdivision of existing farms. Land was being distributed among more and more people (engrossing was practically unknown), and the process was not reversed in Rossendale even in the eighteenth and nineteenth centuries. After the introduction of cotton

[1] Thirsk, A.H.E.W. IV, pp. 409–12; Coke, *op. cit.*, p. 16.

[2] Thirsk, *English Peasant Farming*, pp. 141, 168–70; J. M. Martin, 'The Parliamentary Enclosure Movement and Rural Society in Warwickshire', A.H.R., xv, i, p. 20.

[3] Thirsk, A.H.E.W. IV, pp. 400–6.

[4] Mary Brigg, 'The Forest of Pendle in the Seventeenth Century', *Trans. Lancs. and Cheshire Hist. Soc.*, CXIII, 1961, p. 72.

[5] Jennings, ed., *op. cit.*, pp. 147, 171–2.

manufacture, holdings became more, and not less, minutely subdivided. A rough calculation suggests that the proportion of holdings of less than fifteen acres was two-fifths in the seventeenth and two-thirds in the nineteenth century.[1]

In other pastoral areas comparisons over time are not possible, but it is clear that at the time of the Parliamentary enclosures many pastoral parishes still had a remarkable number of small proprietors. At Foleshill in Arden, Warwickshire, in 1775 794 acres were divided between 107 different proprietors. In the fenland of Holland, Lincolnshire, Gosberton had 160 landowners in 1798, Quadring over 150. Small peasants were not noticeably losing their hold on the land, and in some places they were strengthening it in the sense that more people were acquiring a small stake in the soil.[2]

Most writers in the second half of the seventeenth century explicitly or implicitly held the belief that pasture farming was more profitable than corn growing. Charles Davenant, using Gregory King's figures on land use and yields, offered the opinion in 1699 that "it seems more to the national interest of England to employ its land to the breeding and feeding of cattle than to the produce of corn."[3] This general supposition invites belief because it accords with the general trend in agriculture throughout western Europe between 1650 and 1750.[4]

In England pasture farmers enjoyed an assured and relatively stable market for their produce, and solved the problem created by the dwindling size of their holdings by undertaking more industrial employment. These developments caused some writers to press the novel argument that pasture farming supported a larger population than corn. Reckoning in the work created by crops like wool, hemp, and flax, it was plausible. A Gloucestershire agriculturist who had promoted hemp and flax growing argued the case from his own practical experience. He calculated that forty acres of flax would employ more than 800 people for a year, and, even allowing a wage bill of 8d. a day for 300 men, 6d. a day for 300 women, and 3d. a day for 200 young people, it would still yield more profit to the sower than 160 acres of corn or grass.[5] Sir Richard Weston claimed that one acre of flax was worth four to five acres of corn; and

[1] G. H. Tupling, *The Economic History of Rossendale*, Chetham Soc., n.s., 86, 1927, pp. 76, 235, 95, 227–9.
[2] J. M. Martin, 'Warwickshire and the Parliamentary Enclosure Movement', Birmingham University Ph.D. thesis, 1965, pp. 80–1; David Grigg, *The Agricultural Revolution in South Lincolnshire*, 1966, p. 84. Cf. the saying that the Isle of Axholme had so many freeholders that whoever got the Isle could get the county.—Francis Hill, *Georgian Lincoln*, p. 30.
[3] Charles Davenant, *An Essay upon the Probable Methods of Making a People Gainers in the Balance of Trade*, 1699, pp. 88–9.
[4] B. H. Slicher van Bath, *The Agrarian History of Western Europe, A.D. 500–1850*, 1963, pp. 206–17.
[5] P.R.O., SP 14/180, no. 79.

to prove that pastoral regions generally provided more work than corn lands he turned to the examples of Normandy, Picardy, and Lombardy in France, Holland, Friesland, Zeeland, and Flanders—all pastoral regions which, he claimed, were the most populous places in Europe. Dairy farms occupying 100 acres of land employed many more hands than 100 acres of the best corn land; even sheep keeping, while it depopulated the countryside, nevertheless kept a great many people in working the wool into cloth.[1] John Houghton in 1692 argued along the same lines. Did not the wool and skins produced by an acre of pasture create greater employment than tillage? He had made some calculations and promised some time to print them.[2]

While the evidence is circumstantial and fragmentary it seems reasonable to suggest that the pasture-farming regions of the kingdom in the seventeenth century presented a picture of greater economic prosperity for larger numbers of people than the arable regions. The rebuilding of peasant houses in the north and west which took place generally after the Civil War period may perhaps be deemed a further reflection of this prosperity.[3]

The merits of the dual economy of pastoral regions were frequently misunderstood. Defoe gives us one of the few portraits of the farmer-leadminer's life in the Derbyshire Peak. The sight of a family living in a cave with little ready cash filled him with horror. The wife was inordinately grateful when he and his friends tipped the loose change from their purses into her hand. And yet he had to admit that the cave was clean though simple; the children were very bonny, the wife was comely. A close of corn at the door was ready to be harvested. A cow, thin though it was, grazed at hand and pigs rooted about nearby. Bacon hung in the roof. The husband worked in the mines, and when the wife was free, she washed ore.[4] This was clearly a poor family by the standards of pasture-farming communities generally, but it was not the abject hopeless poverty of landless, and frequently workless, labourers who formed a growing proportion (at least a third and more) of the population of arable villages in the lowlands.

The most sympathetic and understanding observer of this economy in the later seventeenth century, however, was the Puritan divine, Richard Baxter. Indeed, he is an explicit exponent of the more general argument advanced in the paper. In 1691 he wrote his last treatise, *The Poor Husbandman's Advocate to Rich Racking Landlords*. Baxter came from Kidderminster in Worcestershire, a thickly populated region of peasant workers of every kind, metal workers, nailers, potters, miners, leather workers, and glass workers. He had also lived in

---

[1] Hartlib, *His Legacie*, pp. 55–6. Hartlib listed the commodities got from cattle (meaning cattle and sheep) as cloth, stuffs, stockings, butter, cheese, hides, shoes, and tallow.

[2] Houghton, ed. Bradley, *op. cit.*, I, p. 49.

[3] M. W. Barley, *The English Farmhouse and Cottage*, 1961, pp. 227, 230, 236, 244.

[4] D. Defoe, *A Tour through England and Wales*, Everyman edn, II, pp. 161–3.

and around London, in Westminster, and in Acton, Middlesex. His plea to landlords to show generosity and mercy to husbandmen was not a petition on behalf of all husbandmen, but only on behalf of what he called the racked poor; *not*, he observed, the market gardeners of the Home Counties who, though they paid double rent for their grounds, had a treble opportunity to improve them. (These are some of our arable farmers producing labour demanding crops.) "Nor do I speak of those tenants that have some small tenement of £5 or £10 per annum and have besides a trade which doth maintain them." He instanced here weavers, butchers, tailors, joiners, and carpenters. Elsewhere he spoke of the comparative security of life of the nailers, spurriers, swordsmiths, scythe-smiths, and sword makers around Dudley, Stourbridge, Birmingham, Walsall, Wednesbury, and Wolverhampton. In short, his was an impassioned plea not for peasant-workers in pasture-farming regions, or for arable farmers grow-ing special cash crops, but for the poor husbandmen in the traditional corn-growing districts, whence the small landowners were fast disappearing, and whence, in his view, small tenants were also being driven by rack-renting land-lords.[1]

One of the questions that follows from this analysis of social and economic trends in the seventeenth-century countryside is how and why the dual econo-mies in pastoral regions stimulated technical innovation in industry. It is plainly anomalous to expect agricultural innovations of an expensive kind from these regions. The pressure upon industry seems to derive from the very suc-cess of the dual economy. As the market for industrial goods expanded, it met labour shortages which peasant workers could not, or would not, satisfy, and which are reflected in the rapid rise in textile wages in the first half of the eight-eenth century.[2] For peasant workers to turn wholly to industry meant sur-rendering their hold on the land and surrendering, moreover, a life of varied labour as well as independence.[3] The advantage to the national economy of factory-based industries may seem clear enough if we take a sternly economic view excluding other considerations, but it was purchased at the price of a traditional, and in many respects congenial, life centred upon a smallholding of land, with its industrial annexe. Throughout the seventeenth century, at least,

[1] F. J. Powicke, ed., *The Reverend Richard Baxter's Last Treatise*, John Rylands Library Publica-tion, 1926, pp. 25–8.

[2] Professor Crouzet suggests in a recent essay that one of the two most powerful stimuli to techni-cal innovation was the shortage of labour in the handicraft industries of S. Lancs., Yorks., the Midlands, and in the metal-working industries of the Black Country.—F. Crouzet, 'Angleterre et France au XVIIIe siècle. Essai d'analyse comparée de deux croissances économiques', *Annales E.S.C.*, 21e année, no. 2, 1966, pp. 286–7. See also E. W. Gilboy, *Wages in Eighteenth-Century England*, 1934, pp. 191 *et seq.*

[3] This is the view of Gilboy, *op. cit.*, p. 143, and is supported by other authorities there cited. See also Crouzet, *op. cit.*, p. 288; N. J. Smelser, *Social Change in the Industrial Revolution*, 1959, p. 77.

the economics of smallholdings in pastoral regions were not such as to drive the peasant worker from the land.

Phyllis Deane has recently described in general terms the causes of the industrial and agricultural revolution. She concluded with certain misgivings about generalizations on a national scale. "The national economy is not always the most convenient unit of economic analysis. The effect of regional variations in economic conditions is that statistics relating to a particular area may give no indication of the comparable movements for the nation as a whole, and that the national aggregates may obscure the trends for regions in which the significant changes are taking place. An attempt to assess the quality and rate of economic change at the national level may not lead to meaningful results whether we are looking for the significant continuities or for the significant discontinuities of history."[1] These reflections justify a first attempt at illuminating "the trends for regions in which the significant changes are taking place." It carries the story only to the end of the seventeenth century. To disentangle regional trends from national aggregates, more detailed local studies are needed which will trace developments in the seventeenth century more precisely and, more important, in the early eighteenth century when a further shift of emphasis took place in the economies of both pastoral and arable regions and the ground was finally prepared for two separate revolutions after 1750.

[1] Phyllis Deane, *The First Industrial Revolution*, 1965, pp. 17–18.

Nonconformity in Country Parishes

By ALAN EVERITT

THE great age of Dissent in England lasted from the Restoration till the First World War. Since then Nonconformity has largely ceased to be the aggressive force in English life that it once was. The historian should be wary of saying that it can never become so again, for society rarely develops along regular lines, but proceeds by unpredictable fits and starts. It is not often possible to be absolutely certain that a human movement has reached the ultimate end of its allotted span of life. The power in recent years of the more extreme sects to attract numerous adherents to themselves, almost alone among Christian bodies outside the Catholic church, is one of the stranger vagaries of the times. Nevertheless, the more traditional dissenting denominations may be said to have come to the end of a certain cycle or phase in their history by the early years of the twentieth century.

Many people might be inclined to date the decline of Nonconformity rather earlier, for example from the days of Darwin's *Origin of Species*. But in fact the major dissenting bodies, despite important ups and downs in their fortunes, generally continued to expand till long after Charles Darwin. In rural areas it is very common indeed to find chapels founded, rebuilt, or extended up to the last decades of Queen Victoria's reign. A lonely Primitive Methodist chapel on the windswept Pennines above Middleton-in-Teesdale, for example, originally built in 1842, was extended and refronted in 1888. The Wesleyan chapel at Naseby in Northamptonshire, first erected in 1825, was enlarged and 'restored' in 1871, while a new Sunday School, nearly as large as the chapel itself, was added as late as 1903.[1] These two examples may be taken as typical of hundreds of others in country districts all over England.

The history of Dissent is one that should therefore be of some interest to the student of local agrarian society. The predilection of large and growing sections of the English population for a locally autonomous form of religion, unfettered by archbishops, popes, or presbyteries, is indeed one of the more striking peculiarities—one might almost say perversities—of English provincial society from the days of Charles I to those of Edward VII. It is one of the many signs that local attachments, far from declining with the growth of national consciousness, were in many ways becoming stronger: a fact which will cause no surprise to an observant reader of novelists like George Eliot and Mrs Oliphant. True, by no means all the traditional English sects placed equal emphasis on the autonomy of the local chapel. Compared with the Congregationalists the

[1] This information is from datestones on the buildings.

Wesleyans, for instance, have always been a highly organized body. Nevertheless the life of every Dissenting sect was centred in the local chapel. Its enthusiasm was the enthusiasm of a nexus of local dynasties, often closely inbred through generations of intermarriage. And without too greatly stretching the evidence, it may be said that the waning of Dissent began with the growth of centralization—in government, in provincial society, and in the organization of Nonconformity itself—during the last sixty or seventy years.

The importance of Dissent in provincial life has, of course, long been recognized, and has given rise to a very considerable literature of a kind. It must be confessed, however, that, faced with the sagging shelves of chapel histories and Dissenting hagiographies, even the most intrepid historian is apt to wilt. Is it really possible to make useful generalizations out of this edifying literature, or to harness its not inconsiderable scholarship to the interests of a more secular age? The work of scholars like Dr G. F. Nuttall has shown that it certainly is. Recently a whole crop of university theses and many local studies have been devoted to various aspects of Nonconformity, both local and national.[1] And in *Devonshire Studies* Professor H. P. R. Finberg himself contributed a witty and masterly study of the development of Nonconformity in the south-west.[2] The present paper makes no attempt to synthesize recent work or to explore the deeper spiritual problems of Dissenting history. It sets out with the limited aim of answering a single elementary question: in what types of rural community did Dissent tend to find a foothold and flourish? Was there any relationship between the differing species of local society and the proliferation of Dissent in certain well-defined areas, or its relative absence in others?

(i) *Nonconformity in 1851*

The remarkable regional diversity in the pattern of Nonconformity in England was first clearly shown to the world by the Census of 1851.[3] This census was the first to record religious allegiance, and because of the wrangles and disputes the results gave rise to, the exercise was never repeated. Although the present paper deals chiefly with the period before 1851, a preliminary glance at the census figures is instructive. These recorded both the numbers of

---

[1] Mr H. G. Tibbutt, for example, has published a valuable series of studies in Bedfordshire Nonconformity, each devoted to the history of a local Congregational or Baptist church.

[2] W. G. Hoskins and H. P. R. Finberg, *Devonshire Studies*, 1952, 'A Chapter of Religious History'. This study relates chiefly to the seventeenth and eighteenth centuries.

[3] For a discussion of the significance, reliability, and limitations of the 1851 census record see Professor K. S. Inglis's important article, 'Patterns of Religious Worship in 1851', *Jnl Eccles. Hist.*, XI, 1960, pp. 74–86. The value of information on religious allegiance was much disputed at the time, but Professor Inglis advances a cogent and balanced case that on the whole it was conscientiously compiled and within its limits substantially reliable. For this paper I have relied on the summaries and abstracts of the census given under each county and parish entry in J. M. Wilson, *The Imperial Gazetteer of England and Wales*, 6 vols., 1870 (hereafter cited as *Imp. Gaz.*).

attendants at services on census Sunday, and the number of 'sittings' available
in churches and chapels. For a variety of reasons, such as illness and bad
weather, attendance at church on census Sunday was unusually low, so that
attendance figures cannot be regarded as very reliable for a comparative guide
to the strength of different denominations. The figures recording the number
of 'sittings' in church and chapel are also open to obvious statistical objections;
but they provide at least some kind of rough indication of denominational
strength. What do they tell us?

Judged by the number of 'sittings' recorded in 1851, 44 per cent of the
English population as a whole at this time were Dissenters, and 56 per cent
Anglicans.[1] The census figures are probably in some areas misleading, particularly in the eastern counties where there were many large parish churches
serving small and dwindling populations. In Norfolk and Suffolk particularly
the number of 'sittings' probably overestimates the strength of Anglicanism by
a considerable margin. It is quite possible that Dissenters may have formed
half, or nearly half, the population in these two counties. Nevertheless, when
all allowance is made, the census figures are of great interest and significance.

By far their most remarkable feature is the astonishing increase they indicate
in Nonconformist numbers since the later seventeenth century. Though at the
time of the Compton Census (1676) some towns had Dissenting congregations
with several hundreds of adherents, the number of these was probably exaggerated by contemporary observers, of Nonconformist leanings, like Defoe and
Celia Fiennes. The typical congregation rarely numbered more than fifty at
this time, and it is doubtful if in any county Nonconformists comprised much
more than 10 per cent of the population. Probably in many counties and most
country districts they were far fewer than this, as we shall see below in considering their distribution in Kent. The great period of expansion came, of
course, with the Evangelical Movement of the later eighteenth and early nineteenth centuries.

The next feature about the 1851 Census figures is the striking regional
differences they indicate in the pattern of Dissent. At a first glance, the analysis
of regional allegiance in TABLE I seems to suggest two principal and not un-
familiar tendencies in this pattern. In the first place Nonconformity appears to
have been more powerful in the north than the south. In the whole of the north-
east, from Derbyshire and Nottinghamshire up to the Scottish border, Dissenters apparently comprised more than half the church-going population, and
in Durham and Northumberland as much as 60 per cent of it. In the counties
south of the Thames, by contrast, they generally formed little more than one-
third of the population. Secondly, Dissenters often appear to have been more
strongly represented in 'industrial' than in 'agricultural' counties. The ten

[1] See TABLE I, 'General Religious Allegiance in 1851'.

TABLE I

GENERAL RELIGIOUS ALLEGIANCE IN 1851

	Total Church and Chapel Sittings	Anglicans		Dissenters		
		Sittings	%	Sittings	%	
1. Herefordshire	68,675	49,312	72	19,363	28	41
2. Rutland	17,299	12,131	70	5,168	30	40
3. Oxfordshire	109,301	74,369	68	34,932	32	39
4. Sussex	160,011	108,076	67	51,935	33	38
5. Surrey	219,094	143,783	66	75,311	34	37
6. Westmorland*	37,239	24,411	66	12,828	34	36
7. Dorset	120,082	77,886	65	42,196	35	35
8. Kent	299,296	194,443	65	104,853	35	34
9. Hampshire	212,161	135,720	64	76,441	36	33
10. Shropshire	143,663	92,435	64	51,228	36	32
11. Suffolk†	224,229	141,417	63	82,812	37	31
12. Middlesex	552,231	344,487	62	207,744	38	30
13. Berkshire	92,737	56,679	61	36,058	39	29
14. Essex	216,113	132,041	61	84,072	39	28
15. Somerset	287,353	174,723	61	112,630	39	27
16. Warwickshire	201,831	123,624	61	78,207	39	26
17. Worcestershire	138,668	85,155	61	53,513	39	25
18. Norfolk†	283,420	168,722	60	114,698	40	24
19. Hertfordshire	93,230	55,193	59	38,037	41	23
20. Devon	332,934	191,710	58	141,224	42	22
21. Staffordshire	279,516	161,217	58	118,299	42	21
22. Buckinghamshire	113,209	64,231	57	48,978	43	20
23. Cumberland	99,783	56,803	57	42,980	43	19
24. Gloucestershire	276,606	156,651	57	119,955	43	18
25. Northamptonshire	150,472	84,816	56	65,656	44	17
26. Wiltshire	158,694	87,843	55	70,851	45	16
27. Lancashire	708,217	383,466	54	324,751	46	15
28. Cheshire	229,711	121,882	53	107,829	47	14
29. Leicestershire	156,678	82,964	53	73,714	47	13
30. Huntingdonshire	45,014	23,568	52	21,446	48	12
31. Cambridgeshire	104,196	52,917	51	51,279	49	11
32. Lincolnshire	279,247	142,844	51	136,403	49	10
33. North Riding	161,062	79,740	50	81,322	50	9
34. Bedfordshire	87,814	42,557	48	45,257	52	8
35. Derbyshire	182,581	87,829	48	94,752	52	7
36. Nottinghamshire	150,024	70,928	47	79,096	53	6
37. East Riding	140,793	64,135	46	76,658	54	5
38. West Riding	665,428	276,910	42	388,518	58	4
39. Co. Durham	167,285	66,319	40	100,966	60	3
40. Northumberland	131,646	52,405	40	79,241	60	2
41. Cornwall	261,684	95,155	36	166,529	64	1
Total	8,359,227	4,641,497	56	3,717,730	44	

* The number of sittings in the four Baptist chapels in the county was not reported. These have been estimated at 1,000.

† The figures for Anglican sittings in these counties are probably affected by the exceptional size and number of ancient parish churches.

counties with the highest percentage of Anglicans—about two-thirds or more of the population—were all predominantly agrarian, including Herefordshire, Rutland, Oxfordshire, Shropshire, Westmorland, Dorset, Sussex, and Kent. In counties with a good deal of industry, by contrast, such as Yorkshire, Derbyshire, Nottinghamshire, and Durham, they formed less than half the population.

These overall tendencies certainly cannot be ignored. They were not entirely an optical illusion. But the more closely they are examined, the more unreliable they appear as generalizations. To some extent the disparities between different counties are merely due to the fact that Anglican churches tended, for reasons of history and settlement, to be more numerous in the south than the far north. West of the Pennines, moreover, in contrast with the east, Dissenters nowhere formed as much as half the population, and in Westmorland the proportion was exceptionally small (34 per cent). In Staffordshire and Lancashire, two of the most industrialized counties in England, the Nonconformist population was markedly lower (42 per cent and 46 per cent) than in agrarian counties like Huntingdonshire, Cambridgeshire, and Bedfordshire (48 to 52 per cent).[1] In the predominantly agricultural North and East Ridings the proportion of Dissenters, though lower than in the West Riding, was still remarkably high by national standards—much higher than in industrial Staffordshire—amounting to more than half the local population. Finally, we must not forget that absolute numbers may be as significant as percentages in assessing the strength of Dissent. And these show that of the thirteen counties with more than 100,000 chapel-sittings in 1851, eight were in the south and only five in the north, whilst four were predominantly industrial and seven or eight at that date predominantly agrarian: Kent, Somerset, Norfolk, Devon, Gloucestershire, Lincolnshire, Cheshire, and Cornwall.

The truth is that there was no simple equation between agricultural society and Anglicanism, or industrial parishes and Dissent. Nor was there any inherent tendency to Nonconformity in the north-country character as opposed to that of the southerner. There were areas of counties like Sussex and Suffolk where Dissent was nearly as strong as in a Nottinghamshire mining village or a West Riding clothing town. Ultimately, what is essential, if we are to explain the pattern of rural Nonconformity in England, is not large-scale generali-

---

[1] It might be thought that the figures for Lancashire would be affected by the size of the Roman Catholic population. In fact, though far more numerous in Lancashire than elsewhere, Catholics were still a relatively small minority. Judged by the number of church-sittings there were 383,466 Anglicans in the county, 324,751 Nonconformists, and only 55,610 Roman Catholics. The latter were outnumbered by both Congregationalists (80,072 sittings) and Wesleyan Methodists (107,983 sittings). Throughout this paper I have excluded Catholics from figures of 'Dissenters'; their case is obviously a special one. In most counties they apparently comprised only 1 or 2 per cent of the population in 1851, though 'sittings' are probably an unreliable indicator of Catholic numbers.

zation but a microscopic examination of the society of these places: of each county's economy as a whole, of the various rural economies within it, of the social structure of each local community in the county, and of the Dissenting sects and chapels within that community.

The 1851 Census also indicates many other regional differences between the various religious persuasions of England. A comparative study of religious allegiance in the four counties of Lincolnshire, Leicestershire, Northampton-shire, and Kent, for example, raises a number of intriguing speculations.[1] Why was it, to begin with, that (judged by the number of sittings) almost 40 per cent of the whole church-going population of Lincolnshire were Methodists, in comparison with only 21 per cent in Leicestershire, and no more than 14 or 15 per cent in Kent and Northamptonshire? Why was it that the old Dissenting bodies of Baptists and Independents formed a much larger proportion of the population of Northamptonshire than in any of the other three counties, three times as large, in fact, as in Lincolnshire? (There were few counties indeed where the Old Dissent was so deeply entrenched as in Northamptonshire.) Why was it that a West Country sect like the Bible Christians, intensely emo-tional and proletarian in character, found no adherents at all in three of these four counties, but more than 3,000 in far-away Kent? Why was it indeed that the more colourful or unusual sects—Latter Day Saints, Huntingtonians, Catholic and Apostolic Church, Lady Huntingdon's Connexion, and a whole crop of nameless 'isolated congregations'—generally found far more followers in Kent than in the other three counties?[2] And why were there more than 20,000 Particular Baptists in both Kent and Northamptonshire, whereas there were only 7,000 in Leicestershire and less than 5,000 in Lincolnshire?

Such seemingly anomalous facts, however trivial they may appear to a secular age like our own, are certainly in some way related to significant differ-ences of local society as well as to more purely personal and spiritual causes. They are not wholly to be explained by different forms of local society. So far as Lincolnshire is concerned, no doubt, the strength of Methodism was due in part to the personal influence of John Wesley; for this was his native county. Yet if the divine fire was essentially personal and unique in its impetus, the way in which it spread was largely dictated by peculiarities of local economy, forms of family connection, and lines of social class. One does not need any profound knowledge of history, or any extensive acquaintance with chapel architecture, to recognize the marked social distinctions between, say, the Primitive Methodists, the Wesleyan Methodists, and the Countess of Hun-tingdon's Connexion, whatever religious principles may have originated their

---

[1] See TABLE II, 'Religious Allegiance in Four Counties in 1851', on p. 184.

[2] Dissenters outside the three traditional groups (Congregationalists, Baptists, Methodists) were three times as numerous in Kent as in the other counties.

TABLE II

RELIGIOUS ALLEGIANCE IN FOUR COUNTIES IN 1851

	Acreage	Population in 1861	Parishes	Anglicans	Independents	Baptists	Wesleyan Methodists	Primitive Methodists	Other Methodists	Other Dissenters*	All Dissenters
Kent	1,013,838	733,887	425	C 479 / S 194,443 / 65%	86 / 27,091 / 9%	107 / 25,668 / 8%	184 / 33,759 / 11%	26 / 2,877	45 / 7,285	52 / 8,173 / 3%	500 / 104,853 / 35%
							255(C); 43,921(S) 15%				
Leicestershire	514,164	237,412	214	C 289 / S 82,964 / 53%	41 / 11,988 / 8%	85 / 24,001 / 15%	129 / 21,739 / 14%	53 / 7,930	20 / 3,523	26 / 4,533 / 3%	354 / 73,714 / 47%
							202(C); 33,192(S) 21%				
Lincolnshire	1,775,457	412,246	621	C 657 / S 142,844 / 51%	38 / 11,508 / 4%	62 / 13,620 / 5%	462 / 78,862 / 28%	221 / 25,164	21 / 4,517	27 / 2,732 / 1%	831 / 136,403 / 49%
							704(C); 108,543(S) 39%				
Northamptonshire	630,358	231,079	303	C 292 / S 84,816 / 56%	56 / 17,444 / 12%	87 / 23,200 / 16%	97 / 18,620 / 12%	16 / 1,759	9 / 992	29 / 3,641 / 2%	294 / 65,656 / 44%
							122(C); 21,371(S) 14%				

C = churches or chapels   S = number of sittings   * Excluding Roman Catholics and Jews

divisions. More intensive study of differences like these would undoubtedly point up many social peculiarities in each region and sect. In the limited space of this article only a few of these differences can be singled out for study, though I hope to discuss others in more detail in a subsequent paper.[1]

(ii) *Nonconformity in the Countryside*

Nonconformity of the older stratum is often supposed to be a predominantly urban phenomenon, but this supposition is not borne out by the facts. In the seventeenth and early eighteenth centuries a great deal of it, almost certainly the bulk of it, was in fact based in the countryside.[2] In many towns, it is true, such as Canterbury and Northampton, Dissent was a powerful force, often much more forceful and vociferous than the mere numbers of its adherents might lead us to expect. It was also, of course, very powerful in London. But if one analyses sources like the subscribers' lists of celebrated Dissenting works in the early eighteenth century, one is likely to find that the truly urban sub-scribers were considerably outnumbered by those from purely agricultural areas and small market-centres. Of the 1,100 subscribers to the first volume of Philip Doddridge's *magnum opus*, *The Family Expositor* (1739), only 2 per cent came from London (where it was published) and 35 per cent from the larger provincial towns like Coventry, Liverpool, Hull, Oxford, Shrewsbury, and Bristol. By contrast 34 per cent came from very small rural market centres like Olney, Oundle, and Cullompton, and nearly 30 per cent from wholly agrarian parishes. Many of the 'urban' subscriptions, moreover, probably represented country people, since they came from booksellers in market towns, whose customers doubtless included villagers as well as townsmen. Probably at least two-thirds of the subscribers, therefore, were really of rural or semi-rural origin.

The country basis of much of the Old Dissent may be further illustrated from the numbers of Nonconformists recorded under each parish in the Compton Census of 1676. These figures cannot be regarded as exact; in some parishes it is clear that they were largely based upon guesswork. But they are the earliest figures of any kind that we have, and broadly speaking they are con-firmed by other types of evidence. For Kent the figures have been edited by

[1] This paper will be based chiefly on a more detailed examination of the 1851 Census, related to forms of local society.

[2] An obvious factor in this distribution is the impact of the Clarendon Code. This is a complex subject which cannot be discussed in detail here. Two points may be made, however. First, the strict-ness of the ban on Nonconformity in incorporated towns varied a good deal with the type of Dissent, the current political situation, and the attitude of the local justices. That many groups, most of the time, in most boroughs continued to exist is undoubted. When licences were taken out under the Declaration of Indulgence, the largest numbers were granted to Dissenting groups in incorporated boroughs. Secondly, it is unlikely that the influence of the Clarendon Code still had any marked effect on local Nonconformity in these respects by George I's reign.

Mr C. W. Chalklin, and the following calculations are based upon his text.[1]

Of the total of 7,037 Dissenters recorded in the county of Kent in 1676, 51 per cent came from wholly rural parishes and 49 per cent from the towns. These gross figures need some care, however, in interpretation. Included among the urban 'nonconformists' in Kent were also the members of foreign congregations (principally French-speaking) in Canterbury, Sandwich, Maidstone, and Dover. The numbers of these groups are not given separately in the census; but in the 1640's they probably exceeded 1,500.[2] Probably, therefore, we must exclude a good third of the 3,464 urban 'nonconformists' in Kent if we are to arrive at a true figure for the native, indigenous Dissenters. This leaves a total of 5,882 local Nonconformists in the county as a whole, and of these 61 per cent lived in wholly agrarian parishes.[3]

We shall probably not be far wrong, then, in thinking that, outside London, at least one-half and probably two-thirds of all English Dissenters before 1740 were countrymen, and not townsmen. It would be foolish to belittle the importance of the urban element in English Nonconformity, but there was certainly nothing essentially urban about Dissent. No one with two eyes in his head and any knowledge of counties like Northamptonshire, Norfolk, Lincolnshire, Suffolk, and Devon could suppose that there was. There are still hundreds of chapels in the rural parishes of counties like these bearing witness to the former extent of Nonconformity in the countryside, though many are now fast going to decay.

The second point to notice about the Old Dissent was that, despite the claims of both its enemies and its champions, it seems to have comprised only a small

[1] See TABLE III, compiled from the parish figures in C. W. Chalklin, 'The Compton Census of 1676: the Dioceses of Canterbury and Rochester', *Kent Records: a Seventeenth Century Miscellany*, Kent Arch. Soc., Records Publication Committee, XVII, 1960, pp. 153–74. For the following calculations I have excluded three or four suburban parishes adjoining London, since properly these appertain to the metropolitan rather than the Kentish economy. It has usually been assumed in the past that the Compton figures refer only to communicants. It is now realized that they vary in their basis, but generally include adults only. The problems of the reliability of this 'census' and the extent to which it underestimates the number of Nonconformists cannot be discussed here. Mr Chalklin gives a balanced assessment (*loc. cit.*), to which the reader is referred. The membership of early Nonconformist churches in counties like Kent, Cambridgeshire, and Northamptonshire was certainly as a rule very small at this time, rarely as high as fifty. The real problem concerns the unknown number of 'occasional' conformists, and whether these should be reckoned as Dissenters or Anglicans.

[2] There were 900 in Canterbury, 500 in Sandwich, and 50 in Maidstone, according to a contemporary account.—British Museum, Thomason Tracts, E.285.6, p. 22. The figure for Dover is not given.

[3] This figure probably underestimates the total, since many 'urban' parishes in Kent (e.g. Maidstone and Cranbrook) included thousands of acres of countryside, with subsidiary villages and hamlets. We do not know how many Nonconformists in these places were in fact countrymen, and I have therefore reckoned all as 'urban' perforce. In emphasizing the strength of urban Dissent in Kent, Mr Chalklin (*op. cit.*, pp. 173–4) seems to have overlooked this fact. He has also included the foreign congregations, which I have excluded as explained above.

minority of the population. Even in Kent, where, to judge from the Compton figures, its adherents were unusually numerous in the 1670's, they represented no more than 8 per cent of the total population, or if we include the foreign congregations, 10 per cent.

TABLE III

DISTRIBUTION OF DISSENT IN KENT IN 1676

	Parishes	Conformists		Nonconformists		Papists	Total
		Number	%	Number	%		
A. RURAL PARISHES							
I. East Kent							
North-East							
Marshlands	18	1,347	98	20	2	—	1,367
Foothills	41	4,639	93	338	7	7	4,984
Downland	42	5,222	97	179	3	2	5,403
Forest of Blean	8	1,165	94	68	6	8	1,241
Romney Marsh	22	1,016	92	82*	8	—	1,098
Total	131	13,389	95	687	5	17	14,093
II. Mid-Kent							
Foothills	20	2,418	99	8	0·3	26	2,452
Downland	18	1,927	98	24	1	6	1,957
Chartland	33	5,107	95	255	5	9	5,371
Weald	33	9,667	83	1,986	17	29	11,682
Total	104	19,119	89	2,273	11	70	21,462
III. West Kent							
Thames-side							
parishes and Hoo	11	1,066	99	16	1	—	1,082
Foothills	12	2,087	98	34	2	3	2,124
Downland	16	1,529	99	19	1	1	1,549
Chartland	17	2,052	97	52†	3	11	2,115
Weald	16	5,483	96	177	4	27	5,687
Total	72	12,217	97	298	3	42	12,557
IV. Unclassifiable							
Rural Parishes	9	1,402	82	315	8	1	1,718
V. All Rural Parishes	316	46,127	93	3,573	7	130	49,830
B. URBAN PARISHES	34	17,535	83	3,464	17	63	21,062
C. ALL PARISHES‡	350	63,662		7,037	10	193	70,892

* Of these, 50 were in Lydd parish.

† Of these, 40 were in Snodland.

‡ The Compton Census, on which the figures are based, does not cover the whole of Kent. There are no surviving returns for 53 parishes, of which the chief group is the 31 parishes of the deanery of Shoreham in West Kent. The 350 parishes covered by the surviving returns therefore represent about seven-eighths of the county.

The Compton figures, it is true, are open to serious question; but when the records of individual congregations are examined, it is clear that, before the Evangelical Awakening, the membership of the typical chapel was surprisingly small. None of the five or six groups of Dissenters in Northampton, at the time when Philip Doddridge accepted the call to Castle Hill Chapel in 1729, numbered more than forty or fifty communicants; and this was not at all untypical. Mrs Spufford has found much the same conditions in late-seventeenth century Cambridgeshire. In Northampton Doddridge built his own congregation up to a membership of three hundred at its maximum; but this was a remarkable feat of skill and industry on his part, prophetic rather of the future Awakening, with its hordes of converts, than of the limited, Puritan past. Although large numbers of people often attended chapels of which they never became formal members, it is clear that, in speaking of the Old Dissent, we are in general dealing with numbers of quite a different order of magnitude from those of Victorian Nonconformity.

(iii) *Nonconformity in the Forests*

How were these groups of rural Dissenters distributed between the different types of agrarian economy alluded to above? The figures for Kent in the Compton Census of 1676 have been analysed in detail and are given in TABLE III. Kent is a county which, owing to geological, climatic, and historical causes, is sharply divided into distinct agrarian regions. Between the Surrey border and Thanet it may be said to fall into three parts: West Kent, Mid-Kent, and East Kent. North and south, it is naturally divided into riverside marshes (separated by the Forest of Blean between Faversham and Canterbury), fertile (often loamy) foothills, flinty chalk downlands, sandy and stony chartlands, the old Wealden forest, and a second extensive area of marshland around New Romney. Altogether there were (and still are) thirteen or fourteen distinct rural economies within the county, and the distribution of Nonconformity varied strikingly between them.

In the rural parishes of East Kent Dissenters numbered 5 per cent of the population; in Mid-Kent 11 per cent; and in West Kent, despite the relative proximity of London, no more than 3 per cent. As between the different types of economy in each division, differences were equally marked. In all the scores of downland parishes in the county, whether in East, West, or Mid-Kent, there were no more than 230 Dissenters altogether, or less than 2 per cent of the communicant population. Dissenters were everywhere most numerous in the forest parishes, and in the Wealden area of Mid-Kent they comprised as much as 17 per cent of the population. In some Wealden parishes the proportions were much higher than this: in Staplehurst 35 per cent, in Frittenden and Sandhurst 39 per cent, and in Smarden no less than 48 per cent. In fact more than 60 per cent of all the rural Nonconformists in Kent were to be found in the Weald, though this area probably comprised only one-quarter of the rural population as a whole.

What is the explanation of this remarkable prevalence of Dissent in the forest parishes and its equally curious absence from the chalk downlands? It is significant that in chalk and limestone regions in other counties at this time, such as the Lincolnshire and Leicestershire Wolds, the Old Dissent often seems to have been conspicuous by its absence. It is equally remarkable how prevalent it was in woodland regions in other shires, such as Rockingham Forest in Northamptonshire and Macclesfield Forest in Cheshire.[1] In the past the predominance of Dissent in rural areas like the Weald has usually been attributed to the cloth industry. Quite why there should be this apparent association between sectarian Christianity and cloth has always seemed, to one student of history at least, something of a mystery. When one looks more closely into the distribution of rural Dissent, however, it becomes clear that it also flourished in many districts where there was no cloth manufacture to speak of. The truth rather seems to be that the link was only an indirect one, and that cloth-making and Nonconformity were probably fostered independently by certain local characteristics peculiar to the society and settlement pattern of these areas. What were these characteristics so far as Dissent was concerned?

In answering this question, the Weald is further examined as a case-study. In other areas of strong Dissent, like the West Riding dales, east Devon, southeast Lancashire, east Cheshire, north Warwickshire, west Leicestershire, and Rockingham Forest, many of the same settlement characteristics appear. But forms of local society are rather echoed than repeated precisely in different regions, and it must be left to other students to examine these different districts in greater detail. In all these areas it seems to the present writer that the proliferation of Dissent was due to a conjunction of favourable circumstances rather than to any single universal cause. Not all the operative circumstances in the Weald were apparent elsewhere, but as a rule two or three elements in the syndrome seem to have been present.

The first characteristic fostering Dissent in the Weald was no doubt the exceptional size of the parishes, especially in the Mid-Kent Weald, where Dissent was strongest. On the downlands of East Kent the average parish extended to less than 1,600 acres, and many parishes were of under 1,000 acres. In the Weald, by contrast, the average parish covered nearly 5,000 acres, and several were twice this size. Goudhurst, for example, covered 9,800 acres, and Cranbrook 10,400 acres; the original area of Wrotham amounted to nearly

---

[1] For information about Macclesfield Forest I am indebted to Dr R. C. Richardson. For Northamptonshire I have relied on contemporary tracts, local chapel histories, and licences under the Declaration of Indulgence.

11,000 acres, of Westerham to 11,100 acres, and of Tonbridge to more than 15,000 acres.[1] In these vast parishes many families lived far away from their parish church, often as much as several miles. No doubt they occasionally worshipped there; but it is impossible to imagine a family with young children, who lived in an outlying hamlet or 'forstal' in one of these parishes, *regularly* attending their local church, especially during winter months when Wealden roads were notoriously difficult to negotiate. In the large parishes of the north of England, subsidiary Anglican chapels were often to be found in dependent settlements like these. But for some reason outlying chapels were very rare in Wealden parishes in the seventeenth century. There is evidence that they had existed before the Reformation; but by the period we are concerned with none at all seem to have remained in use in the great parishes of Goudhurst, Cranbrook, and Tonbridge. Such areas were ripe, therefore, for the development of Dissenting chapels of their own, independent of the established church.

The scattered nature of Wealden settlement was a further factor favouring Dissent. Even today it is not at all unusual to find forty or fifty separate settlements in a Wealden parish. In Smarden, for instance (not a particularly extensive parish, of 5,385 acres), there are still sixty-two distinct hamlets and isolated farms, nearly all of them medieval in origin. In the nineteenth century many new Anglican churches were built to serve outlying hamlets in parishes of this kind, for instance at Kilndown, Ide Hill, Corks Pond, Mark Beech, Bough Beech, and Four Elms. But in the seventeenth century there was only a single instance of any attempt to solve the problem by dividing an ancient parish. This occurred when the 11,000-acre parish of Wrotham, stretching seven miles from its northernmost tip on the downs to its southern edge in the Weald, was divided into three portions during the Commonwealth period. The division was later quashed by the Restoration church, but it had resulted in the remarkable little Interregnum church of Plaxtol, built by the local Puritan squire in 1648, and still almost as Gothic in its inspiration as any medieval church in the county, or the well-known Laudian building at Staunton Harold in Leicestershire, erected about the same time.[2] Nowhere else in Kent, however, was any attempt made to build a new church till Tunbridge Wells became a fashionable spa in the late seventeenth century, and a new chapel was built near the springs and dedicated to King Charles the Martyr. Elsewhere, such additional places

[1] Wrotham and Westerham parishes were not wholly within the Weald, and the original settlement in each case was strictly speaking outside its borders; but most of the area of the two parishes was woodland in character. Originally Westerham included the whole of what is now Edenbridge parish. Though Edenbridge had its own medieval church, and by Hasted's time had been formed into a separate parish, it still remained a dependent chapelry of Westerham.—E. Hasted, *The History and Topographical Survey of the County of Kent*, 2nd edn, III, 1797, p. 188. In many counties forest parishes tended to be larger than fielden. In Warwickshire, for instance, Tanworth-in-Arden covered 9,400 acres, Wootton Wawen 8,700, and Hampton-in-Arden 11,052.

[2] Hasted, *op. cit.*, v, pp. 22–5, 27.

of worship as were built in rural areas before the nineteenth century were, without exception, Nonconformist in origin.

The spread of Dissent in the Weald was further facilitated by the comparative weakness of the local manorial structure. Manorial organization in Kent is generally supposed to have been weaker than in the Midlands; but in the half of the shire to the north and east of the Weald, this weakness had in many ways been offset, particularly under the Tudors and Stuarts, by the growing power of the gentry, both in economic standing and in matters of local government. If the homes of the major county families of Kent in the seventeenth century— knights, baronets, and peers—are plotted on the map, few will be found in the Weald. Their parks and mansions were with few exceptions sited on the chartlands or the downs. Twysdens, Oxindens, Hardreses, Haleses, Scotts, Wottons, Harfleetes, Boyses, Finches, Sackvilles, Tuftons, Filmers, Honywoods, St Legers, Sondeses, Walsinghams, Diggeses: these and a score of other leading county families in the shire all lived outside the Wealden area, though a number of them possessed scattered or outlying property within it. There were gentry in the Weald, but most of them belonged to comparatively minor families, with a modest patrimony, and little power to overawe the numerous clothiers and independent yeomen of the parish.[1]

There can also be no doubt that the changing structure of population in the Weald in the sixteenth and seventeenth centuries was a major factor in its propensity to Dissent. As has been argued elsewhere, one of the striking differences between forest and fielden areas of England generally in this period was that, while the population of the latter often remained numerically stationary or in some cases declined, the inhabitants of forest and heathland districts generally tended to increase in numbers. There is a good deal of evidence that a new and final wave of settlement was taking place in the woodlands of England at this time. Much of the rapid growth in the English population between Henry VIII's reign and the Civil War was probably absorbed by these latter areas: partly because there was still waste land to colonize, partly because the land was poorer and less in demand, and partly because newcomers could more easily squat down without molestation in an area where manorial control was weak.[2]

By 1640 districts like the Weald had become some of the most densely settled in the countryside. Contemporaries like John Norden and William

[1] Cf. A. M. Everitt, *The Community of Kent and the Great Rebellion: 1640–60*, 1966, ch. II. Many of the greater parks of Kent, such as Knole and Squerryes, were situated on the stony, infertile greensands in the chartland belt, or 'Quarry Hills' as the area was called. The Kentish word 'chart' means 'rough common, overrun with gorse, broom, bracken', and is identical with the Norwegian word *kart*, 'rough, rocky, sterile soil'. Much of the land was of little use but for woods and parks.

[2] For this and the following paragraphs see my chapter on 'Farm Labourers', pp. 396–465, in *The Agrarian History of England and Wales*, IV, *1500–1640*, ed. Joan Thirsk, 1966.

Harrison, and many disputes in the Exchequer and Court of Requests, bear witness to the rapid growth of the cottage populations in areas like the Forest of Dean, the Forest of Kingswood, Feckenham Forest, the heaths and woodlands bordering Warwickshire and Staffordshire, and the forests bordering Buckinghamshire and Northamptonshire. Analysis of the Compton Census of 1676 confirms that in Kent the Wealden parishes were by that date the most thickly settled rural areas in the county. There were then less than 8 acres of land to every rural inhabitant in the Weald, compared with 11 acres on the downland, 18 in the low-lying parishes along the north coast of Kent, and 44 in Romney Marsh.

What was the consequence of this rapid growth of forest populations? Many contemporaries believed it led to lawless and semi-heathen communities of squatters and social outcasts.[1] The hostile views they expressed, however, probably tell us only part of the truth. The fact seems to be that by the mid-seventeenth century there were two kinds of community in woodland districts like the Weald of Kent. On the one hand there were the older centres of population, like Goudhurst and Cranbrook, with a powerful core of more rooted, stable, and prosperous families of freeholders and clothiers, who had long been natives of the area. On the other hand there were the newer squatters' communities, settled on sandy tracts and heaths like Ide Hill, Goathurst Common, Kennington Lees, and Seal Chart, largely composed of very poor cottagers, with a substantial leaven of recent migrants. In all probability the strictures of writers like Aubrey and Norden upon forest dwellers were really more applicable to these latter settlements. With the relaxation of local control by the justices of the peace during the Commonwealth period, the lawless inclinations of heathland communities became a frequent subject of complaint. When the earl of Dorset returned to Kent after the Civil War, his steward reported to him that the "poor and of a better sort" on Seal Chart "are yeomen so thievish and unconscionable that all the care [that] can be taken will not, without arresting some of them, and send[ing] them to prison, reform them. I have made many journeys to one poor old justice (and he dwells six miles from me) but to little purpose, the poor of Senoke [Sevenoaks, the adjoining parish] are grown so insolent."[2]

These two types of forest settlement may well have fostered distinct brands of Nonconformity: the older and more stable communities encouraging the more traditional forms of Dissent, already prevalent in centres like Cranbrook and Goudhurst by the time of the Civil War: and the newer, heathland communities

---

[1] Cf. A. M. Everitt, *Change in the Provinces: the Seventeenth Century*, Leicester University, Dept. of English Local History, Occasional Papers, 2nd ser., 1, 1969, pp. 22–3.

[2] Quoted from a document in the Kent County Archives Office, in Everitt, *Community of Kent*, pp. 171–2.

of squatters encouraging the more extravagant and millenarian kinds of sect. It is difficult to prove this thesis conclusively for the seventeenth century; but in the eighteenth and early nineteenth centuries it is certain that Methodism and eccentric messianic sects tended to flourish in 'outcast' settlements of this type, particularly in areas like Kingswood, Wychwood, and the Forest of Blean.[1] It is possible that a comment made by Canon J. J. Raven in 1895 in this connection, no doubt with a certain humorous intent behind it, may contain more than a grain of truth. Discussing the different brands of Dissent in Suffolk he remarked: "High predestinarian doctrine [i.e. of the Old Dissent], chiefly of the Particular Baptist type, seems to flourish more on the heavy soils, while the sudden conversions of various forms of Methodism have been more frequent on the sands and gravels."[2] For it was on the poorer sands and gravels that squatters' settlements tended to flourish.

(iv) *Nonconformity in Boundary Settlements*

We must not make the correlation between Dissent and forest societies too simple, however. Even in the seventeenth century Nonconformity was also found elsewhere in the countryside. Another form of rural community in which it tended to proliferate was the frontier settlement, situated on the boundary between two parishes. Places of this kind tended to be more frequent in forest districts, where waste land was more abundant; but they were not confined to woodlands. In Kent, where they were exceptionally numerous, they were to be found in most parts of the county. In Cowden, for example, a Wealden parish on the Sussex border, there are still nine outlying settlements situated on the parish boundary. In Lenham, a mid-Kent parish straddling the downs and the chartlands, the parish border passes through the middle of eleven distinct hamlets and farmhouses. In Elham, a large downland parish of East Kent, the boundary bisects no fewer than thirteen subsidiary communities. The origins of these settlements are outside the scope of this paper; but most of them certainly go back to the fourteenth century, and probably a good deal earlier; a few, indeed, are recorded in Anglo-Saxon charters. At least seventeen of the thirty-three in these three parishes are mentioned in documents dating from before 1385, and many of the rest, on topographical or toponymic grounds, must probably be assigned to an equally early period.[3]

Dissent was not found in more than a few of these boundary settlements, of course. Most of them have remained solitary farmsteads ever since their foun-

---

[1] For the Forest of Blean see P. G. Rogers, *Battle in Bossenden Wood*, 1961, relating to the followers of John Nichols Tom in this area; for Kingswood, *Imp. Gaz.*, *sub* Kingswood; for Wychwood, R. M. Marshall, *Oxfordshire Byways*, [1949], pp. 146–7.

[2] J. J. Raven, *The History of Suffolk*, 1895, p. 254. I owe this reference to Mr Norman Scarfe.

[3] J. K. Wallenberg, *Kentish Place-Names*, 1931, *passim*; and *The Place-Names of Kent*, 1934, pp. 81–3, 223–7, 431–5.

dation. A number, however, at some period of their history, gradually developed into populous communities in their own right. In Kent these kinds of boundary settlement are often distinguished by characteristic suffixes, such as *common* (e.g. Goathurst Common, on the border of Sundridge and Chevening); or *minnis*, a Kentish word meaning 'land held in common' (e.g., Stelling Minnis and Rhodes Minnis); or *lees*, a word in Kentish usage often referring to 'rough commonland or pasture' (e.g. Challock Lees and Kennington Lees); or simply the word *green* (e.g. Grafty Green, on the border of Lenham and Boughton Monchelsea). Places like these were the kind of boundary settlements that often proved conducive to Dissent. Many, it will be noticed from their names, were situated on common land, shared between two or three parishes, where jurisdictions were difficult to define and tended to come into dispute. Such conditions often fostered independent or (according to one's viewpoint) lawless behaviour; for in such a community it was always easy, on the approach of the parish constable, to claim that the inhabitants in question were not under *his* jurisdiction but that of the next parish.

In Leicestershire, a classic example of such a settlement is the village of Walton, a few miles east of Lutterworth. Nowadays the boundary has been adjusted to include the whole of Walton in Kimcote parish; but originally it passed through the middle of Walton village so that half the settlement lay in Kimcote and half in Knaptoft. Walton is certainly a very ancient settlement, for it is mentioned in Domesday, and is quite possibly older than either Knaptoft or Kimcote. It may have originated as a settlement of British serfs or slaves, for the name may mean 'the *tun* of the Welshmen'. Or alternatively it may mean 'the *tun* in a wood'. Either meaning would explain its subsidiary relationship to Kimcote and Knaptoft, of which it has remained an outlying appendage, with no parish church of its own—though in medieval times there was a chapel—until today. Yet it was large enough to develop a strong community life, with several times the population of Kimcote and many times that of the now vanished village of Knaptoft. In George III's reign there were a number of shopkeepers and craftsmen among its inhabitants, and probably many more framework-knitters than farm workers. How far back the Nonconformist traditions of this boundary settlement go we do not know; but during Queen Victoria's reign there were at least two Dissenting chapels within it, whereas there were none in either Knaptoft or Kimcote.[1]

Another, though much later, example of a Leicestershire boundary settlement with a strong Dissenting tradition is Coalville. It originated in the 1820's,

---

[1] The above paragraph is based on the accounts for Kimcote and Walton in nineteenth-century directories, John Nichols's *Leicestershire*, *Imp. Gaz.*, *The National Gazetteer of Great Britain and Ireland*, [1868] (hereafter cited as *Nat. Gaz.*). I am also indebted for information to the Rev. R. A. Cowling. The Methodist and Baptist chapels were both in Walton village. The former has disappeared; the latter is still in use.

under the name of Long Lane, at the junction of three distinct parishes, Ib-
stock, Whitwick, and Packington, and the separate chapelry of Snibston. By
1838 its first Nonconformist chapel had been erected, by the Baptists, and by
1870 (with a population of about 1,700) there were no fewer than four dissenting
churches, with but a single place of worship for Anglicans.[1] No doubt other
factors than its situation at the junction of three parishes affected Coalville's
propensity to Dissent; yet it is interesting as an unusually late example of the
persistent association between Nonconformity and boundary societies.

Closely similar in character to these boundary settlements were those which
sprang up on extra-parochial tracts and wastes. Typical of these were places like
Dunkirk in Kent and Lye Waste in Worcestershire. Lye Waste, like Coalville,
was a late settlement. According to Lewis's *Topographical Dictionary* (1833),
The National Gazetteer (1868), and *The Imperial Gazetteer* (1870), it had originated on the uncultivated waste of Lye village, and was "settled by a numerous
body of men, who acquired a right of separate freehold on the passing of an
enclosure act..." It consisted chiefly of nailmakers, and of cottagers employed
in the local iron and coal works. Part of the settlement, Carless Green, was
"noted for insurance clubs called Stewpony societies, and for an institution
designed to improve the condition of the labouring classes, called the Stewpony
Allotment Society."[2] By 1870 there were at least four Dissenting chapels on
Lye Waste. The story of this community, with its numerous small freeholders
and many Dissenters, would well repay further exploration. The association between an outlying settlement, independent cottagers, rural industry, and Nonconformist propensities is characteristic of many Midland manufacturing
villages like this in the early days of industrialization. It was an association that
had a very long tradition behind it.

The origins of Dunkirk, in Kent, are more obscure. It has been claimed as an
Anglo-Norman settlement; but there appears to be no documentary evidence
for its existence in the medieval period. According to the *Imperial Gazetteer*
(1870) "the name Dunkirk was first given to it, about the middle of last century,
by a body of squatters, who took free or forcible possession of the land, and
who became notable for smuggling practices." This account, however, seems
to date the origin of the settlement rather too late. More probably, like many
other squatters' communities, it originated during the seventeenth century,
when the Dunkirkers preyed on English vessels round the coast and the term
was synonymous with pirates and outlaws. At all events, by the early eighteenth
century the Kentish place was sufficiently important to be regarded as a dis-

[1] *Imp. Gaz.*, *sub* Coalville; Sarah E. Wise, *Coalville: the Origins and Growth of a Nineteenth
Century Mining Town*, Leicester M.A. dissertation, 1968, pp. 1, 3, 7, 15, 21n., 63.

[2] The name Stewpony was no doubt associated with the local inn called the Stew Pony. Probably
the meetings of these societies were originally held there.

tinct 'ville' or township, and was certainly 'extra-parochial'. Situated within the old Forest of Blean, outside any parish jurisdiction, and within a few miles of the north coast of Kent, it became a notorious centre for smugglers and highwaymen. According to Hasted, writing at the end of the eighteenth century but referring to an earlier period, it was "inhabited by low persons of suspicious characters, who sheltered themselves there, this being a place exempt from the jurisdiction of either hundred or parish, as in a free port, which receives all who enter it without distinction," so that "the whole district from hence gained the name of Dunkirk."[1]

The inhabitants of Dunkirk were probably amongst those whom Wesley inveighed against as 'savages' when he preached in this area after returning from America.[2] In the early nineteenth century the 'ville' became the chief centre of a notorious sect in East Kent, led by John Nichols Tom, the self-styled Sir William Courtenay, who ultimately claimed to be the Messiah. The story of this sect has been more than once described by local historians. It came to a tragic end in 1838, when, after a series of riots and impostures, Courtenay and seven of his followers were killed by the Kentish Militia in the Battle of Bossenden Wood. The desperate poverty and brutality of the area revealed by these events profoundly shocked the local gentry and clergy, and indeed Parliament itself. In an effort to civilize the inhabitants an Anglican church and school were built about 1840, and in the following year Dunkirk was formed into a separate parish. "The process of reclaiming the bad characters of Dunkirk began," says a recent historian, "almost as if a mission had been started in some far-off equatorial jungle, instead of in Kent."[3] In 1888, the Reverend W. J. Springett, who had by then been vicar of Dunkirk for thirty-five years, remarked that "the clergy had had a very uphill work in reclaiming the neighbourhood from the ignorance and immorality which were the results of a long period of neglect." By the time he wrote, however, their efforts had been "crowned with sufficient success to make Dunkirk no longer distinguishable from any other Christian and civilized neighbourhood."[4] The history of Dissenting vagaries in the area, with their strange mixture of idealism and delusion, had come to an end. There was no longer much that was shocking, or

---

[1] Hasted, *op. cit.*, IX, pp. 3–4; *Imp. Gaz.*, *sub* Dunkirk; *Nat. Gaz.*, *sub* Dunkirk.

[2] Quoted in Richard Green, *John Wesley: Evangelist*, 1905, p. 176. Wesley is said to have been preaching at or near Faversham, on the edge of Blean Forest. It is possible he was referring to the townsmen, but more probably to the forest inhabitants, who were notoriously lawless.

[3] Rogers, *op. cit.*, p. 202.

[4] Quoted *ibid.* Possibly, however, the Rev. Springett was too optimistic. About the same time an anonymous local author wrote of this area: "even in this year of 1890, we can positively affirm that it would hardly be safe in the outlying districts surrounding that fatal gathering-place [Bossenden Wood] to mention with a sneer or a rude jest the name of William Courtenay. The descendants of those who followed him—a few of whom are still living there—believe in him to this day."—*Annals of a Fishing Village: drawn from the Notes of "A Son of the Marshes,"* ed. J. A. Owen, 1892, p. 67.

perhaps much that was interesting, about it. Even now, however, the events of those times have not entirely passed out of local memory.

The association between Dissent and boundary settlements or extra-parochial tracts is obviously a subject that needs more extensive study than can be given to it here. It would also be profitable to explore a similar connection between Nonconformity and disputed boundaries in a number of provincial towns as well as rural areas. In late seventeenth-century Leicester, for example, the local justices and the corporation had a good deal of trouble with illegal conventicles in the extra-mural suburb known as the Bishop's Fee. The jurisdiction over this area had long been a matter of dispute between the town and the bishop of Lincoln (and later the county), and it was not finally resolved till the nineteenth century. In all probability there was also a connection in this case between these conventicles and the illicit trading and innkeeping for which the area became notorious. Part of it, still known in the early nineteenth century as No Man's Land, developed as the chief centre of Leicester's great autumnal fair.[1] An association of this kind between a disputed jurisdiction, illicit conventicles, and dubious trading activities seems to have been characteristic of a number of market towns in the seventeenth and eighteenth centuries. In many cases, probably, there was a connection with the fraternity of travelling merchants and factors, by whose means radical religious ideas were readily propagated. Certainly Stourbridge Fair, near Cambridge, was noted not only as a mart of national importance but also as a centre of Puritan disturbance as early as Queen Elizabeth's reign.[2]

(v) *Envoi*

Between the seventeenth and the twentieth centuries Nonconformist chapels were erected in thousands all over England and Wales. Exactly how many there were we shall never know, but at their most numerous, towards the end of the nineteenth century, there may well have been more than 30,000 of them. Certainly at the time of the 1851 census there were about 20,000 in England alone.[3] In Northamptonshire, for example, there were 294, in Leicestershire 354, in Kent 500, and in Lincolnshire 831. In all these counties there were, by Queen Victoria's reign, more Nonconformist chapels than Anglican churches.

Yet of the vast majority of these local chapel communities we know extremely little. Even the whereabouts of many of them are now unrecognized, and of

---

[1] Helen Stocks, ed., *Records of the Borough of Leicester . . . 1603–1688*, 1923, p. 259 *et passim*; C. J. Billson, *Medieval Leicester*, 1920, pp. 114–15; V.C.H. *Leicestershire*, IV, pp. 48, 54, 57–8, 350.

[2] Everitt, *Change in the Provinces*, p. 42.

[3] Again, the exact number is not known to me. This estimate is based on the fact that there were 3,717,730 'sittings' in all Nonconformist chapels, and the average size of chapel was approximately 200. (In Lincolnshire the average size was 164 sittings, in Leicestershire 208, in Kent 210, and in Northamptonshire 223.)

their inner life we know virtually nothing. For many of them there are no surviving letters, no diaries, no personal memoranda: not a shadow survives to
tell us what their members thought or felt or did, their joys and hopes and sor-
rows, or even who they were. How much 'the Chapel' meant to its members
we do know from the bare economic fact that congregations of less than two
hundred members on the average, rarely composed of wealthy people, without
state support, and usually without any kind of endowment, were prepared to
build, finance, and run their chapel and to pay their own minister. Something
of what their religious life meant to them we can also sense from the vast corpus
of hymns they have left behind them—the unexplored, unrecognized folk-
poetry of England.

But all this can tell us nothing about the individual genius of any particular
religious community. And the variety amongst Nonconformist chapels, it
must never be forgotten, was at least as great as were the similarities. One
would like to know the history of a remote rural chapel near Hartlip in East
Kent, for instance, built in 1820, and inscribed in its pediment with the single
eloquent word 'Cardiphonia'—the utterance of the heart. The allusion is to a
once-famous volume of John Newton's letters, published under the title
Cardiphonia in the year 1781. Yet why should the members of this little wayside
Bethel have so revered the Anglican parson's book, with its intense and tender
sentiment, as to name their chapel after it? This is one of those minor yet intriguing mysteries of provincial life whose answer, could we discover it, might
open quite an unsuspected bypath of rural life. There must have been depths
of thought and feeling amongst the folk at Cardiphonia Chapel which the
evidence merely hints at, and then tells us no more. Perhaps, if there had been
a George Eliot to overhear their conversation, we should have found a Dinah
Morris among them, a Mrs Poyser, or an Adam Bede.

Of another chapel, only a few miles from Cardiphonia, in a lonely marshland
spot near Milton Regis, we know more. It originated about the same time, but
its character must have been utterly different. Like many of the smaller religious communities in the countryside, it was founded by a farmer on his own
land and became a kind of proprietary chapel. This is how it was described by a
Victorian writer who had known it as a boy.[1] "Some distance from Philip
Magnier's homestead, on the edge of the marshes, close to the highroad, there
used to be a small but very substantially built farmhouse, on rising ground,
surrounded by barns and other outbuildings. Sheltered from the winds, a little
lower down, was a small orchard well stocked with fruit-trees, which were old
like the buildings, and like them covered with moss and lichens. Ponds of fresh

---

[1] The following account is based on Owen, *op. cit.*, pp. 105–7. The precise whereabouts of the
chapel and farm are not given, but internal evidence shows that the 'Marshton' of this book was
Milton Regis.

water stood round about. Apart from the other buildings was one capable of holding about fifty people. It was Old Grab's chapel, or as the folks called it, his preaching shop." Old Grab, the farmer, said it was a long way for the people to get to the parish church, and he had a notion it was not right for them to live and die like heathens. So he built the chapel at his own cost, and then he preached to them himself.

The farmer-pastor evidently preached to his captive congregation a decidedly grim gospel, and they all became greatly afraid of him. In particular he preyed upon their dread of witchcraft, which was still widely practised in the marsh. They also said that he drank enough smuggled brandy to scald a hog (smuggling was still widespread in the area), and yet he preached to them about rendering Caesar his dues, and the sinfulness of getting drunk, "in a way to make them cry." Then suddenly one day the old farmer went mad. He gave all his workfolk notice, including a carter who had been with him for eleven years, and informed them that he was going to join his son in foreign parts. It was all a pitiful hoax. His own terrors must have caught up with him: he committed suicide instead.

Twenty years later the same Victorian author revisited the spot and found all the farm buildings derelict. "Apparently they had been deserted for some time. The casements had been blown to pieces, only the iron frames were left hanging. Before the door tufts of rushes had sprung up between the flags of the roughly paved path, and small pools were here and there. Most of the old trees in the orchard were prone on the ground, not dead, for their roots were not exposed, but sloped down by the wind. The reed-thatching was blown off or rotten; from a pool that used to supply the house with drinking-water some wild ducks flew up, and one could see, by the tracks on the surface of the reed-covered cattle-pond, that wild-fowl made it one of their feeding-spots."

It was a strange and melodramatic end to a small dissenting community in a Kentish parish in the early days of Queen Victoria. It might almost have been invented by Edgar Allan Poe. And of course it cannot be taken as genuinely characteristic of country conventicles in the provinces. Yet the fierce and introverted life behind the story of this marshland chapel was probably not at all untypical of Nonconformist communities in rural parishes. The history of these Dissenting groups, scattered in their thousands up and down the countryside, provides yet another tract of largely uncharted territory for the student of agrarian society to explore.

Index